FRANK O'CONNOR
An Introduction

FRANK O'CONNOR

An Introduction

MAURICE WOHLGELERNTER

Columbia University Press
New York 1977

Library of Congress Cataloging in Publication Data

Wohlgelernter, Maurice.
Frank O'Connor: an introduction.

Bibliography: p.
Includes index.
1. O'Donovan, Michael, 1903–1966.   2. Authors,
Irish—20th century—Biography.   I. Title.
PR6029.D58Z98   828′.9′12[B]   76-45085
ISBN 0-231-04194-2

Columbia University Press
New York   Guildford, Surrey
Copyright © 1977 Columbia University Press
Printed in the United States of America

for
DEBRA, ELLI, BETH
"look back to look forward"

Contents

Contents

Introduction

"Frank O'Connor will have a biographer."
> —Frank O'Connor in a letter to Sean Hendrick

"After a man's long work is over and the sound of his voice is still," Henry James once wrote, "those in whose regard he has held a high place find his image strangely simplified and summarized. The hand of death, in passing over it, has smoothed the folds, made it more typical and general. The figure retained by the memory is compressed and intensified; accidents have dropped away from it and shades have ceased to count; it stands, sharply, for a few estimated and cherished things, rather than, nebulously, for a swarm of possibilities. We cut the silhouette, in a word, out of the confusion of life, we save and fix the outline, and it is with his eye on this profiled distinction that the critic speaks."

In this introductory study, I have attempted to fix an outline of the distinguished profile of Frank O'Connor, whose long work was over on the afternoon of March 10, 1966. I have concentrated on the "few estimated and cherished things" that I have accumulated over an extended period of time. This is not, therefore, a "life and works" nor a "reader's guide" but, rather, an attempt to cut his silhouette against the confusion of modern Irish life and letters.

In the decade since his death, no critical study—except two unpublished doctoral dissertations, and these only on the short stories—has been made of O'Connor who, in Yeats's view, did for Ireland what Chekhov had done for Russia. O'Connor deserves a better fate. Not only because of what he did for Ireland, which, throughout his life, was—despite his many criticisms and those

scoldings such as take place only within a family—his deepest passion, but also because of his major contribution to Irish letters and
contemporary literature. O'Connor was surely correct, therefore, in
predicting that someday he "will have a biographer." However, I
am not, nor, I fear, was I ever destined to be, that biographer.

What I have undertaken, instead, is to relate O'Connor's main
thought to the historical and intellectual events of his time, placing
it specifically in the stream of Irish literature. Whatever biographical material I have used in the development of O'Connor's thought,
this study may be considered a sort of biography of his mind.

Summing up the achievement of that mind, I have taken two
things, at least, into account: his character and the character of the
circumstances he had to deal with. These sad and terribly difficult
circumstances, which made of his native Ireland a ruined and fragmented country divorced from its past, brought out the very best in
O'Connor's mind and character. For his was, like his friend Yeats's,
the "sort of mind that could build happily among ruins," ruins
which left Ireland the "last country in the world in which to study
[or create] Irish literature."

And what he admired further in Yeats was equally true of himself. Speaking at Drumcliffe at the hundredth birthday celebration
of Yeats, O'Connor commented that Ireland, in all its troubles,
"needed a mind like his, strong and full of sweetness, to build
in this empty house of ours and to see beyond the quarrelling sects
and factions an older Ireland where men could still afford to be
brave and generous and gay." O'Connor was all that and more.
For, again like Yeats, but unlike Joyce, O'Connor refused to flee
the stifling conditions of his native country, whose "greatest single
weakness is its tendency to turn everything [it] loves from [its]
language to [its] religion into a test of orthodoxy," but, instead,
chose to live there for the most part in order to restore in its empty
house the "created" conscience of his race.

Although O'Connor had his roots in Ireland, clinging to his "native earth like a crabtree, tenacious, twisted, idiosyncratic, wild,"
he was freed into his art by a "spacious mind of the spirit, so that
what is earthbound is also liberated and breaks the 'cake of custom.'" To understand that liberated spirit, after his years of in-

volvement in the affairs of men, I found it necessary in my opening chapter to show what was "earthbound" in his personal past from which he had to free himself, eventually, in order to dedicate the greater part of his life to his art. I attempt also to record some of the people who helped shape his mind, from his mother—the one influence from which he seemed never to free himself—to Harold Macmillan, who gave him the most beneficial advice he was ever to receive: to forget his organizational interests and involvement in the theater, and to sit down and write. Sitting down to write, he finally knew where he was going—to where "glory" awaited him. And, in great measure, he was able, fortunately, to find that glory.

Before he found it, however, he became involved, if only briefly and unsuccessfully, in the struggle for power, commonly known as the "Troubles," waged in Ireland in 1922. This involvement gave rise to *Guests of the Nation,* a volume of short stories dealing, in the main, with this war and its aftermath, as well as *The Big Fellow,* a biography of Michael Collins, the charismatic leader at that time of the government forces. These works, as well as other war stories in subsequent volumes, tending to show that the whole of Irish life was vitiated by intolerance, which generated, in O'Connor's words, "a sodden atmosphere of disunion and dissention which makes all positive action appear futile and quixotic," are the subject of Chapter II.

Chapter III is devoted to a study of the role of religion and, more specifically, the clergyman and priest in Irish life and how their lives are reflected in the many stories O'Connor dedicated to them. To be sure, when he discusses priests, or, in other places, lawyers and policemen, O'Connor tries his best, he confesses, not to think of priests or lawyers or policemen as such, for his "business as a writer is to get past the circumstances of the story and to find in each of them the quality that makes him an individual human being and a more professional figure." And that is what gives his stories, in O'Connor's phrase, an "interior perspective" so that instead of a "flat surface you get a texture like life itself, something you can move about in and apprehend at various levels and can at the same time be moved by and smiled at."

But that, of course, does not make O'Connor an adherent of

any particular school of thought, such as, say, the Freudian, for he was forever insistent on maintaining the writer's absolute freedom in the treatment of any subject. As a writer, he hated to be tied down, liking the "freedom of a subject that has no tabs or labels attached to it." Hence, he never approached the subject of Irish life—discussed in some detail in Chapter IV—with any preconceived "labels" but treated it frankly with all the compassion and frustration it evoked in one who experienced it deeply all his years; to this subject, he devoted most of his stories as well as his only two novels, *The Saint and Mary Kate* and *Dutch Interior*.

Besides fiction, O'Connor wrote a great deal of criticism, the subject of Chapter v. He published, in addition to articles and reviews, one short work—*Towards an Appreciation of Literature*—and four major works of literary criticism: *Shakespeare's Progress*; *The Mirror in the Roadway*; *The Lonely Voice*; and *A Short History of Irish Literature*. Though never trained as a formal critic—a fact he publicly lamented—O'Connor in his critical works nevertheless proves interesting, primarily because his views are so unorthodox and refreshingly candid, despite their lack of consistency.

Because he was no less candid in his views on the theater—witness his short volume, *The Art of the Theatre*—and its movers and shakers on the Board of Directors of the Abbey Theatre, I conclude with a chapter devoted to a discussion of his brief tenure as a director of the Abbey as well as some of his ideas on the drama. His criticism and his interest in the theater together also make up a part of the essential "cargo" he carried along the road to fame.

O'Connor also wrote some poetry. But like his plays, that was not his major interest or *métier*, since, aside from his slender volume, *Three Old Brothers and Other Poems*, most of his muse's effort was directed toward translations from the Gaelic, both ancient and modern, his most noteworthy work being his rendition—incidentally, the best ever done—of Brian Merryman's eighteenth-century poem "The Midnight Court." Unfamiliar with Gaelic, I am, unfortunately, unable to assess his contribution to this field; hence, I do not discuss it at all, relying instead on Dr. Brendan Kennelly's splendid essay in *Michael/Frank*, which delineates the "variety and vitality" of O'Connor's translations. Dr. Kennelly shows how O'Connor "brilliantly recreates personalities and situations of an ancient world" and thereby "helps to order and illuminate the world in which we live."

It goes without saying that admiration for a writer does not mean complete agreement with him. When I have disagreed with O'Connor's conclusions I have not attempted always to supply other answers to the problems with which he dealt; rather, I have attempted, where I disagreed as well as agreed, to make clear the implications of O'Connor's positions.

Far more illuminating, however, than his positions or poetry or drama or even criticism was his own personality. It drew much attention and admiration from many friends, as witnessed in the nineteen elegiac essays in *Michael/Frank*, as well as a scattering of biographical reminiscences by friends in various periodicals. Though acquainted with all these and some additional tales told to me by O'Connor's family and friends, I have found myself querying, as this book began taking final shape, just what, in O'Connor, other than his obvious artistry as a story teller, drew my own concentrated attention to him these past few years. I realized soon enough that, to answer this question, like O'Connor himself who always wanted to convey to his readers the "qualities" that lay "behind" his fictional characters, I would have to find those qualities in his personality, oftimes revealed only fleetingly in his works, which served to focus my strong interest in him. It gradually became apparent that I had begun to recognize in his character certain attitudes toward life, the source of all art, which, in some ways, I admire greatly. If, as Matthew Arnold commented, "we become what we sing," I shall record briefly what moved me to "sing" of this man and his art.

The man loved his country. That is not to say, of course, that O'Connor assumed a particular patriotic stance but rather that, as a profound Irishman, "unmistakably a Munster man, inescapably of Cork," he yet remained the interpreter of these conditions rather than an outward symbol. He was "a harp that responded to every wind that blew." And some of those winds, of indifference, of callousness, of disregard for writing, for writers, for libraries, for things permanent—matters which concerned him most—disturbed him deeply. Some of these attitudes of his countrymen he recalled sadly toward the end of his life. In a lecture delivered to the Dublin P.E.N. Club in 1964, he lamented their attitude toward the arts as that of a "famine stricken, beleaguered people who don't seriously believe they have anything of their own to be proud of. . . ." O'Connor believed there was much in his country to be proud of, so that, among its ruins and fragments, he would bring to it, by his personal contribution and involvement, justifiable honor, distinction, and pride.

What ought to have been of greatest pride to his countrymen, according to O'Connor, was their past. The tales, myths, folk stories, and above all, poetry of Ireland were the stuff of which great nations are built. They need only be known and read to be appreciated. To that end, O'Connor mastered not only Modern Irish, but also Old Irish, which is "as far from Modern Irish as the language of *Beowulf* is from that of a daily newspaper." And, in intervals between his own writing, he did an enormous amount of research in these areas in order to transmit that "unknown" past to the present by his translations. These translations of Old, Middle, and Modern Irish, some of which are collected in *The Fountain of Magic*, have, Professor D. A. Binchy attests, "left many a professional scholar gasping with amazement." Blessed with the same "divine spark" which, he claimed, the scholar no less than any other artist needs "if he's to be really good at his job," O'Connor illuminated Ireland's past, giving his countrymen considerable roots for their pride. And all because one cannot, he was convinced, "look forward" without first "looking backward."

What O'Connor was determined to achieve with all his writing and translating was that "no young Irishman would ever again grow up so ignorant of his own past." To that end, he assumed not only the role of translator but also that of teacher. In that role, too, he was eminently successful. Not only were his visiting lectureships at Harvard, Stanford, Northwestern, and Trinity College, Dublin, highly effective—more effective, according to his colleagues, than O'Connor himself, because of his lack of formal education, had thought possible—but he was also an extremely persuasive teacher outside the classroom, in his public talks and appearances, and, of course, in his writings. On such extra-curricular occasions, he would always stress that the true reasons why his countrymen ought "to learn and speak Irish is that it is bound up with our history, that it is a lovely, if difficult, language, and that it contains enshrined in it a wealth of song and story, the loss of which to us and our children would be irreparable."

O'Connor wanted to preserve not only songs and stories but also the relics of brick and mortar which, in the form of cathedrals, abbey, monasteries, cemeteries, and other ruins, dot the Irish countryside. They are the visible symbols of a glorious past that must be preserved, something to which Ireland was giving too little attention. He crossed the country to search for them and to help preserve them, as he recalls so interestingly in *Irish Miles*. No less lamentable for him had been the loss, through purchase by foreign countries, of an equally valuable national treasure: countless thousands of manuscript papers and letters of the modern Irish masters —Synge, Yeats, Lady Gregory, Joyce, and O'Casey—who, if only asked politely, O'Connor contended, would have left them to the various colleges and libraries in Ireland. Instead, they were "allowed to leave [the] country because we could not budge from our attitudes of 1848." The best of men left their treasures on foreign soil so that others might know and admire, more lovingly than the native born, Ireland's rich and vibrant past.

But perhaps his effectiveness as a "teacher" and preserver was the result not only of his scholarship and his striking manner behind the lectern, but also his being himself the "example of what humanity, cultivation, learning and sensitivity could come to in a fully matured writer." Since he embodied the qualities of an ideal instructor, he was able to influence young Ireland to look back at its past with interest, insight, and a sense of indebtedness.

Yet, of all O'Connor's personal qualities, the one that was most noteworthy, I believe, was his humanity. Favoring, at all times, "courtesy, decency and order," he had a natural sympathy with anyone less fortunate or in distress. He did not share in that most fatal of Irish vices, callousness. He was never indifferent, but always deeply involved; he penetrated to the heart of vital issues. And nowhere, it seems to me, is this more evident than in his B.B.C. talk of December 27, 1940, entitled "Across St. George's Channel." In-

vited to broadcast from London, he jumped at the opportunity
because, as he related, "when somebody who's been a good neighbor to you has trouble in his house, you want to show, even if it's
only in a small way, that you haven't forgotten his kindness." To
O'Connor, England was a sort of spiritual haven, "a personified
ideal, an extension of our own personality, that makes us live a
little above ourselves." He then proceeded to tell the English, in all
the agony and suffering of their loneliness, just what it was he admired so much about their national character and country. What
he broadcast then to the English, in order to encourage them in
their "finest hour," obviously says as much about him as about
them, since they were "an extension of his own personality":

*One's impression of a nation, like one's impression of that house one
knew as a child, is a distillation of hundreds of little incidents, too
trifling to repeat. It is the most difficult thing in the world to generalize
about: it is a perfume and one tries in vain to capture it in words. For
me the perfume is compounded of many things: kindness, which is the
strongest ingredient; courtesy, decency, order. Then there is a sort of
simplicity; a singleness of mind and purity of intention; a touch of
knight errantry one loves, even though one pokes fun at it. There is last
of all a mind that looks outwards on life rather than in upon itself, that
does not exploit or dramatize itself, that does not raise its voice.*

Given this temperament, it is not surprising that O'Connor
would, at least twice in his writings, criticize his close friend Yeats
for supporting O'Duffy's blue-shirted Fascists during the Thirties.
And if somewhat muted in his criticism of Yeats, he was quite out-
spoken about what he considered to be the "fascist" tendencies of
the "romantic" D. H. Lawrence. After linking politically "the extreme realists, who are the naturalists, and the extreme realists who
are the communists, and the extreme romantics, who are symbolists,
with the extreme conservatives who became fascists," O'Connor
quoted, after demurring from both attitudes, a disturbing passage
from D. H. Lawrence's *Sea and Sardinia*, which would seem to confirm this link between art and politics. Lawrence could write: "It
is a great mistake to abolish the death penalty. If I were dictator,
I should order the old one to be hanged at once. I should have
judges with sensitive living hearts; not abstract intellects. And be-

cause the instinctive heart recognized a man as evil, I would have that man destroyed. Quickly. Because good warm life is now in danger."

To such a passage and its writer, O'Connor, in his tender passion for humanity, gave an answer filled with obvious disagreement and utter rejection: "Forgive an old-fashioned liberal, and bear with him a little, but I do not like that tone. I do not like it at all. As a liberal, I hate to raise my voice, but I really must say that I think, in the words of Mr. Woodhouse in Jane Austen's novel, that 'that young man is not quite the thing.' "

If what Lawrence said is not "quite the thing," what O'Connor said, on a not unrelated matter, is most decidedly "the thing." It concerns World War II and the greatest tragedy of modern times —the Holocaust—which occurred during those catastrophic years of the early Forties. That these awesome tragedies as well as the destruction of innocents everywhere would concern him is hardly surprising when we bear in mind his brilliantly moving story "A Minority," on the Holocaust, dealing with the "delinquent" and "despised" but tenacious Willie Stein who, for clinging to his identity, is "transformed by a glory." Further, Michael MacLiammoir, recalling O'Connor's compassion for humanity at large and for children and poor people, tells us:

"At some time during the Hitler war, he spent, I remember, an afternoon with us. He had just returned from a visit to London in the darkest hours of the blitz; he was shaken with pity for the sufferings of the English people who were living through the bombardment of their capital city. . . .
'To see a people crucified . . . crucified!' he said again and again."

Again and again, he would read of how the Nazi beast stalked the earth, devouring innocents alive, news which would "shake his frame from head to heel."

What also moved O'Connor, in addition to his passionate concern for these, like other "submerged populations," was his profound understanding that, as a result of the Rising in 1916, which, uniquely and effectively, linked arms and a literary renaissance, Ireland must become conscious of its inheritance of the remains of an Indo-European civilization. This, O'Connor believed, would invest it with a mystique that "has made of us, for the most part unwillingly, a People of the Book. It is as though we could no more escape from the burden of tradition than the Jews have been able to escape from the Pentateuch." Overcome by that mystique, O'Connor, after looking back, was able to look forward to the glory of his country and its books.

Such a man, obviously, deserves a study of his own.

The writing of this book has placed me under many happy obligations. I am especially indebted to Joseph L. Blau, Chairman, Graduate Department of Religion, Columbia University; Kevin Sullivan, Director, Irish Institute, Queens College, City University of New York; James L. Clifford, William Peterfield Trent Professor, Emeritus, Columbia University; Emile Capouya, Literary Editor, and Grace Schulman, Poetry Editor, *The Nation*; Dean Doner, Vice President for Academic Affairs, Boston University; Seymour Lainoff, Department of English, Yeshiva University; and Raymond J. Porter, Department of English, Iona College, who carefully read the manuscript amid their own pressing work, giving me the advantage of their criticism and encouragement. To Andrew Lavender, Department of English, Baruch College, City University of New York, for giving every draft a detailed and affectionate reading and for his abiding concern for my welfare, I owe more than I can hope to express.

Among my former teachers at Columbia University, I owe the greatest debt to William York Tindall, who taught me, among many other things, not only how to read but also how to write a book. To this work, as to everything else I have ever written, he, together with his wife, Celia, has been generous with his time and devoted concern. For all his genuine interest in me as teacher and writer, beginning with my years as student in his graduate courses and seminars at Columbia University, I am abidingly grateful.

To Clyde Wingfield, President, William Monat, Vice President for Academic Affairs, and Arthur W. Brown, Dean, Baruch College, I offer thanks for their encouragement and their many kindnesses. I am ever mindful of Dean Brown's careful reading of this book and how much I benefited from his editorial comments. I deeply appreciate the opportunity granted me by my good friend Edward M. Potoker, Chairman, Department of English, to share the pleasures of working with and for a department deeply committed to teaching and research. To Michael Wyschogrod, Chairman, Department of Philosophy, who remembered when so many others had forgotten, I am richly indebted.

To my revered teacher Rav Joseph B. Soloveichik, of Boston, and Yeshiva University, scion of a great and glorious tradition, who, from the day I first entered his classroom to become his student over three decades ago, has guided and moulded my spiritual life and thought, I owe a profound debt of gratitude. I have never ceased to be impressed by his vast erudition, his genius for clarity, his uncanny ability to initiate enthusiasms, to clear paths and inculcate discipline. His voice, after all these years, is still just. His most serious triumph as a teacher is, I believe, the uniquely impressive one that his son and my trusted friend Rav Chaim Soloveichik, Dean, Bernard Revel Graduate School, Yeshiva University, is able to wear, with similar dedication, the many colored mantle of his father's tradition.

I am also indebted for ideas, facts, corrections, encouragement, and other aid to many colleagues and friends—William F. Bernhardt, Michael Bernstein, George Cohen, Eric Gruen, Esther Guttenberg, Jerry Hochbaum, Frederick M. Keener, John V. Kelleher, Joseph Kestner, Shirley Lebowitz, Louis Levy, William Turner Levy, Joseph Lowin, Albert Marrin, Aliza Mishkoff, Marjorie Hope Nicolson, Stephen Nordlicht, Jack Prince, Myron Plaut, Myron Schwartzman, Harriet Sheehy, and Donna Walsh. I need hardly add that, in spite of these many obligations, I alone must bear the responsibility for the pages that follow.

I am deeply grateful to my devoted friends Arthur and Arlene Reiss, Trustees, Isidore Reiss Memorial Foundation, for a grant that helped further the completion of this book. And to my dedicated friends Tobias and Miriam Heller, who answer my every call, I owe much, for all too much.

The librarians of the Columbia University Library, New York Public Library, Bancroft Library of the University of California at

Berkeley, National Library, Dublin, and Baruch College Library were most helpful. Many publishers have allowed me to quote from works for which they hold the copyright; their names are given on the page following this note.

To my wife, Esther, whose acute observations, salutary comments, abiding faith, and loving concern have made the writing of this book, like so much else, possible, I owe more than I could ever possibly hope to record. I shall, therefore, remain in her eternal debt for "every *other* reason."

The traditional last sentence of this brief introduction is reserved for our children Debra, Elli, and Beth, to whom this book is dedicated with much love—briefly expressed in the dedication—and with much hope.

M.W.

Baruch College of the
City University of New York
February 1, 1976

Acknowledgments

The following have generously granted me permission to quote from the works for which they hold the copyright:

Iona College Press for the first chapter, "A Portrait of the Artist as an Only Child," which originally appeared, in somewhat different form, in *Modern Irish Literature: Essays in Honor of William York Tindall*, 1972, ed. Raymond J. Porter and James Brophy.

The Bancroft Library, University of California at Berkeley, and Harriet O'D. Sheehy for the letters from Frank O'Connor to Sean O'Faolain. Mrs. Sheehy also provided the photograph, taken in 1964, for the jacket cover.

John V. Kelleher for the photograph, taken c.1941, facing the title page.

Alfred A. Knopf for Frank O'Connor, *An Only Child*, *The Mirror in the Roadway*, *More Stories by Frank O'Connor*, *A Set of Variations*, and *My Father's Son*.

Capricorn Books, a division of Putnam's Coward, McCann & Geoghegan, *and* Cyrilly Abels Agency, % Joan Daves, for Frank O'Connor, *A Short History of Irish Literature*.

Templegate Press, Springfield, Illinois, for Frank O'Connor, *The Big Fellow*.

Thomas Y. Crowell for Frank O'Connor, *Shakespeare's Progress* and *The Lonely Voice*.

Fridberg Publishers, Dublin, Ireland, for Frank O'Connor, *The Art of the Theatre*.

Macmillian Co., and A. P. Watt & Son Ltd., London, England, for lines from Yeats's poems "A Municipal Gallery Revisited" and "The Man and the Echo," and the play *The Herne's Egg*.

Brendan Kennelly for lines from "Light Dying."

FRANK O'CONNOR
An Introduction

CORK

I know you by your bitter face,
I think you are the Sovereign Race,
And for the suffering on your brow,
Sovereign soul, to you I bow.

● ● ● ●

O Ireland, mother, Ireland, nurse
O heroes, but their nurse no more,
The wolves, the wolves are at thy door. . . .
The devil waste you with his curse!

—Frank O'Connor, "Unpublished Poem"

ONE

A Portrait of the Artist
as an Only Child

My parents were poor and I was an only child.
—Frank O'Connor, *Towards an
Appreciation of Literature*

When as kids we came to an orchard wall that seemed too high to climb, we took off our caps and tossed them over the wall, and then we had no choice but to follow them.

I had tossed my cap over the wall of life, and I knew I must follow it, wherever it had fallen.

—Frank O'Connor, *An Only Child*

Of all the species of writing, Samuel Johnson once remarked, none "seems more worthy of cultivation than biography, since none can be more delightful, or more useful, none can more certainly enchain the heart by irresistible interest, or more widely diffuse instruction to every diversity of condition." True of biography, this comment is truer of autobiography, for, Johnson added, "every man's life may best be written by himself." [1]

Truer of autobiography, it is truest of Frank O'Connor's two autobiographical works, *An Only Child* and the posthumous *My Father's Son*, which, because they are so delightful and useful, are most worthy of our attention. They are his portrait of the artist as an only child and as a young man. This young man, to whose portrait we are irresistibly drawn, laid claim to Cork as his dwelling place, Ireland as his nation, and heaven as his expectation.

If another one of the expectations of an artist is to be read, then

O'Connor has surely achieved some of his heaven. Already during his lifetime, many of his stories, collected in some ten volumes— *Guests of the Nation, Bones of Contention, Crab Apple Jelly, The Common Chord, Traveller's Samples, The Stories of Frank O'Connor, More Stories, Stories by Frank O'Connor, Domestic Relations,* and *A Set of Variations*—were widely anthologized. And today hardly a volume of collected stories tumbles off the presses, especially those used in undergraduate or graduate courses, without one or another of O'Connor's contributions gracing its pages. In addition, the few critical estimates of his place in contemporary Irish life and literature, appearing as long ago as 1934, have increased somewhat since his death in 1966, the most notable being *Michael/ Frank,* an excellent collection of studies edited by Dr. Maurice Sheehy, University College, Dublin. But it is not with endings that we are concerned here, only beginnings.

And it all began in Cork in 1903. Frank O'Connor was born Michael O'Donovan, the only child of Minnie and Michael O'Donovan. The mother, to whom a good deal of *An Only Child* is devoted, worked as a maid and was an excellent cook and first-rate housekeeper. She was clean, neat, and tidy, the "sort of woman who is always called in when there is trouble in a house." Though herself once an orphan, to whom little of the agony of an orphan child was unknown, she never lost her passion for gaiety and maintained always "a certain simplicity of mind that is characteristic of all noble natures" and "never really understood the hatred common natures entertain for refined ones." [2] Her faults were apparently few; the only two O'Connor recalls were that "she was vain and obstinate." Otherwise, her nature was that of a child, completely without self-consciousness. In short, she was, to her only son, the ideal, the unique, the only mother, the mother with the "thin, virginal face."

The father, on the other hand, was different, terribly different. Tall, fine-looking, he was, despite his love of music, a "brooding, melancholy man" who made his home his cave. Often drunk, he would borrow till he had exhausted his credit, and then, whining and maudlin, would force his wife to pawn her possessions and his clothes in order to satisfy his insatiable need for more drink. In fact, one of the son's saddest memories—an experience which so seared his childhood that he repeated it in both volumes—is the father, mad and uncontrollable because he was unable to get money from his wife, flinging both mother and child out into Blarney Lane in their night clothes. The son describes the nightmare:

. . . we shivered there in the roadway till some neighbors took us in and let us lie in blankets before the fire. Whenever he brandished the razor at mother, I went into hysterics, and a couple of times I threw myself on him with my fists. That drove her into hysterics, too, because she knew that at times like that he would as soon have slashed me as her. Later, in adolescence, I developed pseudoepileptic fits that were merely an externalization of this recurring nightmare.[3]

The father was "sour and savage," and never gay because he "had no integrity."

Consequently, early in his childhood, O'Connor was forced to make an exacting choice between his mother, whom he idolized, on the one hand, and his father's family, every member of whom he hated because of their "drunkenness, dirt, and violence." The families represented the "two powers that were struggling for the possession of his soul." [4] Between the two, the youngster could not but choose his mother's side and, as he unashamedly admits, became "the classic example of the mother's boy." Small wonder, therefore, that years later, when he had to be careful not to involve his employers in his literary activities and so assumed a pseudonym, he took his mother's maiden name and became, as writer, Frank O'Connor.

One Christmas—the "worst time of the year" for him—O'Connor's mother, after buying him a toy engine, took him to a nearby convent. There young O'Connor saw the Holy Child and, distressed that Santa Claus hadn't brought the Infant anything, he put the engine between its outstretched arms. And he tells why he did so: "Because somehow I knew even then exactly how that child felt— the utter despondency of realizing that he had been forgotten and that nobody had brought him anything, the longing for the dreary, dreadful holiday to pass till his father got to hell out of the house, and the postman returned again with the promise of better things." [5]

II

The postman's ring promising better things would come, O'Connor learned early, only with education. His hopeless situation could be alleviated by reading and study. He would get nowhere without an adequate education. And if such an education implied nice manners instead of coarse, he would, after contrasting the manners of his mother and father, read and study. So he began by using his pocket money to buy his favorite penny papers and boys' weeklies which, together with his vivid imagination, brought him closer to the established ideals of the public school code. In fact, he adopted this code on his own by refusing to tell lies or inform on other boys or yell when beaten.

And then, while O'Connor was enrolled at the local St. Luke's school whose headmaster Downey "combined the sanctimoniousness of a reformed pirate with the brutality of a half-witted drill sergeant," [6] there arrived one day an assistant with "a lame leg" who not only impressed the youngster deeply but also had a powerful and lasting effect on his life and thought. This man was Daniel Corkery. From him, O'Connor borrowed Irish books and a collection of Browning's poetry, and, of equal significance, he was inspired by him to become proficient in language and literature, especially the literature of Ireland's past. [7]

In order to further his intense knowledge of the country itself, Corkery suggested to O'Connor that he enroll in the Gaelic League Summer School in Dublin to be trained to teach Irish. Then he could roam the country as an instructor and learn all about Ireland. But these classes in the Irish language were less significant than the Irish songs he learned there. Suddenly O'Connor realized that the "Irish race had gone to hell since saga times, and this was what had enabled the English to do what they liked with us." [8] Like all the Irish people of the late nineteenth and early twentieth centuries, he was receiving "more of an education of the heart and not enough of the head or intellect." [9]

To be sure, formal schooling was never meant for O'Connor. His imagination was too vivid, his interests too varied, his loneliness too deep for him to be saddled with regular classes and structured lessons. Instead, he developed a fierce passion for people, and Corkery was "his first and greatest love." He worked for a while as a clerk and, after being sacked, turned to reading Goethe. He taught himself German, having already learned French on his own. His wide reading also included the nineteenth-century English, French, and Russian novel, resulting much later in his fine study of the genre of that period, *The Mirror in the Roadway*. Turgenev was his favorite author, and he managed to win a national competition once with his essay in Irish on that Russian master.[10]

Immersed in literature, O'Connor also read much Irish history and found much of it horrifying. He began listing the atrocities the British had committed against his homeland in the previous one hundred years. Though horrible, his list did not fire his revolutionary zeal. "It is only in the imagination," he claimed, "that the great tragedies take place, and I had only my imagination to live in." [11] The real and the imaginary worlds apparently were totally unrelated.

III

But the uprising of April 1916 and the Civil War some six years later changed all that for O'Connor. During that "patriotic frenzy," Corkery, O'Connor's authority for everything, warned him: "You must remember there are more important things in life than literature." [12] By which he meant, of course, that his pupil, in his initial gropings with words and meanings, should not exalt art above life but should rather equate art with experience and assume that the true artist is one who lives not less but more fully and intensely than others. Or, as O'Connor was to discern, if only vaguely at the beginning but more fully later, the "imaginative improvisation of the community had begun to dominate the imaginative improvisation of the artist and made its fires seem dim by comparison." [13]

And what, indeed, could be more significant than the community of Ireland which, after centuries of British misrule, would now gain its rightful independence? Or than the fact that, after the Anglo-Irish Treaty of December 1921, with the British gone, the Republic, first declared in 1916, would eventually re-emerge with peace in the land. But history is not often that kind. With the British gone, the nation was divided between the Free State Party and the Republicans. And men, previously united in quest of Freedom's grail, began to fight old comrades, even brothers.

In this fratricidal war, O'Connor chose the Republican side not only because of Corkery's stand but also because his mother favored it, "doing errands herself, carrying revolvers and dispatches." Of course, the young man's role was somewhat circumscribed. He tells us that "on the sole basis of an intimate acquaintance with Tolstoy's *Sebastopol*," [14] he was cast in the role of war correspondent.

So, carrying dispatches from Liam Deasy, the Republican divisional O.C. whose headquarters was in Buttevant, to Kilmallock, O'Connor and two companions were captured by the Free State troops. Thereafter, we learn the following:

Escorted as a prisoner to a nearby farmhouse where the National Army had set up a temporary post, O'Connor was soon dodging Republican bullets as his own friends besieged the farmhouse. His captors had been ready to leave on lorries when the Republicans appeared and had dashed back into the farmhouse, leaving the engines running. . . . The garrison wanted to surrender but their signal went unobserved, so O'Connor obtained permission to run to his friends waving a white handkerchief. An officer of the National Army opened the door for him and closed it after him. Surrender was accepted and O'Connor was put in charge of the prisoners who were taken back to Buttevant.[15]

Constantly on the move, he and Sean Hendrick, his close friend, were forever dismantling and reassembling their printing machine.[16] Paper was a problem, too, difficult to obtain and heavy to hump around the country. When Cork fell, they narrowly escaped death while riding in a lorry from there to Macroom.

All this baptism of fire, however, did not make of O'Connor an

apostle of revolution. Despite his experiences and Corkery's admonition, he still saw life, even in war, through a veil of literature.
Lacking his teacher's self-control and the unique ability to unite
self-control with humanity, austerity with sweetness, O'Connor
became tired of the war and wanted to go home. Unable to pay
the price such self-control demanded, he found the reading of
poetry and the nineteenth-century novel more suited to his temperament. In fact, when Erskine Childers, one of the most romantic figures of the period, was executed, he "wrote the date over
Whitman's lines on the death of Lincoln in the copy of *Leaves of
Grass* that he always carried with him at the time—'Hushed Be
The Camps Today.'" [17]

And it is surely not without significance that O'Connor also admits that he was carrying a copy of Dostoevsky's *The Idiot* in his
pocket when captured. He favored both these authors at the very
instant when he should have been actively concerned with bombs,
detonators, and explosives. Or, at the very least, reams of Republican propaganda. As he reflected on the "romanticism" of war, especially when one of the youngsters he was protecting in captivity
was senselessly shot, O'Connor began to think that all it really
amounted to was "a miserable attempt to burn a widow's house, the
rifle butts and bayonets of hysterical soldiers, a poor woman of the
lanes kneeling in some city church and appealing to a God who
could not listen, and then—a barrack wall with some smug humbug
of a priest muttering prayers." [18] Such reflections "changed something forever in him."

Not only was O'Connor disillusioned with war but also with the
worship of martyrdom so pervasive in Irish life and thought. A
martyr, he began to feel, was "merely trapped by his own ignorance
and simplicity into a position from which he couldn't escape."
What was needed was an affirmation not of death but of life.
Something should be said in favor of living. And life, as he began
to dream it in the midst of death, meant "to live, to read, to hear
music, and to bring my mother to all the places that neither of us
had ever seen, and I felt these things were more important than any
martyrdom." [19]

Small wonder, therefore, that at this very period he developed a significant interest in grammar and its importance in reading and writing. But grammar was more than rules, declensions, and conjugations; it was an image of human life. And if grammar was the "father" of language as usage was the "mother," then it must, like all fathers, forever return "to its thankless job of restoring authority." And for an emotional young man like O'Connor, "authority" was the operative word. Life, like language, demands order. Hence, politics and revolution, however noble their purpose, only obliterate authority and, obviously, disassociate the sensibilities of the literati. Or, as he himself confesses: "Maybe it was the grammar that started me off, or maybe the grammar itself was only a symptom of the emergence from a protracted adolescence, but I was beginning to have doubts about many of the political ideas I had held as gospel." [20]

Trying desperately to think things through, O'Connor came to the further conclusion that "mystical religion" was no less exasperating than "mystical nationalism." When he returned home from "captivity," his mother, with characteristic insight, remarked: "It made a man of you." What that meant became apparent soon enough. The Sunday after his return, he no longer wanted to go to Mass. She had discerned, in her motherly glimpse of him, that he had somehow "crossed another shadow line." He began, in fact, to wonder whether he should ever again be "completely at ease with the people [he] loved, their introverted religion and introverted patriotism." [21] What was certain was that he would never be the same again.

Hence, O'Connor also began to question Corkery's assertion at the outset of hostilities that "there are more important things in life than literature." Perhaps the contrary was true: that art exists above life, that the artist can make use of life only if he stands aloof, that by turning, finally, to story-telling, the artist might celebrate the immortal souls who cannot ever be diminished or destroyed. What he was seeking, in short, was freedom, a freedom to do not what one pleased but what one thought was right.

IV

What was immediately right, on being released from internment at twenty years of age, was to get a job. Learning from Corkery that Lennox Robinson, the dramatist, who was secretary of the Irish Carnegie United Kingdom Trust, was organizing rural libraries and looking for young men and women to train as librarians, O'Connor applied and was appointed to the librarianship at Sligo and, after six months there, to a similar post at Wicklow. To be a librarian was important to him because never before in his life had he had enough books to read. He seized the opportunity.

At Wicklow, his immediate superior was Geoffrey Phibbs, an Irish Protestant with an English education who gradually became O'Connor's "dearest" and best friend. The young librarian was completely taken by him, not only because of his "animal beauty and animal cruelty" and his intense love of English poetry, but also because he wrote poetry "without the pains and aches of composition." [22] As a result of this friendship, life for O'Connor changed for the better.

Despite his personal comfort, O'Connor began to recognize, in those early years of his librarianship, the restrictiveness of the life around him. The priests controlled almost all of Irish life and they would not allow the establishing of new libraries. They feared lest the fresh air of ideas ventilate the minds of men. The young librarian felt the first pangs of frustration.

And yet, O'Connor would not be deterred, despite George Russell's explicit warnings to the contrary, from moving on to, of all places, Cork. Like his father, he was a "one-city, one-house" man and his weakness for his birthplace outweighed the inevitable restrictiveness of that city. And it was not long before Russell was proved correct. O'Connor just couldn't "stand the damn place." For not only was he appalled by the pettiness and viciousness of the local Cork County Council, but, what is worse, he also began to discern that "Ireland was no longer the romantic Ireland of the little cottages and the hundred men, but an Ireland where everyone was searching for a pension and a job." The youthful dreams about his homeland were totally unlike the reality of his young manhood. He didn't enjoy Cork because it "was no longer the place he had known." [23] It was threatening to suffocate him.

But why, if so restricted and unhappy, did O'Connor not flee that place? Why did he dissipate his youthful energies in fruitless meetings with local councils when he could more profitably have been reading Turgenev and Tolstoy? Such questions did cross his mind. And with a refreshing candor that makes both his autobiographical works so unusual, O'Connor answers them: "Nothing could cure me of the notion that Cork needed me and that I needed Cork. Nothing but death can, I fear, ever cure me of it." [24]

Never really cured, O'Connor applied nevertheless for the municipal librarianship of Dublin and, with the aid of Russell, landed the job and left Cork. And yet, despite his advancement to the big city, he frankly admits that he remained a "provincial in Dublin." In his heart, he was always, apparently, the man from Cork.[25]

If never fully adjusted to the big city, O'Connor nevertheless profited greatly from meeting and knowing the notable figures of contemporary Irish literature who lived there. Among them were George Russell (AE), Osborn Bergin, Richard Hayes, Gogarty, Higgins, and, of course, Yeats. And the major interest of *My Father's Son* is the absorbing miniature portraits that O'Connor paints of these men and a host of other personalities.

O'Connor was fascinated by Russell. He considered AE a first-rate mind. Nevertheless, O'Connor couldn't understand why, as father of two quite attractive sons, Russell suffered from a "frustrated paternalism towards younger men." And O'Connor understood even less his being such a terrible creature of habit, "the sort of man who all his life will sit at the same table of the same restaurant to eat the same meal, and be ill at ease when waited on by a waitress he is not acquainted with." [26] Another puzzlement was that Russell, when repeating his poems—and he repeated them endlessly—"never changed a word or an intonation." Yet he possessed a virtue which alone made him the father of three generations of poets—a virtue O'Connor himself nurtured so well—the ability to devote any amount of time towards helping anyone in whom he detected even a small talent for writing. For, however bad a poet he may have been himself, "he was a poet, and he simply knew."

Aware of O'Connor's self-educated interest in Old Irish, Russell introduced him to Osborn Bergin, the greatest of Irish scholars, who "knew more Celtic than anyone in the world." O'Connor was awed by this brilliant man, finding him to be at the same time fiercely emotional and possessive and consumed with obscure hatreds for such as George Moore, Yeats, and Joseph O'Neill, another "good Celtic scholar." What he and AE had in common, O'Connor reveals, was that "both were European figures who in their hearts never ceased to be anything but small town boys." [27]

Of the "big time" boys, of course, none loomed larger than Yeats. As a friend, he could give "admiration, tolerance, and absolute loyalty" but never, alas, pity, for he was "as pitiless with others as he was with himself." O'Connor became his "devoted slave" not just because Yeats had memorized all his poems but because Yeats was "generous and utterly loyal." A shy and rather lonely man who "desperately wanted to be friends," [28] Yeats hardly ever spoke with malice about anyone except those—George Moore and Padraic Colum are notable examples—who he thought had injured either Lady Gregory or Synge.

Of Yeats's principal weakness, O'Connor found two that were outstanding. First, he was easily bored and made no effort to conceal it. And that "cost him the affection of people who would have been better friends than some of those he made." [29] Among those he made were Higgins and Gogarty, whom O'Connor considered malicious gossips prone to betray the most intimate confidences. They succeeded, however, in holding Yeats's attention because, as O'Connor generously points out, they "broke through the barriers he could not help erecting about himself."

Second, because Yeats was a "natural organizer, never happy unless he was organizing something or somebody," he tended to be a "bully." So when he organized his Academy of Letters in 1932 to encourage, in part, young poets to publish without benefit of priestly censorship, he included Russell, Higgins, Robinson, O'Sullivan,

Gogarty, and O'Connor, and, true to character, tried to "bully" the last only to find, to his surprise, that O'Connor gave him "the lip, almost on principle." [30]

In fact, when O'Connor was also elected to serve on the Governing Board of the Abbey Theatre, he had a row with Yeats that amounted to a showdown. They differed, principally, as regards the style of acting the players should adopt. Yeats believed in the "Abbey tradition," or a continuation of the Senecan style of acting "in which words were important, nobody spoke while moving and nobody moved while someone else was speaking for fear of distracting attention from the words." After all, for Yeats a play was "two chairs and a passion." This theory, of course, stood in contradistinction to the later English naturalistic convention "in which beautiful speeches are chopped up and fitted into bits of stage business." O'Connor, like Hunt, who was brought in to revive a theater fallen into desuetude because of Lennox Robinson, a despondent and ineffectual, though personally brilliant, director, wanted an all Irish theater in the later tradition. Hence, when Yeats criticized Hunt's production of *The Playboy of the Western World* without having even seen it, O'Connor "stepped hard on his toes," accusing him of spreading "green room gossip." As O'Connor puts it: "No one but myself would stand up to him in one of his bullying moods." [31] But though Yeats never forgot a rebuke, they remained fast friends until he died.

After Yeats died, O'Connor resigned from the Board, deeply regretting his having to leave the theater. He could not, he felt, stay on to fight the current members who, removed from the ideals of the founders, would no longer, after Yeats's death, be bound to defend themselves. For genius is often, O'Connor notes with remarkable insight, "a light by which we occasionally see ourselves and so refrain from some commonness of thought or action that time allows." With the "light" extinguished forever, there was too much commonness for O'Connor to contend with. Furthermore, he had to leave because "It takes a large heart to hold even a small country and since Yeats's death there has been no other that could hold us with all our follies and heroism." [32]

V

What held O'Connor together, in addition to his friends and the lonely curate Tim Traynor, was ultimately, his mother and father. To be sure, he never made peace with the latter. If he titled his second autobiographical volume *My Father's Son*, it is apparent that he did not mean it as a reconciliation. All it does mean is that, having risen in the world of arts and letters, having received the approbation of his peers, and having acquired the financial security that comes with such recognition, the son had not turned into the liability the father had prophesied. O'Connor's hope, expressed early in his career, that "somehow, somewhere [he] would be able to prove that [he] was neither mad nor a good-for-nothing" was fulfilled.

What O'Connor also fulfilled was the hope, nurtured as an only child, that he would someday take his mother on holiday. During her convalescence after a fall, he took her to Switzerland and Italy. And it is not without justifiable pride that he tells us what he felt about that grand tour:

It was like the fulfillment of a prophecy, the accidental keeping of promises made to her as a small boy, when she came in exhausted by a hard day's work and I airily described to her—all out of a guidebook and a couple of phrase-books—the wonderful journeys we should make when I was older and had come into my own. And the enchantment was only sharpened by the feeling of quiet we both had when we worried about my foolish father staggering home to Harrington Square when the public-houses shut.[33]

To the very end, apparently, he was "mother's boy."

Having accomplished all that, O'Connor faced one final decision. It came, interestingly enough, after a discussion with his publisher, Harold Macmillan, who, aware that O'Connor was trying to be a librarian, run a theater, and write, all at the same time, said to him: "You've reached the stage where you must decide whether you're going to be a good writer or a good public servant. You can't be both."[34] It was manifestly true in O'Connor's case and he knew it.

All Macmillan did was to give him a push in the direction he had already decided to take. What Corkery had once claimed, that there was more to life than literature, might apply to those like Yeats, who because of their genius might engage actively in both. It didn't, O'Connor was convinced, apply to him. He best describes his dilemma and ultimate decision:

It was in war-time England sometime later that I came to realize the full significance for me of Yeats's death and my resignation from the Abbey. I was staying with Leonard and Sylvia Strong and had a dream one night which a psychiatrist friend of theirs sought to interpret for me. Suddenly I knew perfectly well what the dream meant and that it was a warning never again to allow the man of action in me to get on top. There was more wisdom in Harold Macmillan's advice than I had thought. Before Yeats died he told me that the time had come to decide whether I wanted to be a good writer or a good public official, and I had resigned my job as librarian. Now I saw that the man of action was still on top; with nothing like Yeats's talent I had been playing Yeats's game. At once I resigned from every organization I belonged to and sat down, at last, to write.[35]

And what O'Connor wrote, from his first published volume of stories, *Guests of the Nation,* to the last story, "The Mass Island" in the posthumous collection *A Set of Variations*—including, of course, the autobiographical *An Only Child* and *My Father's Son*—certainly enchains the heart by irresistible interest and useful delight.

TWO

Patriotic Frenzy

A patriot frenzy enduring too long
  Can hang like a stone on the heart of man
And I have made Ireland too much of my song;
  I will now bid those foolish old dreams to begone.
                                        —Frank O'Connor, *My Father's Son*
. . . They're restless, and at last they burst out in some crazy bloody
racket like the Civil War. Anything to let off steam!
              —Frank O'Connor, "What's Wrong With the Country?"

What is, of course, irresistibly interesting in O'Connor's work is the imaginative writing that resulted from his irrevocable decision "never again to allow the man of action in [him] to get on top." And yet, as with many of his contemporaries, it was precisely out of his experience as a "man of action," during the most fateful period of his country's modern history, that he fashioned his early writings about man at war.

It could not be otherwise. For, as Eavan Boland reminds us, "history cannot be generous in supplying the meaning of an individual until it has supplied the meaning of a nation." [1] And because O'Connor was an abiding student of Irish history, it follows that we must necessarily review, however briefly, some of that history, which, inevitably, shaped his thought and gave so much meaning to him as an individual and as an artist.

Ireland, oppressed for centuries of English misrule, was the first among nations to launch one of the most successful revolutions in the twentieth century. It was led by a group of individuals faithful to the ancient Cuchulainn tradition of heroic forms of patriotism, which was revived in modern times in Wolfe Tone at the end of the eighteenth century and extended through the Irish Republican Brotherhood of the mid-nineteenth century to the Sinn Fein movement of the early twentieth century. They openly defied the superior English forces, offering their blood sacrifice for Ireland's sake. For it was clearly evident to these individuals and their followers that, in order to give meaning to their nation, there could be "no peace between the body politic and a foreign substance that has intruded itself into its system; between them war only until the foreign substance is expelled or assimilated." [2]

Assimilation was, naturally, impossible. Only war, the militant nationalists believed, would effect the separation, more or less complete, of Ireland from Great Britain. In the very midst of World War I, therefore, these separatists resolved that Ireland assert itself in arms; and in making their resolve "they were moved less by any calculation of the prospects of success than by a feeling that, if such an opportunity were allowed to pass, the reality of Irish national aspirations might be called in question." [3] With only some 1200 troops in Dublin, the seat of oppression, these few planners of the insurrection, recognizing in advance the impossibility of their task during Easter week, 1916, challenged the larger, better-equipped, better-organized British army. After a week of deliberate self-sacrifice, the insurgents succeeded in reading from the steps of the Central Post Office their famous Proclamation. They proclaimed, among other things, "the right of the people of Ireland to the ownership of Ireland, and to the unfettered control of Irish destinies, to be sovereign and indefeasible." [4] But, despite the invocation to their Most High God for His blessing on their arms, they were crushed, with little success and even less sovereignty to show for their dubious battle. Ireland's meaning seemed meaningless.

Yet, historically, it was quite the contrary; their effort was terribly meaningful. For the British committed the mistake of executing fifteen of the insurgent leaders, including all the signatories of the Proclamation—Thomas J. Clarke, Sean MacDiarmada, P. H. Pearse, James Connolly, Thomas MacDonagh, Eamonn Ceannt, and Joseph Plunkett. As a result, public opinion, generally hostile to the revolutionaries, was horrified by this action of the government. The people's "horror turned to anger against the government and admiration for the insurgents." As Shaw warned at the time, the British were "canonizing the prisoners." For Ireland was "quickly passing under the most dangerous of all tyrannies—the tyranny of the dead." [5]

Among the "canonized" was, of course, Padraic Pearse, poet and schoolmaster. His canonization resulted not only from the fact that it was he, as leader of the Rising, who read the Proclamation from the steps of the Central Post Office, but also because he, like Yeats and the other literary revivalists of his time, "personified Ireland as Dark Rosaleen, or Deirdre of the Sorrows or Cathleen Ni Houlihan—a poor old woman who would become a Queen once more only when men became gallant as the knight of Gaelic Ireland and thought her worth dying for." [6] Pearse was able, apparently, to merge the "meaning" of his nation with the "meaning" of self, a prototype for future Irish leadership in art and politics. Or, as he once declared in one of his poems: "I am Ireland . . . I that bore Cuchulainn the valiant. . . ."

Small wonder, therefore, that, as Desmond Ryan tells us, Pearse would always remind his students at St. Edna's, the school for boys he founded in 1908, of the motto emblazoned round a fresco in the school: "I care not if my life have only the span of a night and day if my deeds be spoken of by the men of Ireland." [7] And deeds for Pearse, because his, like every other, Irish mind was influenced to the point of obsession by the deeds and passions of the past, meant immediate sacrifice. Cuchulainn inspired him to exclaim to all the Irish citizens of his day and, perhaps, all days: "We must accustom ourselves to the thought of arms, to the sight of arms, to the rise of arms. We may make mistakes in the beginning and shoot the wrong people; but bloodshed is a cleansing and sanctifying thing, and the nation which regards it as the final horror has lost its manhood. There are many things more horrible than bloodshed; and slavery is one of them." [8] What Pearse apparently forgot, however, was that war, like poetry, has its metered cadences, and to enter battle without adequate planning and strategy, as actually happened, may "cleanse" and "sanctify" but rarely, if ever, achieves victory.

Nevertheless, Pearse and his dead succeeded in "tyrannizing" the living to carry on in their, and Cuchulainn's, spirit. The valiant must never submit to an oppressor even in a peace effort. Hence, the British, relying chiefly on the wily Lloyd George to enter negotiations toward a settlement of the "Irish Question," again met with stiff opposition. Negotiations dragged on for almost two years, from 1916 to 1918, but, in the end, achieved no results. These negotiations "had about them, at least in retrospect, an air of unreality; for the surviving leaders of the revolutionary movement took no part, and it was they, rather than Redmond, leader of the Irish Parliamentary Party, who now represented the dominant force in Irish politics." [9] History again proved that the vanquished, when valiant, became victors.

Victory, however, was not yet in sight. Different plans and a better strategy needed to be developed if their martyrs' blood was ever to be redeemed. Hence, during the period of these fruitless negotiations, the Irish Republican Brotherhood was making plans, in early 1917, to reconstitute the Volunteers, while Sinn Fein emerged as the political wing of the revolutionary movement. Furthermore, at a national conference held in Dublin in October of that year, Arthur Griffith stepped down from the leadership of Sinn Fein in favor of the new, untried de Valera, who, a month later, was also elected president of the Irish Volunteers. Thereby, the political and military wings of the revolutionary movement were brought under the control of one man. The main source of de Valera's strength, it would appear, lay in "a firm tenacity of purpose, combined with a flexibility of method; his weakness, in an unwillingness to work with those who would not subordinate their own views to his." [10]

The other leader to emerge from this conference was Michael Collins, who was to prove, eventually, that he would not subordinate his own views to anyone. Unlike his counterpart, Collins was usually "at boiling point and burst out in earthquakes, thunderstorms, and showers." [11] Nevertheless, he was efficient and straightforward, and most always the supreme realist. And, as a realist, it didn't take him long to realize what it was that reduced the Easter Rising, despite all its valor, to "a wistful tragi-comedy." He said so in no uncertain terms:

They have died nobly at the hands of the firing squads. So much I grant. But I do not think the Rising week was an appropriate time for the issue of memoranda couched in poetic phrases, nor of actions worked out in a similar fashion. Looking at it from the inside (I was in the G.P.O.) it had the air of a Greek tragedy about it, the illusion being more or less completed with the issue of the before mentioned memoranda. Of Pearse and Connolly I admire the latter the most. Connolly was a realist, Pearse the direct opposite. There was an air of earthy directness about Connolly. It impressed me. I would have followed him through hell had such action been necessary. But I honestly doubt very much if I would have followed Pearse—not without some thought anyway.[12]

Henceforth, it would be a different war: guerrilla tactics would replace direct action. The Irish Volunteers, reconstituted early in 1919 as the Irish Republican Army, would not engage in open assault but operated "in flying columns, fifteen to thirty strong, conducting a war of raids and ambushes." A new kind of war was declared on England, a war called "The Troubles."

If Pearse is the hero of the "Rising," Collins is the hero of the "Troubles." And if imagination had been far beyond reality in the "Rising," reality caught up with a vengeance in the "Troubles." For Collins' program was "as simple as it was unpoetic; to bring about a general state of disorder." Unable to cope with this "invisible" army which, through the cleverness of Collins, would strike the British from all directions and, often, when least expected, Lloyd George and his government thought they would subdue the Irish by shipping over the "Black and Tans," a force "to inspire terror in a population less timid and law abiding than the Irish." [13] They robbed and killed and blackguarded wholesale. But to no avail. They failed in their attempt to destroy the Irish will to survive, and what was most humiliating to them was their inability, despite repeated efforts, to capture Collins, dead or alive. And all because, fearless, he would walk among them undetected.

Besides, during the "Troubles," "fact replaced myth, and realism, idealism, and the Irish Republican Army did things the noble and stoical Fenian John O'Leary had said one must not do to save a nation." But, as Yeats once lamented, romantic Ireland was with

O'Leary in the grave. And into that grave also went, eventually, the old English rule and its oppression.

II

Before final burial, however, the British, reluctant as always, like most other global powers, to recognize other people's sovereign aspirations, agreed, after many assassinations and wanton bloodshed, to implement, at least partially, the Home Rule Bill. A delegation headed by Arthur Griffith, Michael Collins, Erskine Childers, Eamonn Duggan, Robert Barton, Gavan Duffy, and five others went to England to negotiate with Lloyd George, Austin Chamberlain, and Winston Churchill. Under political duress, the Irish delegation signed the agreements on December 6, 1921. Among the stipulations contained in that agreement there was one, at least, which, were it not for the pressures of the moment, would never have been agreed to—the partition of Ireland into two states: "Northern Ireland," consisting of the six Ulster counties whose exclusion from home rule had been proposed in 1916, and "Southern Ireland," consisting of the remaining twenty-six counties.

Upon the return of the delegation from England, not only the country but the people were divided in bitter controversy as a result of this treaty. Besides, Childers, because of his abiding hatred of Imperialist England, and Brugha, Minister of Defense, and Stack, Minister of Home Affairs, because of their personal animus towards Collins, all influenced de Valera to oppose the Treaty signed by their own plenipotentiaries. Their main objections were, ostensibly, that

> . . . it was a betrayal of the 1916 Declaration of an Irish Republic and all it stood for, in so far as it accepted the partition of Ireland, permitted the presence of British naval bases on Irish soil, a governor general in Dublin representing the Crown, and, above all—the telling symbol— introduced an oath of allegiance to the Crown to be subscribed to by every member of the Dail. More generally, it was felt, in the words of one of the most active leaders of the Republican Resistance, Liam Mellows, that only the commercial interests and the merchants were on the side of the Treaty. We are back to Wolfe Tone, and it is just as well, relying on the men of no property.[14]

The whole thing, it seemed to these men, was a "betrayal of political dreams, primordial values, and the centuries old struggle of the dispossessed poor against the exploiting Empire." [15]

Responding with all the force at the command of his explosive personality, Collins defended his position and that of his colleagues. He argued, first, that the element of duress was present; not so much the personal one at the signing as "when we agreed to the truce, because our simple right would have been to beat the English out of Ireland. There was an element of duress in going to London to negotiate." [16] In other words, it was the acceptance of the invitation which forced the compromise.

Second, the fact that the British refused to allow the declaration of an Irish Republic but insisted, instead, on the term *Irish Free State* did not disturb Collins greatly. Admitting that the term "Republic" was only a symbol, a resistance device, he argued, further, that the

Irish struggle has always been for freedom—freedom from English occupation, from English interference, from English domination—not for freedom with any particular label attached to it. . . . When I supported the approval of the Treaty at the meeting of Dail Eireann, I said it gave us freedom—not the ultimate freedom which all nations hope for and struggle for, but freedom to achieve that end. . . . With the evacuation secured by the Treaty has come an end of British rule in Ireland. . . . We shall have complete freedom for all our purposes.[17]

Collins' speech was effective. The heated debate, "marked by vituperation and spite rather than logic and detachment," ended with a final vote of 64-57 in favor of the Treaty. And in the ensuing election to determine "whether the Treaty was acceptable to the people of Ireland," the pro-Treaty panel candidates won 58 of 128 seats, while the de Valera opposition won only 35, with the remaining seats divided among Labor, Farmers, and four members of Dublin University.[18] What the vote really meant was the matter of peace or war.

Given the intensity of the emotions on both sides, it meant war. A war, O'Connor once remarked, "that was really anticipated by anyone with sense because it was merely an extension into the fourth dimension of the improvisation that had begun after the crushing of the insurrection in 1916." [19] Revolution, apparently, breeds Civil War. And the saddest part of it all was that men who had once stood so valiantly together now tried to rip each other apart. The Nationalist movement had split up into the Free State Party, which accepted the Treaty, and the Republicans, who opposed it by force of arms. What is so terribly ironic is that neither side really wanted to fight. Calton Younger confirms the fact that, despite the ten thousand Republicans captured by the government forces and the seventy-seven executed, the war was, to use O'Connor's artful phrase, "a patriotic frenzy." Indeed, only a hair's breadth of principle divided the opposing sides:

. . . there was among many Republicans a lack, not of conviction or courage, but of heart in the fight. They wanted to make their protest as urgently as they could and to keep on making it: they wanted to stop the Provisional Government from working the Treaty and building up an administration. They did not want to take life if they could avoid it, and neither did most of the Provisional Government's troops, and so flights of bullets hurtled through the air as migrating birds. The air above Ireland was criss-crossed with easy bullets with no particular object in view.[20]

These "easy bullets" flew from June 28, 1922, to April 30, 1923. Then, with the civil war ending at last, seven long years of external and internal struggle beginning with the Easter Rising in 1916 came to a close. The "migrating birds" rested. And they even began to sing again of the meaning of an Irish nation that could only achieve "peace by ordeal."

However, let us recall that while the bullets were still flying, O'Connor was one of those thousands of prisoners captured by the governmental forces. And he realized soon enough that he never really was, nor was he ever meant to be, a soldier. In fact, he is quite candid about that part of his life. For, when questioned years after the conflict, during the *"Paris Review* Interview," about his life in the Irish Republican Army, he responded frankly:

My soldiering was like my efforts at being a musician; it was an imitation of the behavior of soldiers rather than soldiering. I was completely incapable of remembering anything for ten minutes. And I always got alarmed the moment people started shooting at me, so I was a wretchedly *bad soldier, but that doesn't prevent you from picking up the atmosphere of the period. I really got into it when I was about fifteen as a sort of Boy Scout, doing odd jobs for the I.R.A., and then continued on with it until I was captured and interned for a year. Nearly all the writers went with the extreme Republican group. People like O'Faolain, myself, Francis Stuart, Peadar O'Donnell, all the young writers went Republican. Why we did it, the Lord knows, except that young writers are never capable of getting the facts of anything correctly.*[21]

Not only was he incapable of getting the facts of soldiering straight, but once, when accidentally finding himself wearing "a dead boy's blood-stained cap," his attitude toward the entire Civil War and its aftermath became one of loathing and revulsion.

Reflecting further on that bizarre war with its "romantic idealism" and "Cuchulainn valor," he reduced his entire experience—his and that of his countrymen—to one painful conclusion: that this was a war between hysterical soldiers, committing atrocities unworthy of all men, let alone Irish men, and all because they were in a disgusting state of "patriotic frenzy." As a result, "something changed forever" in O'Connor. This change was the consequence of his decision to be done with soldiering forever; now that history had given nothing to his country, he would see how history would shape his "meaning as individual."

As an individual, O'Connor, rejecting war, did not, however, reject its history. His involvement in it, however minor, affected him artistically. Those seven years, the "Embers of Easter," inspired O'Connor, like so many other Irishmen, in his classic art of storytelling. "The individual alone in his study, or even transported in his vision, is not out of history, for history is the imagery of his vision as language is the expression of his thought." [22] Yeats, late in life, pondered:

> All that I have said and done
> Now that I am old and ill
> Turns into a question till
> I lie awake night after night,
> And never get the answers right.
> Did that play of mine send out
> Certain men the English shot.[23]

For O'Connor the obvious answer to the poet's musing was a re-
sounding "Yes." That play of his *Cathleen ni Houlihan* did send
out certain men to be shot, but the circumstances of history had, of
course, "placed them in a frame of mind to be sent out, and these
are the things that had placed Yeats in a frame of mind to write
the play." [24]

Similarly, these are the things that placed O'Connor in a frame
of mind to write his early stories about the war. For what impressed
him later about the revolution was, in his own words, "its imaginative quality—its improvisation, gaiety and make-believe." He obviously gained more than the "atmosphere of the period"; he gained
his imaginative powers. For O'Connor tells us that "a revolution
had begun in Ireland, but it was nothing to the revolution that had
begun in me. It is only in the *imagination* that the great tragedies take place, and I had only my imagination to live in." [25] Apparently the thousand or so farmers and clerks, ill-armed but re-
sourceful, who set themselves up against an Empire, and, thereafter,
set themselves up against each other, not only gave meaning to
Ireland as a nation, but also gave meaning to the imaginative individuals who relived their country's tragedy and triumph in their
art.

III

Out of O'Connor's imagination, where so much Irish history
lived, came a series of short stories about the war, collected mostly
in *Guests of the Nation,* and *The Big Fellow,* a biography of
Michael Collins, the "powerhouse of the revolution." One readily
understands the reason for the stories, but, the reader may rightfully
ask, why Collins? After all, hadn't O'Connor served with the opposition, or the "irregulars" as they are called, or the Republican
side, and not under Collins, the leader of the Free State or government troops, the "regulars"?

O'Connor, himself troubled by this question, provides some of
the answers. In the "Foreword," he tells us that this biography was
"a labor of love." As the fever of the Civil War died down, he became more and more attracted to Collins as a character. What

O'Connor set out to achieve, therefore, was not a fully documented story of this hero, but rather "a sense of the man behind the documentation." This is not a full portrait but, in O'Connor's apt word, a "snapshot," a "snapshot" of a "living man."

Second, O'Connor wished to take on a role which, eventually, he was actually to assume, often, during his visits to America and in his native country, namely, that of a teacher. A whole new generation of Irishmen was growing up to whom people like Collins were becoming "inhuman shadows," heroes who, in their illustrious pantheon, never seem to have made the mistakes of mortals. To that generation, men like Collins were, indeed, becoming "boring immortals." O'Connor, the teacher, felt he had to rectify that situation. He would write a work which would present such mortals as far from boring, but, who, like the younger generation, "took a drink, swore and lost [their] temper." In other words, Collins was, like them, a vibrant Irishman, and, therefore, worthy of study.

And, third, as an ardent student of Irish history, O'Connor could not but observe that among the three major episodes in the Civil War—"the death of Michael Collins, the excesses of National Army soldiers at Kerry, and the executions" [20]—the first would, for historical, pedagogical, inspirational, and personal reasons, seem most natural to demand his writing attention. In death, Collins achieved apotheosis, for his charismatic personality and forceful deeds remain a living legend to this very day. Besides, O'Connor knew all the history firsthand, something obviously of great importance to a biographer. He had personally experienced that awesome period in Irish history. Moreover, he waited some fifteen years after Collins' death before publishing the biography, which should have given him the necessary "distance" with which to view his subject objectively. Above all, O'Connor did not rely on memory alone. He read all the accumulated documentation then extant and readily acknowledged these sources in his "Foreword."

And yet, despite his having assimilated all of this material—the *Naturwissenschaft* element in the study of history—O'Connor was not primarily interested in a "scientific" approach to his subject. In point of fact, Rex Taylor and Margery Forester in their biographies of Collins, for example, are more convincing than O'Connor ever was, by their accumulation of the "externals of fact." In contradistinction, O'Connor was more concerned with "the projection, the dramatization of that life in words." O'Connor would surely agree that his biography "is not *about* a man's life; it is the simulation of that life in words." In other words, O'Connor developed a simulated life relationship with his subject. He had, obviously, a deep feeling for this giant who strode all too swiftly over the Irish landscape. Not only has O'Connor given us an appealing biography, but he has also established a life-giving "symbiotic relationship" with his subject, achieving, thereby, "an indefinable but unmistakable kinship with his man." For the inner spirit, the true genius of history, A. L. Rowse reminds us, is not in the "intellectual aids" which are external but in "the spirit of man, the flame of life itself. The appropriate rendering of that can only be given by art." [27] And what we learn, therefore, from O'Connor's "kinship" with his man tells us, artfully, as much about the biographer as his subject, as much about O'Connor as about Collins.

That man was called "The Big Fellow," a sobriquet given him by his companions when they wished to sum up "the extremist side of him they most disliked in one scornful phrase. . . . 'Collins thinks he's a big fellow,' they repeated. Henceforth, he was the Big Fellow, and the story of his brief life is the story of how he turned the scornful nickname into one of awe and affection." [28] The task O'Connor set for himself was to trace the major elements that accomplished that change. "Big," to O'Connor, meant not the pejorative "bigshot" we associate with "bigness," but, as we shall see, the "big" we link in praise with "greatness."

What indeed, according to O'Connor, made Collins great? One cannot escape the feeling, on reading this biography, that "greatness" consisted primarily in "violent contraries," or, those polarities in the human personality which, though difficult to comprehend and, at times, even more difficult to tolerate, prove most fascinating. It was precisely that "dichotomy" of his personality which made Collins so truly interesting: "Just as this big, blustering violent nature transmutes itself in the feminine precision and delicacy of his relationship with people who are poor or in trouble, so does the man whom Churchill saw as if straight from a backwoods camp turn his violent emotionalism into labor so exact and detailed that it seems to have been performed under a mental microscope." [29] It was Collins' ability to hold within himself these and other "contraries" that ultimately made him attractive to O'Connor and made him an undying hero worthy of the adulation of future generations of Irishmen.

And what are some of the other "contraries" that frame the essence of O'Connor's biography? What the ambivalences? What the polarities? A careful reading of *The Big Fellow* will reveal that over all others O'Connor stresses three major "ambivalences." First, Collins was a vital, fiery, tempestuous person, impatient of all restraint, even that imposed from within, exploding in jerky gestures, oaths, and jests while being, simultaneously, "the most warm-hearted of men with what for such a healthy animal can only be described as an extraordinary refinement of emotion, and even a hint of poverty, loneliness, illness or old age was sufficient to bring tears to his eyes . . ." [30]

Second, though Collins had often resorted to "bullying" people and was terribly impatient with anyone below his rank who displayed inefficiency in the execution of his duties, whereupon he would immediately display his bad temper, yet, on the other hand, "no one could attract or hold devotions as he could." "He took the simplest men, men whom no one in the world had ever attached importance to, and made them feel that the smallest task they performed was a matter of life and death. Before him, after him, none could give the same sense of responsibility, and their devotion to him was no greater than his to them. Passionate, vibrating, that tenderness of his runs through the whole story of his brief life, and each time one discovers it with a queer thrill." [31] O'Connor observes that even Brugha, his bitterest enemy, was forced to admit that "Mick is so kind, he thinks of everybody." Small wonder, therefore, that when, as participant in the Easter Rebellion, he noticed that ordinary resources had failed, "he contrived to help some of the down and outs of the Rising out of his own miserable salary."

Third, what O'Connor found even more remarkable was the conflict in Collins between the cold realist forever involved in the minute details of finance, army logistics, and the intricacies of spying—whose genius was one of detail, insisting on supervising every little matter, on keeping in his files "receipts for the lodging of political refugees side by side with those for sweeping brushes and floor polish" *and* the romantic idealist who was "filled with a sense of idealism which embraced all the forms of life, music, literature and art," [32] who would spend evenings, while the British were making him the prime target of their massive searches and raids, enjoying himself at the Abbey Theatre where art imitated life.

How fascinatingly this rapid change in character appealed to O'Connor! Consider, for example, how this romantic idealist, this committed revolutionary, ready to further his cause or protect the lives of his friends by calculated assassination, reversed his role when peace talks began with England on October 11, 1921, to become the realist again, "a political leader and man of peace, ready to strike a bargain with the shrewd dealers of the international market place." [33] And one of the bargains he struck with the British, normally unthinkable to any romantic idealist, was the agreement to accept some allegiance to the crown because, O'Connor tells us, he "did not give a button for the symbols over which de Valera worried." For the realist in him felt certain that given control of men, army, money, and arms, he "could have all the symbols he needed." [34]

And yet, this very same practical driver of hard bargains saw that the ultimate "path to freedom" lay not so much in the bargains gained at the counters of political expediency but, rather, in the need "to restore our native tongue, to get back our history, to take up again and complete the education of our countrymen . . . to renew our strength and refresh ourselves in our own civilization to become again the Irish men and the Irish women of the distinctive Irish nation." [35] Such sentiments, the sincere statements of a romantic idealist, further prompted Collins to quote Thomas Davis, an earlier revolutionary zealot, who argued that "a nationality founded in the hearts and intelligence of the people would bid defiance to the foe and guile of the traitor." [36] And these people, in turn, would inspire the poets and artists of "the future Gaelic Ireland."

Fourth, O'Connor stresses that in the life of Collins we must take note of yet another polarity. While he enjoyed being boisterous, gregarious, pugnacious, and argumentative, and engaged in many a wrestling match with his companions, Collins was also, at the same time, reflective, thoughtful, and, what to O'Connor is so highly significant in his own life and fiction, terribly lonely. "Till his death," O'Connor notes sadly, "he was to have no home; he who adored children would never play with his own children at his fireside; the romance which his ardent temperament cried out for was denied him." [37]

But what may have been for O'Connor the saddest aspect of Collins' life was the vast difference between himself and the people he was struggling to free. It slowly dawned on him that not everyone he worked with, or for, shared his idealism, his purpose, his total sense of dedication to the goal he was aiming to achieve. And O'Connor takes pains to point this out, at least twice, in this biography. There were men under Collins, unfortunately, to whom petty gains were far more significant than the creation of a "Gaelic Ireland." And Collins, who showed great sensitivity to the needs of his people, who risked his life countless times to serve them, who, if any of his men were killed, would immediately attempt to retaliate in kind, who appreciated greatly the courage of his men, found, nevertheless, that they were, to use O'Connor's metaphor, "Lilliputians":

Collins, with his elasticity and brilliance, often forgot that these whom he looked on as heroes were sometimes vain, simple, uneducated men. They did not understand the demands he was making on them. He was asking them to rise above Lilliput; they were concerned with petty jealousies, with rank and precedence. Even within the new army, which was (more or less) loyal, there were endless squabbles. When yet another officer appeared at Beggar's Bush with the insignia of a general, Mulcahy protested to Collins. 'Ah, for God's sake,' growled Collins good humoredly, 'let the bloody baby have his stripes.' [38]

What Collins failed to recognize—and this, apparently, is a failing in all good men like himself—was that he was really dealing with an Ireland of shopkeepers, priests, solicitors, hired hands, who were more involved with their own parochial vanities and affectations than with the establishment of a great nation. After all, hadn't they "black-guarded Synge, scoffed at books, let Larkin down" and, to use O'Connor's searing comment, "believed it was all settled in the Penny Catechism"?

And those few, like Collins, who had freed themselves from the restraints of the "Penny Catechism" find, ultimately, that they are, at all times, alone, with shadows falling across their path. Such men often seem to have a premonition that their lives, because they are so overcome with idealism, may be cut short before their last mile. In fact, Collins had such fears that, toward the end of the Civil War, he once remarked, gravely, to his friend Cosgrave, "Do you think I shall live through this? Not likely!" [39] He didn't.

While on an inspection tour of his forces at Beal na mBlath, near Cork, his birthplace, on August 21, 1922, his convoy was ambushed and he was shot dead. Some years later, de Valera was accused of having conspired in Collins' death. And even if we were to accept de Valera's denial, it is still possible that, because he actually was in that area at the time and never did utter a word of condemnation of the terrorist act, de Valera might "well have known that Collins was in danger of his life." [40] Whatever the case may be, there was nothing more, apparently, that Collins could have done for Irish freedom but to die for it.

But of one thing O'Connor is certain: "the greatest oak in the forest had crashed." The historical process, however, goes on. Other, if smaller, men took his place. These men were able, in time, to enthrone life, which is, ultimately, the goal of every historical process. What marked Collins' death is not only, as O'Connor cogently comments, the fall of a genius, but the "tragedy of men who must go through life marked indelibly by their contact with magnificence. Collins had spoiled them for lesser men. . . . Collins's death left normality enthroned." [41]

One of the "marked" men Collins left behind offered a final tribute which seemed to imply that the manner and matter of his death were not without some personal value, other than helping in the creation of a modern Irish Republic or the achieving of that legendary status which made him the subject of many biographies and studies. Another genius, G. B. Shaw, had dined with Collins some three days before the ambush, and, hearing of his valiant death, wrote a brief letter of consolation to Johanna, Collins' sister. The genius in Shaw recognized what had, for some time, troubled the genius in Collins: the fear, in working with Lilliputians, of future disappointments: "So tear up your mourning and hang up your brightest colors in his honor; and let us all praise God that he had not to die in a snuffy bed of a trumpery cough, weakened by age, and saddened by the disappointments that would have attended his work had he lived." [42] No mean consolation for the spirit of the volatile Collins. And, indeed, one of the bright colors later unfurled in his honor is surely O'Connor's *The Big Fellow*.

IV

It must now, therefore, be determined what further meaning the struggle for Irish independence gave to O'Connor the artist. It is quite obvious, as already indicated, that his experience during the "Embers of Easter" surfaced in his art. Such was the case not only with many, if not all, of his contemporaries but also O'Connor himself. For, as Thomas Flanagan has cogently remarked, "the singular adventures, spiritual and public, out of which the literature of modern Ireland issued, made of its greatest writers exemplary figures, arguing within their art and outside it the meaning of the Irish experience." [43] Hence, some of O'Connor's public experiences, first in the guerilla war and then in the Civil War, serve as a clear inspiration to some sixteen stories, most of which appear in his collection *Guests of the Nation*. In these stories, he argues the meaning of these experiences, seeking to express, artistically, the reaction of his countrymen to the agonies at the birth of their nation.

This collection, O'Connor carefully notes, was originally written "under the influence of the great Jewish story teller Isaac Babel," [44] by which, he means, of course, Babel's *Red Cavalry*. Yet that O'Connor, who read widely in European literature, should, of all authors, come under the influence of Babel is not, on further reflection, at all surprising. For, in both these collections, we perceive "the writer's intention to create a form which shall in itself be shapely and autonomous and at the same time unusually responsible to the truth of external reality, the truth of things and events." [45] The truth of the events, it should be added, inescapably contains moral issues with which both artists were, personally, deeply involved.

One of the prime moral issues for many in war, we know, is not whether one can endure being killed, but whether one can endure killing. Though neither Babel nor O'Connor could endure killing, they were, nevertheless, greatly interested in the impulse to violence which seems innate in all men. This impulse has been especially strong in the twentieth century in which violence and killing pervade so much of life. And what he discerns about man is his ambivalent attitudes to war and violence. Hence, the artist, ever conscious of the realities of life, seeks to determine the ultimate effect of such realities on the nature of man. On the one hand, man is drawn to bloodshed, to murder, to the insanity of killing, to the monstrous inhumanity which makes him destroy even the innocent in order to satisfy his destructive element; on the other hand, man is appalled by violence, seeking, instead, to acquire the stillness, the solitude, the tenderness of peace that appears so elusive and even illusory. Hence, we find both Babel and O'Connor juxtaposing violence and repose, action and vision, in all their stories about war and violence.

Consider, for the sake of comparison, Babel's "My First Goose," the story of a young boy's initiation into the brotherhood of Cossacks. To be accepted, the boy kills a goose roaming his yard. "The lad's all right," one of the soldiers says winking. He has experienced violence and should, as a result, prove himself a welcome comrade. But then, after he asks the landlady where he is quartered to cook it for him, she exclaims in horror: "Comrade, I want to go and hang myself." Later, the six soldiers go to sleep after their feast, their feet "intermingled," as if true brothers in murder. The young boys' heart, however, is "stained with bloodshed, grated and brimmed over."

Such "grating of the heart," obviously, can only result from a conviction that man's fascination with and participation in violence is loathesome and haunts the heart in secret revolt. When such violence strains the credulity even of a society steeped in killing, one's immediate reaction might be like the landlady's, to go off and end it all by hanging oneself in mortal shame. There is a need in man, Babel claims, to resist violence, even if, as often occurs, such resistance meets with failure. If, like all men, Babel may have been fascinated by violence, he was, at the same time, revolted by it. And both these reactions appear constantly in his Red Army stories.

Similar reactions are found in O'Connor. One of his earliest war stories published in the *Irish Statesman* but not included in *Guests of the Nation* is entitled "War." In it, an army Commandant of the Free State troops has succeeded in capturing his first prisoners and, trying to withstand the incessant four-hour attack by the "irregulars," displays considerable heroism and daring. But suddenly, in the midst of it all, he "thought of home, and felt a great longing to be there and away from all this thing. It revolted him; it was drab and stupid and unreal—unreal, that was the word." [46] O'Connor, like Babel, apparently was always placing war and peace, violence and repose, side by side to show man's unending dilemma in having to choose between the two, though fascinated by both. This is what we see in this early story, even prior to O'Connor's acknowledgment of Babel's direct influence.

But, O'Connor seems to be adding, even when man chooses war, he can change nothing. For the Commandant continues to reflect that "nothing he could ever do would change the course of things. Even let him not return, his sweetheart would be just the same as she had always been, the same woman with no shred of difference because of anything in the world that might happen." And even when man decides to fight for whatever cause, there remain forces that cause things to happen "outside him" which will rob him of any effect he thinks he may have on the course of things. It was all so futile; it was so "unreal." Small wonder, therefore, that when the Commandant is wounded and one of his men offers him some relief for his pain, all he would cry, in the midst of his frenzy was: "Let me alone! Go away and let me alone!" Like Babel's landlady, the Commandant wants no more of violence and man's fascination with it. Death is preferable, if that is the only means of escape, or choice.

Not only does war reveal to man the "unreality" of his fascination with violence, but also, O'Connor suggests in many of the stories in *Guests of the Nation*, war shows man how removed the real is from the ideal; however widening is the gap between what actually is happening or has happened to his hopes and plans and what he thought he was fighting for. This situation troubled O'Connor terribly, as it had Collins. Consider, for example, "The Patriarch," one of the loveliest of these stories. In it, O'Connor makes this his theme: the vast difference between the idealism generated, say, by the Gaelic league which, in turn, inspired the Rising, and the banalities and the incessant sniper's fire on the streets of Cork. It tells about a small shopkeeper who has spent long decades dreaming of rebellion and worshipping and the Gaelic language. One day a young boy, the "narrator" in this story, recites for him an Irish chorus learned from his grandmother. Whereupon the shopkeeper exclaims passionately: "I'd give five years of me life to know it. . . . The kings and priests and prophets of our race are speaking to us, they're speaking to us out of the mouths of children, and they might as well be speaking to that counter there." When asked, the boy translates the chorus literally as he had heard it from his grandmother: " 'O my wife and my children and my little spinningwheel. My couple of pounds of flax each day not spun— two days she's in bed for one she's about the house, and oh, may the dear God help me to get rid of her.' " To which the patriot, assuming, because he had expected more, that this chorus must have some hidden, some deeper meaning, responds: "Believe me, there's a message in that you and I don't see. They wrapped up their meanings in dark words to deceive their enemies. . . . England, the bad wife—oh, how true it is! Dark songs for a people in chains." [47]

The narrator, who, in this, as in so many other stories, may possibly be O'Connor himself, understands that such songs as he sings could surely never have been meant to be the source of the Gaelic revival, its intense preoccupation with Irish history, myth, and folklore and the deplorable state of Ireland. Like the Patriarch, he is disturbed by fighting in the streets of Cork. What began as an idealistic battle for freedom has now degenerated into something entirely different: "Fighting of this sort is a filthy game in which obstinacy and the desire for revenge soon predominate." [48] And one cannot but recall hearing echoes here of the voice out of the darkness in another war story, "Nightpiece with Figures," which asks, dolefully: "Where is the sovereign Irish. people we used to hear so much about a year or two ago? . . . we haven't any heroes left but we can always find you a few informers." [49] Men and times change, leaving the old Patriarch only his private dreams.

Far more disillusioning for O'Connor than the ever-widening gap between the ideal and the real, resulting, in part, from a war that was a "cruel," silly thing, is the fact that many of his countrymen also lost the meaning of honor, decency, and fair play. And nowhere is this more powerfully revealed than in "Guests of the Nation," the famous war tale he deemed worthy of reprinting in *More Stories by Frank O'Connor*, the second volume of his collected stories, and the story so well known to readers of modern short fiction. Hawkins and Belcher, two British soldiers, are being held hostage against the impending execution of rebel prisoners. The guards, Donovan, Noble, and the narrator, become friends with the hostages. When some rebels are shot by the British, Donovan brings word that Hawkins, the perky little Cockney, and Belcher, the sweet-tempered Tommy, must be shot in reprisal. Hawkins is angry, but Belcher, unruffled, becomes instead the lonely voice that in measured tones condemns the lack of honor and fair play among men, especially their captors:

'You understand that we're only doing our duty?' says Donovan.
Belcher's head was raised like a blind man's, so that you could only see his chin and the tip of his nose in the lantern light.
'I never could make out what duty was myself,' he said, 'I think you're all good lads, if that's what you mean. I'm not complaining.' [50]

But at the moment Donovan shoots him, the narrator hears the birds "shrieking" over the bogs. The bloody stars are all far away and the narrator begins to feel "somehow very small and very lost and lonely like a child astray in the snow." Like Babel's boy, the narrator's heart here begins to grate.

This tale touches the reader not only because of its intrinsic beauty and power but also because it shows O'Connor's understanding of man's nature, especially when man loses all sense of self and his humanity. Above all, it has a universality, the ultimate achievement in fiction, because it transcends the bounds of time and space. If such lack of fair play, of honor, of decency toward men, not really enemies but only of the enemy camp, prevails, then how much more poignant is this story for our times when millions are slaughtered because of that unknowable, undefined, almost idolatrous notion of "duty"! The debasing of man is not limited apparently, to those engaged in the Irish guerrilla war against England. It exists everywhere. "Duty," as O'Connor projects it in the stories, becomes a shield for monstrous acts of evil—and all because of man's failure to see as O'Connor does what abstract terms or forces, or even dispassionate governments, can do, and often actually succeed in doing to his moral nature. Reading "Guests of the Nation," the sensitive reader actually feels "lost" and "astray in the snow."

But not every narrator in O'Connor's war stories, one must hasten to add, is led astray. Nor is every character bedevilled by his own inhumanity and coldness. Nor does every protagonist feel the dark power of melancholy surging within him. There are forces in the lives of men which help them retain their humanity, sanity, and probity. One such force in man is, of course, love. In "September Dawn," Keown and Hickey, having led fourteen "irregulars" across the countryside, decide to disband their men because they wish "to live for Ireland, not die for it." They flee, are pursued, and, finally, find a temporary shelter above Glanmanus Wood, where they go to bed. Keown has a drunken nightmare while Hickey, listening to the raging wind, reflects sadly on his "irregular" life:

He lay back and watched the window that seemed to grow brighter as he looked at it, and suddenly it became clear to him that his life was a melancholy, aimless life, and that all this endless struggle and concealment was but too much out of an existence that would mean little anyhow. . . . If they won, of course, the army he knew would not content him for long, for soldiering at best was only servitude. . . . At that very moment he had felt something explode within him at the inhumanity, the coldness of it all. . . . the feeling of his own loneliness, his own unimportance, his own folly.[51]

To offset all his folly, O'Connor offers man the humanity of love. After this dark night of his soul, Hickey tiptoes down the creaking stairs to the kitchen where Sheela, stirring, put the "seed of fire on the hearth." Suddenly, it lights up. And there is warmth and light:

He watched her, the long golden plait hanging across her shoulder, the young pointed face taking light from the new-born flame, and as she rose he took her in his arms and kissed her. She leaned against his shoulder in her queer, silent way, with no shyness. And for him in that melancholy kiss an ache of longing was kindled, and he buried his face in the warm flesh of her throat as the kitchen filled with the acrid smell of turf; while the blue smoke drifting through the narrow doorway was caught and whirled headlong through grey fields and dark masses of trees upon which an autumn sun was rising.[52]

The rising sun would resurrect man's love and, despite the ravages of war, direct him toward his humanity once again.

"September Dawn" is not the only story in which O'Connor introduces the virtues of love and kindness opposing brutality and hatred. We find, for instance, similar sentiments expressed in "Jumbo's Wife," *Soirée chez une jeune fille*, "The English Soldier," and "Androcles and the Army." Of these, the best and the most humorous is "Androcles and the Army." John Cloone, the circus lion tamer, decides suddenly to leave his job for the army because of "pure, unqualified, bloodthirsty patriotism." Healy, the circus manager, hires D'Arcy, the "strong man," as substitute lion tamer. But, on the night the circus plays for a house filled partly with soldiers, the curtain rises and there, sprawled on the ground before the howling mob, is Cloone, embracing the "lions Jumbo with one arm and Bess with the other." D'Arcy finally forces the lions into the back of the cage and Cloone, after striking his substitute for being a "big bully," escapes the inevitable police chase. They catch up with Cloone, however, who, after pleading "It's my lions" and "I'd never shame the uniform only for them," loses his stripes at the court martial.

Once more, O'Connor is presenting the dichotomy between two worlds: the world of armies with the "same oldmaidish preoccupation with their own dignity" and the simple lion tamer's, who, unlike the bullish D'Arcy, but filled with tender consideration, trains even lions to love. Hence when men like Healy wonder aloud "if anybody has ever succeeded in turning a soldier into anything that was the least good to God and man," O'Connor has Cloone conclude that such men as Healy must surely be "lacking in idealism." Even an army cannot destroy, at times, the basic human instincts of love and kindness.

So, when a soldier, and, by extension, any man allows his instinct for the jugular, for senseless killing, to subvert his deeper instincts toward humanity and concern, O'Connor would dismiss such a person utterly. In particular, he reveals this attitude in the story "Jo." Jo Kiely, an "irregular," and a "real, nice, good-natured fellow," also has a "wild streak in him." The narrator, after telling us how Jo shot the Marshal for tearing up a few rails, concludes that, because the marshall, an only son to an old man, really wasn't a "bad sort" and should have been spared, "somehow I could never bring myself to be pally with Jo again. Though, as I said before, he was an imaginary man, and didn't always mean what he said, there was a terrible wild streak in him." [53] Apparently, for O'Connor, people, however "imaginary" in the art of politics or war, who use guns needlessly, are more than suspect for their "wildness"; they are to be shunned entirely. This is not only in keeping with O'Connor's character, with his "sensitivity and tenderness," but with the general artistic pattern of his war stories—each of them a humorous and ironic commentary on the foibles of men and their experiences in, during, and after the fateful years of the Rising and, because his stories are universal, on every battlefield.

It should also be noted at once that, in all of his stories, O'Connor's humor consists essentially of his rare ability to see simultaneously the dual aspects of life—good and evil, love and hate, peace and war, the beautiful and the ugly. In other words, his humor in the "synthetical fusion of opposites, the gift of saying two things in one, of showing shine and shadow together." And since life, surely, contains both good and evil, the "very will that discriminates them practically gives a deeper poetic endorsement to them both." And whenever O'Connor wrote about his countrymen—the provincial world of publicans, doctors, priests, small merchants, builders, chemists, and solicitors—he saw at once the "shine and shadow" of their lives which he recorded with discriminating insight, followed so often by "volleys of silvery laughter."

That insight, as regards revolution and war, can best be summarized finally in the question and answer O'Connor presents in the wildly humorous tale "The Eternal Triangle." He begins questioningly:

Revolutions? I never had any interest in them. A man in my position have to mind his job and not bother about what other people are doing. Besides, I never could see what good they did anybody . . . And who pays for the damage? You and me and people like us, so that one set of jackeens can get in instead of another set of jackeens. What is it to me who's in or out? All I know is that I have to pay for the damage they do.[54]

The narrator then proceeds to tell us how he, a watchman, is guarding the train when in wanders Cummins, a woman of thirty-five, who doesn't know what all the shooting is about and worries only, in the midst of all the ringing gunfire, about her need for "a bit of sugar for me tea." She proceeds to ask the narrator: "But what are they shooting for, mister? . . . Is it for Ireland?" When the narrator makes some nasty remark about some of the cadets who are doing the wild shooting, she stoutly defends them and Ireland, with, by God, "a tear in her eye." Whereupon the narrator, in one of the most bitingly humorous remarks in the story, a remark that focuses in one sentence O'Connor's conception of the "shine and shadow" in the lives of his countrymen says: "That is the kind of women they are. They'll steal the false teeth from a corpse, but let them lay their eyes on a green flag or a child in his First Communion suit, and you'd think patriotism and religion were the only two things ever in their minds."[55]

Small wonder, too, that when a drunk stumbles into the tram, all he can shout about the sounds of flying bullets is "I'd cut the throat of any bloody Englishman." It makes no difference that he may be shot dead so long as he can give utterance to his abiding prejudice. Prejudice precedes even self-preservation. And Cummins, finally, couldn't care less about a victory for the Ireland she so fiercely defended a little while ago. For all she ever dreams of is, to use O'Connor's favorite metaphor, her Lilliputian request: "If I was only in my own little room this minute, you could have the rest of the city—with my compliments."[56]

If in this story O'Connor questions the meaning of "revolution," he also gives us his answer: every man drowns his highest ideals in the tea of his own petty wants, dislikes, needs, and foibles. We are not surprised, therefore, that at the end of the story when Cummins, peddling her "wares," invites the narrator up to her room for a "cup of tea," he refuses because he was "to disgustcd." In fact, he adds that he "was never so disgusted with anything in [his] life." Is this not of a piece with O'Connor's triggered response to war, violence, man's inhumanity to man: total disgust, a disgust at man's inability to recognize the inevitable results of his fascination with violence.

That disgust with all that he saw happening to his country and countrymen may well explain why O'Connor, like, say, Yeats and Joyce and O'Casey, "had long ago decided that Ireland was morally bound to live up to his expectations." That may also explain why these giants carried on a life-long lover's quarrel with their country, with its "introverted religion" and "introverted politics." But since Ireland, for them, never did live up to their expectations, they were at ease with it only in their poems, plays, and stories. In them, they could weep and laugh, often doing both simultaneously.

And if O'Connor, like some of his contemporaries, found the political life of his country difficult to bear, it is clearly evident that in his stories of war and revolution he was, at least artistically, at ease. And these stories, on careful reading, are irresistibly interesting, precisely because "O'Connor loved those from whom he was alienated." Loving them, he naturally placed them prominently in his art.

THREE

Island of Saints

... the feeling of their own integrity as priests; the thing which gave significance and beauty to their sacrifice.
—Frank O'Connor, "The Wreath"
The whole Cross had become a place of mystery—the grey light, drained of warmth . . .
—Frank O'Connor, "The Face of Evil"

Alienated from politics, O'Connor was no less alienated from his church. Unable, after his internment during the Civil War, ever again to be at ease with his country's "introverted religion," as with its "introverted patriotism," especially since both religion and politics are in Ireland forever hopelessly entangled, O'Connor, on the Sunday following his return home, refused to go to Mass. "Life without freedom," the freedom, that is, to assert his will, he felt "is nothing." And to be free, in this instance at least, meant that he would willingly renounce the "immortality" vouchsafed the faithful adherent to his religion.

He was firm in this decision. Toward the very end of *An Only Child*, after bidding farewell to that part of his life sheltered by the faith of his country and, specifically, his mother, O'Connor goes so far as to consider that kind of "immortality" as decidedly vain. The eternity he is compelled to seek is of a totally different kind; it results from a dedication to art, not religion:

All our arguments about the immortality of the soul seem to me to be based on one vast fallacy—that it is our vanity that desires eternity. Vanity! As though any reasonable man could be vain enough to believe

*himself worth immortality! From the time I was a boy and could think
at all, I was certain that for my own soul there was only nothingness. I
knew it too well in all its commonness and weakness. But I knew that
there were souls that were immortal, that even God, if He wished to,
could not diminish or destroy, and perhaps it was the thought of these
that turned me finally from poetry to storytelling, to the celebration of
those who for me represented all I should ever know of God.*[1]

Such declarations, however fearless and forceful, are often truer,
we know, in theory than in practice. Though, to be sure, a notori-
ous opponent of the "church temporal," O'Connor nevertheless
practiced in his personal life some of the moral teachings of his
"church eternal." Any reading of the dedicatory essays in the memorial volume *Michael/Frank* will surely convince the reader that
the honesty, courage, wisdom, concern for students, dedication to
friends, and an abiding intolerance of all intellectual dishonesty and
moral cowardice by which the contributors attest he lived and
breathed, made him, in the words of Brendan Kennelly, into one
who "looked like a king, felt like a poet, spoke like a god." [2] And,
because he wanted to build a bridge between traditions to show
that "where many saw division, he could discover unity," he was
not only a passionate man but a "religious" one as well. If he
made a formal break with his church, he never really broke with its
traditions. And for that he might very well have achieved the "immortality" he renounced.

Whether in fact O'Connor finally achieved it, now that he is
gone, is not for us to know. What we do know, however, is that
he did celebrate, in his writings, those people who "for him represented all he should ever know of God," thus achieving the "immortality" that does not derive, according to him, from "vanity."
Among the celebrants were, of course, his mother, as well as his
contemporaries, some of the poets and novelists of the past, and,
most emphatically, the clergy. No less than twenty-two of his stories
are devoted to Bishops, parish priests, and curates of the Irish
church. As one of his friends correctly argues, "no other Irish writer
has written with such persuasive warmth of the community of
priests." [3] Religion, indeed, wends its way through much of his
writings.

In truth, it could hardly be otherwise. No Irish writer, either because of upbringing, personal conviction, or intellectual interest, could possibly escape the pervasive influence of the Church, even if he formally renounced it. True of Joyce, this is surely so of O'Connor. A student of Irish history and tradition, he was certainly aware that ever since the coming of Patrick during the reign of Laoghaire in 432, the destiny of his country was inextricably bound up with the Church. Even when, during the Reformation, especially after the Act of Supremacy, the whole Irish ecclesiastical structure was destroyed and the Church was for a long period of time unable to reach its full spiritual promise, it still wielded enormous power over the people. For the people wanted this authority. As one modern observer of the Irish scene says of the Church: "The sterner it is the more we love it, and we ask nothing better than rules for the regulation of the minutest details of our lives." [4]

Perhaps, because of this stringency and its historical isolation from the rest of Europe, Ireland was able to create a Church uniquely its own. It was a church

neither Western nor Eastern, a Church with its own ritual, its own government, its own monasticism. In the cycle of church seasons it was unique. Its hymns and psalm singing, its tonsure, its architecture, were all its own, unlike those of any other church. Its monks were neither Benedictine nor Basilian. . . . It had its schools and its scholars, its saints whose names we still revere, though we have long ceased to understand their lives. It sent its missionaries abroad, apostles of an evangel and a culture strange in the lands to which they went. About its creed and doctrines we can but guess, knowing little except that it was neither Catholic nor Protestant.[5]

And if this Church, so rich in promise, failed, because of the accidents of history and because, perhaps, "men who were not of its spirit sat down in its high places," to change the face of Christendom, it surely changed the face of Ireland. If, on the international scene, it remained a case of "arrested development," the Church still controlled the faith and destiny of the Irish. For, almost alone among Western nations, in Ireland, to this day, religion is still a central reality of life.

All of which may have wisely moved G. B. Shaw to declare, even if we are to discount some of his usual wit and hyperbole, that the "island of saints" is no idle phrase. Religious genius is "one of its national products, and Ireland is no bad rock to build a church on. Holy and beautiful is the soul of Catholic Ireland." [6] Hence, too, when O'Connor chose selections for his *A Book of Ireland*, one in a series of national anthologies by many hands published in England more than a decade ago, he inevitably included a goodly sampling of religious writings. The Church was and is Ireland; Ireland was and is its Church.

A significant paradox, it must be noted, is that the Irish Church, despite one of the greatest missionary traditions in Christendom, should have a particularly inward-looking Catholicism. There is in that Catholicism, as already suggested, a complete reliance upon authority, a repression of individuality, and a complete shifting of the moral center of gravity to a future existence. Such postulates, of course, tended to stunt the growth of self-reliance, and resulted, instead, in a kind of fatalism, with resignation as its permanent virtue.

"Why," the reader may justifiably ask, "did this happen?" The reasons, of course, are many. Among them, one modern Irish historian has written, three main ones account for the shift of the Irish Church from universalism to parochialism. First, this inward-looking nature of Irish Catholicism may be due "to traces of Jansenism which made their appearance after the foundation of Maynooth and the employment there of French professors driven from their country by revolution." [7] And Jansenism manifests itself in "a censorious holier-than-thou attitude." Its practitioners claim "to have a special devotion for, and insight into, the mind of God."

Second, since the Romans never came to Ireland, "Christianity came to the country later and to a different soil than elsewhere in Europe." Furthermore, because it was practically the only Christianity during the dark ages that was totally insulated from the mainstream of European life, "it inevitably developed an ethos which from the start was severe," an ethos with a purgative tradition which grafted upon secular life a quasi-monasticism. In addition, up to and during, and indeed after, the Reformation, "it was the one unifying force in a country ravaged by invasions and quarrelling chieftains." Hence, it gathered strength from looking only inward to its country and people, inevitably adding to its parochialism.[8]

Finally, such continuing particularism gave rise "to a strong streak of conceit," especially since the Irish Church never forgot that "it was the only light in the west amid the encircling gloom of pagan barbarism." Subjected, besides, to the penal laws, it assumed the added dimension of martyrdom. And martyrs develop attitudes of superiority that result in their considering themselves the selected, the elected, and the perfected of all mankind, too great to mingle with lesser souls.

So strong, indeed, was this superior attitude that there have been times, past and present, when the Irish Church has even challenged Rome. There were always, apparently, as Bede long ago noted, extensive hagglings "over Celtic versus Roman usages and rites." And it was, we know, Pope Adrian, viewing the Irish Church's luster dimly, who prompted Henry II's Irish expedition in 1177, "the beginning of seven hundred years of oppression." Years later, Innocent XI gave his "endorsement" to William of Orange's expedition "to wrest control of the three kingdoms from the Catholic King James II." In addition, anyone acquainted with Irish history of the eighteenth, nineteenth, and early twentieth centuries, when the Irish people sought their freedom from British tyranny, will recall how Rome, as perceived by the Irish, became "remote," "unhelpful," and "insidious."

Little wonder, therefore, that when, in 1904, Shaw, at the request of Yeats, made "a patriotic contribution to the repertory of the Irish Literary Theatre" by submitting *John Bull's Other Island* for production, he had Laurence Doyle, the Irishman who returns to his homeland after years of absence in England, exclaim: "I would have Ireland compete with Rome itself for the chair of Saint Peter and the citadel of the Church; for Rome, in spite of all the blood of the martyrs, is pagan at heart to this day, while in Ireland the people is the Church and the Church is the people." [9]

Similarly, when O'Connor decided to include, naturally, some religious poetry in *A Book of Ireland,* he made sure to select carefully from the many extant poems a short one by an anonymous ninth-century poet which shows, obviously, the superiority of the Celtic Church over the Roman. In his own translation from the Irish, it reads:

Ireland v. Rome

To go to Rome—
    Is little profit, endless pain;
The Master that you seek in Rome,
    You find at home, or seek in vain.[10]

II

What O'Connor sought at home, however, was not to discover the theological differences that separated Ireland from Rome. He was not, despite his keen interest in the clergy, a theologian nor ever pretended to be. In fact, in his stories, with the possible exception of "The Custom of the Country" and "My First Protestant," and even here only superficially, there is no concern with matters of dogmatic theology. Hence, what he was looking for, in his own country, were the "Masters" of the local villages, towns, and cities who, from the beginning, served as God's servants of their people.

For central to all religious life in Ireland is, we know, the priest. This is especially clear when we bear in mind that the "hierarchy in Ireland is probably the most powerful in the world." [11] Since Ireland is today the world's last "non-post-Christian" society, everyone, with few irrelevant exceptions, is either Catholic or Protestant. Small wonder, therefore, that there still exists a special reverence for, and trust in, the person of the priest. "A joy inconceivable to non-Catholics possesses an Irish family when a son of the house enters holy orders." [12]

This reverence for the priesthood prevailed even in earliest times. Again, in his *A Book of Ireland*, O'Connor quotes a passage from Bede, describing the work of the Irish missionaries in England, which confirms the reverence with which they were held by the people of the countryside: "the religious habit was at that time held in great veneration; so that wherever any clerk or monk went, he was joyfully received by all men, as God's servant; and even if they chanced to meet him upon the way, they ran to him, and with bowed head, were glad to be signed with the cross by his hand, or blessed by his lips." [13] The tradition established ever since then, therefore, was for the priest to be, in deed and in fact, a person almost disingenuous in simplicity, pious, charitable, meek, and long-suffering.

Such reverence would lead, inevitably, to the "joy inconceivable" that overcomes a mother whose son enters the priesthood. No more striking passage describing this unending pleasure appears than in the once popular novel, *The Valley of the Squinting Windows*, by Brinsley MacNamara, not especially known for his approval of the Irish clergy. Mrs. Brennan, the mother who sinned, finds comfort, in all her marital unhappiness, in her son John, who is studying for the priesthood. One day, riding next to the valley cabbie, she listens approvingly to him describe for her the ultimate in human happiness:

'I suppose,' said he, 'that it's a fine thing to be the mother of a young fellow going on for the Church. It must make you very contented in yourself when you think of all the Masses he will say for you during your lifetime and all the Masses he will say for the repose of your soul when you are dead and gone. . . . 'And, Mrs. Brennan, woman dear, to see him say the Holy Mass, and he having his face shining with the Light of Heaven.' [14]

But not every priest's face, either then or now, shines with the "light of heaven." Some prefer, instead, the good earth; they become avaricious, love hunting, get drunk, swear, wear expensive habits, pray perfunctorily, and, in general, are derelict in their priestly duties. Some, especially since the mid-nineteenth century, turned their interest to politics. Maynooth, for example, the training ground for most of the Irish clergy, was unswervingly loyal to the Crown. Others were swept up eventually in Daniel O'Connell's struggle for Catholic Emancipation. By 1850, Sean O'Faolain reminds us, "that terrible bogy-man of the nineteenth century all over Europe, the 'Priest in Politics' had arrived in Ireland." [15]

Some writers, Liam O'Flaherty in particular, looked upon that turn of events with foreboding and disgust. In his *A Tourist's*

Guide to Ireland, which deals little with tourism but much with his critical analysis of the Irish, he tells us that

in fact, properly speaking, no parish priest has any conviction on politics. At the back of his mind, he regards the state as an enemy that has usurped the temporal power of the Pope. Being an enemy, the state must be exploited as much as possible and without any qualms of conscience. Because of this innate and perhaps unconscious hostility to the state as an institution, the parish priest cannot see that it is his duty as a citizen to endeavor to make political life as morally clean as possible. He cannot see that the community as a whole must always come into the forefront of every citizen's political consciousness and that personal interests must be sacrificed to the interests of the nation. No. The parish priest regards himself as the commander of his parish, which he is heading for His Majesty the Pope. . . . As far as the Civil Power is concerned, it is a semi-hostile force which must be kept in check, kept in tow, intrigued against and exploited.[16]

Nevertheless, even he, on second thought, was forced to admit that the parish priest is not a monster or evil genius but a poor "grown up child" who is the victim of his environment; who errs "through crass ignorance rather than through a natural predestination toward evil." And if he boldly claimed that Ireland impresses one "as a beautiful, sad-faced country that is being rapidly covered by a black rash," it is, at the very same time, a country where the "priest is a kindly soul."

Needless to say, every writer views the priesthood according to his own prejudices. But most writers, if they do not follow such extreme lines in their description of the Irish clergy, "see the priest in one of three aspects—the jovial, hunting, hearty priest, who is really a good fellow in clerical garb; or, the rigorous unbending, saintly and generally rather inhuman ascetic—the patriarch of his flock; or, the man whose life is a long psychological problem." But, however they are depicted by those who knew and lived with them closely, one thing is certain: the priests bulk very large on the Irish scene. That, in fact, is the first thing that strikes a visitor from any other country. What is the reason for this?

Of course, the reasons may be many. But, of all those advanced, it would appear that the ones presented by Arland Ussher in his perceptive book *The Face and Mind of Ireland* are the most plausible. Chief among them is the argument that ever since the Penal Laws, resulting for a long time in Catholics becoming spiritually, nationalistically, politically, and educationally disenfranchised, the "priesthood in Ireland have continuously been united in sentiment with the people rather than with the gentry or the government; in their clergy the Irish race have had that rare thing, a popular aristocracy or elite of learning, a class to speak for them and suffer with them." [17] The poor, therefore, even in the deepest abjection, never feel abandoned. This helped create a kinship between the two which, despite outbursts of disagreement, disappointment, and disillusionment, was ultimately based on reverence. And because, further, the priest himself was of peasant extraction, the two, priest and peasant, were, emotionally at least, on one level.

What may also add to this kinship is the fact that the priest has generally been looked up to as a kind of jack-of-all-trades, always conveniently at hand. We must remember that, despite the transformation taking place in the last few decades as regards educational opportunities, there have been too few Irish who could assume positions of leadership. Hence the priest, as in O'Connor's story "Peasants," must inevitably take on the job of chairman or patron of the local football and hurling club as well as sundry other organizations. Involvement in so much organizational life, perhaps more in the city than in the country to be sure, gives the priesthood added power over matters distinctively secular. This real power notwithstanding, the Irish priest is paradoxically considered a humble, shy man, with a good sense of humor, and not the browbeating forbidding character he may in fact often prove to be. Otherwise, it might be difficult to explain why, on any given Sunday, some half a million Catholics still march to Mass in Dublin. And, "the over all heterogeneity of mass goers is . . . as startling as their numbers: the pious old women are jostled by far from pious-looking young men, the bourgeois share pews with the beatniks—there are as many beards and mini-skirts as there are serge suits and demure mantillas, or bonnets and shawls." [18] And all that is due, in the main, to the power and the glory of the priesthood.

To be sure, of late, things are changing significantly, however slowly and laboriously. Among the younger generation, Sean Mac-Réamoinn observes, a lot of idealism, "previously channelled into purely spiritual or devotional activity, into para-missionary organizations like the Legion of Mary . . . or into the priesthood and religious life," has presently shifted to social issues at home and abroad. There rages in Ireland now "a crisis not of faith but of communication, of language, or a conflict between immediate relevance and traditional values." [19] These crises are not so much *of* morality as *in* morality.

But such crises *in* faith need not concern us here. For the faith which looms large in O'Connor's stories, especially those twenty-two or so dealing specifically with the priesthood, was written still with an eye to the old image of the priesthood as more or less that of a benevolent despotism. He wrote of an era when paternalism was still one of the hallmarks of the Irish clergy; when bishops and parish priests tended to hand down decisions without being questioned; when every matter pertaining to the welfare of man was still "the priest's job"; when there was little outward imbalance between Catholic doctrine and life; when one found God's servants always close to home.

III

What O'Connor observed and then recorded in his stories about the servants of God and the servants of the servants of God, such as their housekeepers, is rich in understanding, meaning, and humor. That he had early renounced his formal relationship with religion did not prejudice him, in his extended writings, against the Irish clergy. In point of fact, it gave him a certain objectivity not always available to the committed. These servants—bishops, parish priests, and curates—appear in O'Connor's stories as subject to the same strains and stresses in all their dedication to the "higher" life as those involved in the "lower" life. And the description of the priests that finally emerges from these stories, therefore, contains a keen insight not only into the Irish priest's professional posture but also his own personality. At times these two elements in his nature are in a conflict which gives added meaning to the artistic quality of the tales.

Such conflict need not surprise us. For, as Sean O'Faolain has cogently remarked, we cannot fully appreciate the role of the priest, especially in Irish society, unless we see him in this permanent state of conflict:

The key to the nature of the priest is that he is elusively twofold. His secret is that of all the arcane professions. It is impossible to isolate, in any of his acts, his personal from his professional elements. . . . Each one makes a sacrifice of his personal liberty, of the single-mindedness, or unity of his personality, in order to achieve the enlargement of power that comes with membership of a great professional caste. . . . Because of this sacrifice one can never see the priest exclusively as priest: his human personality is dedicated but not suppressed. But neither can we see him exclusively as a man: he has risen superior to normal values, intercourse, and sympathies. And he is cut off from the lay world by celibacy.[20]

And it is this dual image of the priest that is "canonized" so interestingly in O'Connor's stories about the "saints" on his Irish island.

Before analyzing some of these tales, however, it is necessary to record that, despite his sophistication and avowed commitment to the freedom of the soul, O'Connor was impressed with tradition. It could indeed hardly be otherwise. For as a student of history, O'Connor was well aware that central to the Irish ethos is the tradition of religion, mysticism, legend, mystic charms, and superstitions. Witness, for example, his incorporation of so much of this material in *A Book of Ireland* as well as his own numerous translations of the same from ancient and medieval sources. And among these traditions, the priesthood is, needless to say, strongest. After all, there have been priests in Ireland for well over a thousand years.

Nowhere in O'Connor's stories is this serious regard for tradition more apparent than in that hauntingly sad and moving tale "The Long Road to Ummera." An old lady, Mrs. Driscoll, disregarding the strong suggestion of her son, "an insignificant little man, jealous of the power the dead had over her," that she remain with him, demands to return to Ummera where she wishes to die and be buried. Furthermore, the return must be by the long road around the lake and when she passes near her little house, her son must tell her neighbors, "this is Abby, Batty Heige's daughter, that kept her promise to ye at the end of all." [21] One night, on seeing a vision in

which her dead husband returns to her, she ignores her son's ulti-
matum, rents a car, and returns, dying en route. Her son finally
executes her last will, reciting the words she had requested to be
said about her.

Her dying wish is obviously not due to a stubbornness resulting
from senility but is rather the cherished dream of one, long separated
from her past, who is anxious to be united finally not so much with
the dead but with a past, the memory of which has never dimmed
even in a strange environment. This story might well be symbolic
of Ireland herself. For we need only substitute for Abby Driscoll,
the names *Eire, Banba, Fodhla, Cathleen ni Houlihan, Roisin
Dubh, Dark Rosaleen;* what O'Connor could then be saying, sym-
bolically, is that Ireland, like the old lady, is drawn irresistibly toward its ancient beliefs and customs, its mystical dreams and mystical terrors which for centuries have captivated her imagination.
Surely, O'Connor felt or believed this. Like the old lady, Ireland,
too, on its long, if not final journey, is saying to its traditions: "I'm
a long way from you but I'm coming at last." [22]

It is not surprising, of course, that O'Connor, because of his
strong interest in tradition, would examine the priesthood so extensively. Taken as a group, his priests are, like all men, both "good"
and "bad." Some lack compassion, engage in trickery unbecoming
their exalted station, are too vain, or subject to violent prejudice.
Others are just the opposite: considerate, friendly, charitable, and,
despite being wedded to divine Love, desperately starved for human
love. Throughout, however, whether he is praising or condemning
them, O'Connor wrote about them with that understanding and
even fondness, which, because of his own generous nature, he possessed in good measure. He seems forever to be smiling, at times
critically, at other times approvingly, but at all times knowingly, at
the strengths and weaknesses of an arcane profession which, despite
its awesome habits, could not hide its inner self from his restless
and piercing eyes.

And this is what he saw.

In "Peasants," Father Crowley, a parish priest, "tall, powerfully
built, but very stooped, with shrewd, loveless eyes that rarely soft-
ened to anyone except two or three old people," refuses to forgive

Michael Cronin for stealing money from the local Football and Hurling Club. Despite the pleas of the committee members, "all religious men who up to this point had never as much as dared to question the judgments of a man of God," petition Father Crowley to write a letter of recommendation so that the thief might leave for America; for this trip they, in turn, are prepared to make a large contribution to the parish fund. Accusing them of bribery with an attempt to force him to perjure himself, he remains adamant. Cronin finally goes to jail. And Father Crowley, despite some forty years of service, becomes "useless" to his congregation and is soon thereafter shifted to another post. The thief, even after being released from jail, resorts to money lending and usury and is hardly changed, something that might only happen if heaven would send to them "another Moses or Brian Boru to cast him down and hammer him in the dust." [23]

Far more culpable than the evil of the thief, who hailed from a line of thieves, O'Connor seems to be saying, is the hardened personal nature of the priest. Had he been more compassionate, he might have shown the way, as did Moses and Brian Boru, in convincing Cronin of his bad ways. How sad, therefore, that after all those years when no one could have accused him of any lapse of conduct, the priest now finds himself the village outcast. In truth, all are peasants who, terribly narrow in outlook, cannot change in changing circumstances. Neither priest nor layman ever rises above his peasant origins, lacking, among other things, some Christian charity.

Rigidity of a somewhat different kind comes under criticism in "Requiem," when Father Fogarty, "a young man with a warm welcome for the suffering and the old . . . with a heart like a house," refuses the sole request of a little old lady who wishes mass said for her dog who "was like a son to her." [24] For the fulfillment of this desire, of course, she is prepared to give the church her life's savings. The priest, reacting immediately to her "sacrilegious" request, refuses, raging against the rich and "their pampered pets." She, lonely and distraught, argues that her little Timmy had a soul, for "anything that can love has a soul"; hence he is worthy of a mass. Father Fogarty still refuses. With a final admonishing word, she tells him that someday "we'll all be together again," presumably as one vast soul of love.

What O'Connor is obviously lamenting is not only that Father Fogarty is rigid but also that, apart from the formal legalisms that obviously deny masses for dogs, the priest fails to understand the heart of his religion: love. Bound by discipline, he cannot, despite his owning "a heart like a house," soothe the stricken feelings of a simple old woman who, unaware of theological meanings, understands love as a binding of all those who share it. As a result, as O'Connor would have it, she might even understand its true significance better than her priest.

If Fathers Crowley and Fogarty fail, so does, for a somewhat different reason, Father Ring in "The Miser." He is rapacious. Mr. Devereux, the "last of a very good family who had once been merchants," has the reputation of being a miser who, with his servant Faxy, lives in abject poverty and in filth. But he is reportedly resting in his last illness on a tin box in his home which, supposedly, contains a fortune. Father Ring, with his "hairy hands," wants to change all that: first, by importing two nuns to care for his body and, second, by writing Devereux's will, whereby the priest will care for his soul. The church, its orders, and Faxy will all receive their due compensation. At the man's death, the priest and the servant tear up the entire house looking for the box. But, alas, it contains nothing more than "old screws, bolts, washers, bits of broken vases and an enormous selection of pipe bowls and stems." Bitterly disappointed, Father Ring can only lament: "I'm afraid, we were had. We were had, boy, all of us. 'Tis a great disappointment, a great disappointment." [25]

However, the greatest disappointment of all, O'Connor would have us believe, is the sly, dubious method Father Ring used in subverting the will of a "remarkable man." To be sure, the priest receives his "just reward." But that is surely no way for a servant of God to act. Might not O'Connor be saying, to be sure, in a light, humorous, and even forgiving way, what Liam O'Flaherty said caustically and not without a touch of venom: "Himself born to poverty and forbidden by his Divine Master to accumulate wealth, [the priest] gets rich furtively and the secrecy of his penny-gathering inspires him with the distrust, with the glowering eye and the dreadful yellow lust of the miser"? [26] Although Father Ring might have been seeking only little, if anything, for himself, he does acquire the "lust of the miser," which, in the end, leaves him a far less "remarkable man" than the miser himself.

Furthermore, in "An Act of Charity," O'Connor seems to say that a little trickery, a touch of pressure, and even a bit of blackmail, when resorted to by a priest for some "higher" purpose, yields even less remarkable men. Father Maginnis, "a smart man with no nerves and no hysterics," does not like his second curate Father Gavin, "a thin irritable and intense man who worried himself over small embarrassments and what people would think of them." [27] The latter, unable to cope with the persecutions of his superior, commits suicide. To shield the family, the dead priest, and the church from any scandal, Father Maginnis suggests to Dr. Carmody that he certify that Father Gavin's death came naturally. The doctor, out of strictness of conscience, refuses. After failing to convince the doctor of the charity of signing, the parish priest, assisted by his first curate Father Fogarty, threatens to bring to the parish another doctor, an act which, in effect, would ruin Dr. Carmody's practice. Needless to say, the doctor signs, consoling himself in a later discussion with Father Fogarty that it might have been "an act of charity" after all.

Most disturbing to the doctor, however, is not "what" he did but "how" it was done. It dawns on him that his priest was not, indeed, acting charitably. Furthermore, he begins to realize that, had the parish priest acted charitably to Father Gavin while he was alive, all this might not have been necessary. And even the doctor, O'Connor believes, had he been more understanding, might have shown more courage and not capitulated so quickly. An inquiry might have got at the whole truth. How else, then, does one explain Father Fogarty's final thought: "What lonely lives we lead"? Unhappily, even a man of the cloth sometimes substitutes a dubious act of charity for a real one.

An even more dubious "act of charity" is performed when a priest compounds the sin of prejudice by the sin of lying. In the story "The Sentry" the consequences are serious, albeit in the ways

of O'Connor not without traces of humor. Father Michael Mac-
Enerney is a lonely man who, for lack of friends, talks only to the
three sisters in the convent, especially Sister Margaret, herself a
lonesome woman. Father MacEnerney, owner of an onion patch
next to the English military base situated in his parish, suspects
the sentry of stealing his onions. A confrontation follows, and after
accusing the sentry of being a "bloody little English thief," the
priest beats him up because all the MacEnerneys were like that:
quiet, but once you gave them occasion, "they'd fight in a bag, tied
up."

Despite the encouraging words of Sister Margaret for his standing up to the English, the priest is ashamed, for not only did he
behave disgracefully but "after all his talk of charity he had in-
sulted another man for his nationality, hit him when he couldn't
hit back, and all for a handful of onions worth about sixpence.
There was a nice behavior for a priest!" [28] Surprisingly, however,
when Howe, the camp inspector, comes to investigate the "crime,"
Father MacEnerney lies about the beating, claiming it never really
happened. The inspector, of course, doesn't believe him but invites
him to a dinner at the mess anyway. The poor sentry therefore
stands officially condemned. When the priest tells all this to Sister
Margaret, she claims it isn't a sin but an "act of charity" on behalf
of the poor because the English won't allow the poor as much leni-
ency as they do the rich. She starts a novena on his behalf at once.

Clearly, O'Connor is criticizing the clergy for the same faults he
finds in the laity: a blind Irish prejudice against the English. Having previously deplored the same prejudice in "Guests of the Nation," he does so again but here even more satirically when dealing
with the priesthood. For they ought to know better. And what irony
that a nun should offer a novena so that when Father MacEnerney
visits Howe he "might be able to get around him." And even if
Father MacEnerney's own father "also perjured himself in the interest of a neighbor," that is no excuse for the son who, after all,
is also a sentry, if of a different sort. Since a sentry's duty is to
stand guard over the unguarded, he cannot afford to let his guard
down. Against such sins of omission, novenas are of little meaning
and less value.

But, of all the sins anyone can commit, especially a priest, vanity is surely the worst. Since, O'Connor remarks, "vanity is the besetting sin of people in religion," Dr. Gallogly, the Bishop of Moyle, and formerly a professor of Dogmatic Theology, sinned terribly in the story "Vanity." Forever fearful, at eighty-six, that his young coadjutor, Bishop Lanigan, is plotting to retire him, Dr. Gallogly decides on a trip to Dublin to visit the bedside of young Father O'Brien, that he may prove his youthfulness. When the elevators fail to work, he insists on climbing the stairs; whereupon he slips on a flight of six steps, because, as always, "pride goeth before the fall." He hurts himself. Subject to stretcher-bearers, doctors, and nurses for the first time in his life, he feels humiliated. So that his pride not be hurt further, he orders that all hospital personnel, except the head nurse and the two nuns who stand guard at his door, be excluded from his room, lest word of his injury get back to Moyle. Assuming a different name in the hospital, he is willing to believe that people will now consider him to be some rich businessman or politician whose illness must be concealed from his enemies. The deception doesn't help much, however, for when he returns to Moyle, everyone already knows. Aware that his secret is out, he blames the leak on the nuns who could never be trusted.[29]

In this story, perhaps more than in the others, O'Connor sums up some of his criticisms of the clergy. For, during his stay in the hospital, the Bishop does learn a few important lessons which, if understood by the priesthood generally, might have benefitted them greatly in their roles as servants of God. First, while supposedly anonymous, Dr. Gallogly becomes aware that the "religious life was too sheltered"; that "women tell dirty stories"; that there is much that the laity thinks and says and does which, if known to the priests, might change their habits for the better. Second, and more important, he learns that he was becoming attached to his anonymity; that what began as vanity ended in humility; that since the "great temptation of religious people is vanity," priests might benefit from a period of anonymity during which people would consider them as they are rather than as they ought to be; that, since "one of the drawbacks of having been almighty God" is the intense dislike of being contradicted, it stood the Bishop well to hear the doctor resist one of his demands. And only anonymity could have given him that experience. Because a priest always maintains a superior position in the public eye, vanity is inevitable. It is necessary, therefore, for the priest to withdraw from the public glare, to hide from public praise, and, for a while at least, listen to the criticism of the laity, adjust to their needs, learn from others. In short, to expunge the sin of vanity. Otherwise, the priest fails and falls.

Another failing of the Church, which, O'Connor believes, renders it more vulnerable than any other institution is the priest's housekeeper. He calls this woman the "Achilles' Heel" of the church. His objection is not to their sexlessness but rather to the fact that they "accept chastity for a higher end—the subjection of some unfortunate man to a degree unparalleled in marriage"! One such unfortunate man in "Achilles' Heel" is again the Bishop of Moyle, whose housekeeper, Nellie Connoly, not only wields enormous power over him but engages in smuggling food and other goods across the border in obvious violation of the law. Tim Leary, the local customs officer, visits the Bishop to inform him of her smuggling ring and of the fact that not only she, but he, too, was under suspicion, Tim producing a ledger to prove that she bought liquor in his name for smuggling purposes. Aghast, the Bishop nevertheless requests that she be allowed to go free lest the scandal widen to include his marrying her. Besides, he promises henceforth to control her actions.

After Tim Leary and the officials leave, the Bishop engages in some serious thought, reflecting, surely, O'Connor's personal view of what is essentially wrong with this institution of housekeeper, the supposed servant of the servant of the Lord: "Like all bishops, he was addicted to power, but he saw now that a bishop's power, like a bishop's knowledge, was little better than a shadow. He was just a lonely man who was dependent on women, exactly as when they had changed his napkin and he had crowed and kicked his heels. There was no escape." Unable to escape such omnipresence priests become little playthings in the hands of the housekeepers, who do with them literally as they please. They learn further, as the Bishop of Moyle learns in this story, that when housekeepers prepare a poor meal and wish to remedy it with some substitute, they make matters worse. So that when Nellie, a notoriously bad cook, makes such an offer to offset his indigestion, he realizes that "it could not lift his sorrow; that whenever a woman says something will make a new man of you, all it means is that, like the rest of her crooked devices, it will make an old man of you before your time." [30] So these priests become both children and old men all at once, a sad combination and an even sadder reflection on their domination by such "strange" women.

Not all priests, to be sure, were subjected to O'Connor's criticisms; there were priests who merited praise, especially when they displayed their human rather than their institutional side. Consider, for example, the priest in "First Confession," a story often anthologized, in which young Jackie tells of his experiences in the confessional booth. The narrator, unable to tolerate his old, unkempt grandmother and harrassed constantly by his sister Nora to a point where he actually began to wonder whether, because of her malice, "all religious people were like that," tells the priest that he tried to kill his sister with a knife. Whereupon the priest, with a touch of sympathy and humor, tells Jackie that "there's lots of people I'd like to do the same to, between ourselves, but I'd never have the nerve. Hanging is an awful death." [31] The boy concludes that such a priest, from the moment he opened his mouth, "was exceptionally intelligent." Besides, the priest's demeanor, his jesting, his ability to converse freely and pleasantly, and to walk jovially with the youngster in the yard is so impressive that Jackie found him to be the "most entertaining man [he'd] ever met in the religious line." In fact, he finds it difficult to part from him.

Would that more priests proved so "entertaining" by showing the human side of their calling! How much greater and more beneficent their influence would be over a generation of young people preoccupied with the vast and rapidly moving changes in their world order. They would capture the hearts of many of the uncommitted and the priesthood would not, therefore, be looked upon so strangely by so many.

In addition to the priests' general lack of open heartedness, O'Connor observed that some of the priesthood also lacked convic-

tion or genuine feeling in the performance of their duties. One such
case is Father Fogarty in "The Teacher's Mass." Father Fogarty is
a man whose "temptation was toward action and energy" but who
feels constantly frustrated in his duties because, "though he loved
and admired his people, he could do little or nothing for them."
This resulted in fits of suicidal gloom in which he takes to the
bottle. He never understands the cause of this frustration. He would
say his private Mass very early in the morning, assisted by Considine, a retired schoolmaster who cannot fathom why Father Fogarty
would rather spend time with "illiterate peasants rather than himself." Although Considine suffers a heart attack, he insists on showing up each morning because, he says, he wants "to die in harness
. . . and the day wouldn't be the same to me if I had to miss
Mass." After a number of such incidents, it suddenly occurs to
Father Fogarty that Considine possesses something he himself does
not have, a "passion of will":

*There was obstinacy there and plenty of it, but there was something else,
which the curate valued more; something he felt the lack of in himself.
It wasn't easy to put a name on it. Faith was one name, but it was no
more than a name and was used to cover too many excesses of devotion
that the young priest found distasteful. This was something else, something that made him ashamed of his own human weakness and encouraged him to fight depression, which seemed at times to overwhelm
him. It was more like the miracle of the Mass itself, metaphor become
reality.*[32]

So when, one day, Considine actually suffers an attack during the
Mass, Father Fogarty completes his prayers but, doing so, realizes
that although he "was actually aware of every detail, every sound,
he had no feelings, he was lacking in concentration." That sudden
transformation is what as a priest he needed, the merging of the
human spirit with the divine, the silent ecstasy, for only that will
keep priests from the frustration Father Fogarty feels at every station along the way. No greater glory could come to any man than
to serve God with feeling. Thereafter, nothing is lacking, so that,
continuing his Mass, while Considine lay dead at the altar, Father
Fogarty could only echo at that moment the rubric: "Then, having
adored and thanked God for everything, he goes away." It is when

metaphor becomes reality that fulfillment of the priest's mission is certain.

There are other priestly frustrations. Chief among them, O'Connor believes, is celibacy. If too difficult or perhaps impossible to handle with polemics, O'Connor felt he might touch upon it in a story which he entitled, significantly, "The Frying Pan." It tells of Father Foley's confrontation with human love. During the course of an evening's visit by his classmate Tom Whitton, a teacher, and his wife, Una, Father Foley learns that Tom has all these years been jealous of him, that Tom, too, had always wanted to be a priest, that he despises Una for standing in his way. In fact, so unrelenting is this desire for the priesthood, that in his relations with Una, "it was never anything but adultery with him, and he goes away and prays for strength to resist it." [33] Because Una appears in Tom's eyes as an adulterous woman, she confesses to Father Foley that she would want someone to make her feel "like a respectable married woman for once in [her] life." All this, of course, occurs while Tom rushes out suddenly to some meeting. Alone together, Father Foley admits he loves her and when she kisses him to the cry of "Darling!" their "unspeakable loneliness mingled." But, at that very moment, Father Foley thinks of "sin" and "adultery," meanwhile hearing the "loud double knock of the old postman, Conscience, at the door."

In this story, as in "The Wreath," also dealing with a priest's need for human love, O'Connor seems convinced that were priests permitted to marry, their lives, instead of suffering so much loneliness—a condition O'Connor was so often concerned with in his stories—would achieve a fulfillment otherwise denied them. Not only would marriage mitigate their consuming loneliness but would remove another form of desolation from their hearts—the lack of children. After accompanying his guests home, Father Foley returns to his own empty house to ponder this very subject with added sadness. Wondering what his "own life might have been with a girl like that," he reflects on it with heavy heart as he ascends to his bedroom: "he remembered that there would never be any children there for his footsteps to wake, and it seemed to him that, with all the things he bought to fill his home, he was merely trying desperately to stuff the yawning holes in his own big empty heart." [34]

However, since celibacy obviously cannot be removed from church canon, other pleasures are often substituted as compensation. Such pleasures, when practiced clandestinely but innocently, were elevated by O'Connor to the category of "song," as in that charming story "Song Without Words." Two monks—Brother Arnold, big, innocent, good-humored, with a pair of blue eyes that always have a twinkle in them, and Brother Michael, "a dour, silent sort of a man that kept himself to himself"—each has a private vice. Brother Michael reads the racing forms on the sly each day and is such an expert at picking winners that Brother Arnold is "filled with wonder to think that where so many clever people lost, a simple little monk, living hundreds of miles away, could foresee it all." [35] Then Michael teaches Brother Arnold how to read the forms so that they begin to bet with each other, paying off their debts in prayers. Brother Arnold, on the other hand, is an expert at cards, and he, naturally, whips his partner; he also has a weakness for a drop of stout which never really did him any harm. As "saints," they are bound to try to improve each other, for "that is the nature of things among saints." And all without a word between them. What emerges from this story is, plainly, the moral O'Connor intended: the hierarchy as well as the laity must be tolerant of such "vices."

Second, these monks, like other men, carry within themselves some hidden failings which are kept from the eyes of their fellow men until they are found out on judgment day. With this basic difference, however: priests, unlike other men, can rationalize the necessity for these "vices" to compensate for their celibacy and the other worldly pleasures they must renounce. Brother Michael expresses the argument best in a moving prayer:

'O Lord . . . a fellow gives up the whole world for You, his chance of a wife and kids, his home and his family, his friends and his job, and goes off to a bare mountain where he can't even tell his troubles to the man alongside him; and still he keeps something back. One little thing to remind him of what he gave up. With me 'twas the horses and with this man 'twas the sup of beer, and I daresay there's fellows inside that have a bit of a girl's hair hidden somewhere they can go and look at it

*now and again. I suppose we all have our little hiding hole, if the truth
was known, but as small as it is, the whole world is in it, and bit by bit
it grows on us again till the day you find us out.'*

These monks are relieved, therefore, to learn that each is subject to
human foibles with which they "improved" each other. This discovery gives rise to an inner song which closes with each of them
saying "Thanks!" to the other. Grateful for their newest discoveries, "they gathered them up between them, the cards and the bottle and the papers, hid them under their habits to avoid all occasion
of scandal and went off to confess their crimes to the Prior." [36] Ultimately, however, the divine must always prevail over the human.
Hence, by the rules of their faith, they are finally forced to reveal
the "words" of their "silent" song.

These, then, are some of the priests who inhabit O'Connor's "island of saints." Not all of them are "good"; neither are they all
"bad." Like all men, they number among them "saints" as well as
"sinners." To be sure, in O'Connor's view, there are more of the
latter than the former. But that is no matter. What does matter is
that even with the "sinners," O'Connor deals kindly, wisely, under-
standingly, and almost always humorously. Unlike his contemporary, Liam O'Flaherty, he harbors in his stories no rancor against
them, even though his irony touches many of their deeds and mis-
deeds. To O'Connor, not unlike, say, Chaucer, they are men of the
flesh as well as the spirit, and the tales he told about them are alternately sad and humorous, and, at times, both simultaneously. What
he tried to do was best expressed by the Irish poet Brendan Kennelly, who, in his elegy on the death of O'Connor, laments:

> You knew the evil of the pious curse,
> The hearts that make God pitifully small
> Until He seems the God of little fear
> And not the God you desired at all;
> And yet you had the heart to do and dare.[37]

FOUR

Naked to the Wolf of Life

What fools people are to embitter their lives about nothing. . . . we have only a few short years on the earth; we come and go like the leaves of the trees, and instead of enjoying ourselves, we wear our hearts out with planning and contriving.
—Frank O'Connor, "A Thing of Nothing"

He loved her as purely and faithfully as he could love anyone after his mother.
—Frank O'Connor, "Lofty"

O'Connor depicts in his art some of the ambivalent phenomena of Irish family life. Not only was his lively intelligence engaged in portraying the religious and political life of his countrymen, but also the difficult and tragic conditions prevailing in their homes and personal lives. Hence, in his two novels—*The Saint and Mary Kate* and *Dutch Interior*—and in, at least, some seventy-odd short stories based on family life, he conveys a feeling of sadness or despair or a mournful note of frustration mingled, as always, with humor and irony. The disarray of Irish domestic relations is central to O'Connor's writing.

To be sure, not all the Irish are hapless in their domestic relations. No doubt some have achieved the *desideratum* of family life, once defined in these hopeful terms:

The Ireland which we have dreamed of would be the home of a people who valued material wealth only as a basis of a right living, of a people who were satisfied with frugal comfort and devoted their leisure to things of the spirit; a land whose countryside would be bright with cosy homesteads, whose fields and villages would be joyous with sounds of industry, with the romping of sturdy children, the contests of athletic youths, the laughter of comely maidens; whose firesides would be forums for the wisdom of old age. It would, in a word, be the home of a people living the life that God desires men should live.[1]

Such idealism as de Valera's certainly stoked the fires of some Irish homesteads.

But what is also certain is that many others, despite regular attendance at Mass, did not live as God desired. Certain conditions prevalent in Ireland seriously interfered with the lives of these "athletic youths" and "comely maidens" and misdirected their quest for the good life, making possible only countless late marriages or no marriages at all. Ireland remained, despite de Valera's vision, an unfulfilled, unhappy, and uninhabitable paradise.

What, indeed, were some of the causes for the failure of this vision? First, and perhaps most significant, is the basic paradox of Irish life which, though "a social system centering so strongly round the institution of the family, condemns a large portion of its members to celibacy and long-preserved virginity."[2] A quarter of all Irishmen never marry. In fact, Ireland holds the "record of possessing the highest percentage of unmarried men and women in the world."[3] Although the average young man expects to marry, he does not get around to it until his thirtieth birthday or later.

Significantly, this surprising number of men and women who pass their lives in celibacy may be due, Sean O'Faolain argues, to a deep psychological repression in the Irishman. Commenting on a disturbing letter from a young correspondent, he writes that "Irishmen have been conditioned into a state of sexual frigidity and expression because for generations we have clothed the sublimity of love in shrouds of taboo, false prudery and an attitude of Victorian Puritanism that has given to the act of sexual union the blasphemous nature of something offensive."[4] All of which gives ordinary Irish men and women a rather distressing appearance "of immaturity, of social gawkishness and sheepishness, of physical uncouthness and malaise."

Part of that malaise may have been produced by the strictness and narrowness of their religious upbringing. The Irish are so overcome with piety that much of the joy and innocence of human love is shrouded in the blackness of "sin." For many, God, in creating the desire for woman in man, "may have been guilty of a lapse in taste." So Ireland became a country where marriage has been defined as "permission to sin." However varied the results, one thing is clear: for many, the Church imperial had a most deleterious effect on love and marriage.

Emphasizing this view, O'Connor wrote a number of stories, among which "The Cheat" is perhaps the most representative. In this story, two "optimists," Dick Gordon and Barbara Hough, after exchanging their marriage vows at the registry office in London, enjoy some ten years of happy marriage until one day the wife, without breathing a word to her husband, decides to take religious instruction and turn Catholic. Her action is considered by Dick's friend, Ned Murphy, comparable to "having an affair with another man." To allow the Church "to enter" a household which had previously enjoyed freedom, innocence, and pleasure would prove, O'Connor implies, its undoing. For, "an adulteress rather than a wife would, thereafter, reside there." And the reader's attention is immediately drawn to Ned's final comment that there was "something uncomfortably apt about the analogy." [5] The wife becomes nothing more than a cheat who, ironically, is in turn cheated out of a husband by his terminal illness. O'Connor's analogy is not only uncomfortable; it is frightening to all, especially the young.

Equally uncomfortable and frightening were some of the other contributing factors to the delayed marriages, ruined hopes, and shattered dreams among the unmarried Irish. Consider, for example, one of the older ones among these in time: the Great Famine. That terrible mid-nineteenth-century tragedy, in which half a million died of famine and some fifty thousand families were evicted from their homes, permanently scarred, it would seem, the Irish psyche. As a result, as Arland Ussher comments, the Irish of even our time are "somber, likely to be suspicious and reserved, puritanical to the point of regarding marriage itself for any other motive but worldly betterment as an almost reprehensible weakness." [6]

To advance their worldly needs and desires, partners to a marriage—and even more the parents of the partners, who really had the final word—would engage in serious and protracted confer-

ences concerning their financial responsibilities. The amount of
the dowry was finally arrived at through bargaining between repre-
sentatives of the two families: "It has three principal provisions: a
statement of the amount of the dowry to be paid by the bride's
father; the stipulation that the groom's father retain no proprietary
interest in the shop; and the provision that in the eventuality of the
death of the husband, his wife becomes the heir-at-law. In this way,
the shop is secured for the wife and her children, and their future
is safeguarded." [7] Such consciousness of the economic burdens of
marriage has been, apparently, so intense and constant that it inevitably discouraged early marriages.

Such hindrances to early marriage and happy domestic relations
were not the only detrimental results of the Famine. Of equal significance with the search for economic stability was the vast and
unending emigration of the young from Ireland. "The Famine,"
John A. O'Brien affirms, "had the catastrophic proportions of a
continuing earthquake that shook the inhabitants from their ancient moorings in the green island and sent them scurrying in
headlong haste to . . . all countries of the world." [8] In pre-World
War II times, most Irish immigrants went to America; today, the
greater movement is towards England. This wild, frantic, unbroken
flight from their native land has continued strangely undiminished
to our day. Whatever the reasons for this exodus—the decline of
agricultural life and its resultant movement towards the crowded
cities, then the loss of jobs—the final result is the great imbalance
between marriageable men and women, leading to an ever-increas-
ing number of bachelors and spinsters.

What further impedes early, that is, healthy, marriages are certain customs, in accordance with which parents retained ownership
and administration of their property even into their seventies and
eighties. Only the grave terminates their rule. Consequently, the
eldest son, who usually remains behind after others have fled, is
destined to inherit the shop or the farm. Into such a household, he
dare not bring a new girl because in the eyes of his parents he is
still a "child." Since old Irish never die but only slowly fade away
at such an age when their offspring can hardly be expected to start a
life of their own, one will remain "a boy forever as long as the old
fellow is alive." [9]

That men in Ireland remained "boys" almost permanently was caused not only by the longevity of the "old fellow," but also by the "old lady." The mothers of Ireland are as responsible as the fathers, if not more so, for their marriage-shy and sex-denying sons. "The Irishman," declared a keen observer of the Irish scene, "is the world's prime example of the Oedipus Complex." [10] The elderly Irish mother has been described as the "most jealous and unreasoning female on the face of the earth." If this should perhaps appear too harsh a judgment, one cannot, nevertheless, escape the conclusion that, because of her matriarchal possessiveness, the Irish mother gives credibility to such a severe view. As Maura Laverty comments:

In this matriarchy, men cannot help being motherbound. Mothers prize their sons far above their daughters—and they have no compunction in showing this favoritism while their sons are young. . . . Sisters are taught at an early age that their duty is to dance attendance on their brothers. . . . The inevitable result is that the Irish boy grows up with an exaggerated affection for and dependence on his mother and with a contempt for all other females.[11]

In consequence, one might expect to find that a good many Irish boys turn out to be something less than full men.

Small wonder, therefore, that O'Connor should appropriately call one of his many stories dealing with parent-child relations "My Oedipus Complex." As one of his most celebrated stories, like "My First Confession," often and widely anthologized, it is cited at least as much for its incisive insight into Irish life as for its charming humor. Larry, the young narrator, who as a child habitually climbed into his mother's bed, realizes one morning, after waking his father, that the old man was really jealous of him. They become, Larry admits, "enemies, open and avowed," and conduct "skirmishes against one another, he trying to steal my time with Mother and I his." [12] Till one day, another son, Sonny, arrives and the two of them—the father, because Mother had "no consideration for anyone but the poisonous pug," and Larry, because of "simple sibling rivalry," become friends.

One cannot escape the conclusion that, though casting his protagonist as a little fellow, O'Connor is here aiming his satiric humor not only at the oedipal relations which make every chap, falling in love with an attractive mother, want to murder his father, but also at the whole tragic condition of Irish life which finds boys, from their early adolescence, severely tied to their mothers' love. And, despite the final act of reconciliation and mutual understanding between son and father, what Larry now really seeks is, ironically, the attention and affection of his possessive mothers. Boys, forever anchored to their mothers, can give little thought, and less attention, to the demands of manhood, let alone marriage.

True of urban life, to which O'Connor directed most of his literary attention, this condition is no less true of the rural areas. There, too, we are told,

the son who remains on the land after his brothers have gone off to the towns or overseas may be discouraged from seriously contemplating marriage until middle-age or else discouraged from marrying at all because mother cannot stand the thought of a rival female in the household with whom she must share her boy's affections. At the same time, those of his sisters who have not emigrated may have surrendered themselves to spinsterhood and a life of waiting on their parents, brother and whatever elderly relatives may be in the household.[13]

Of such maternal possessiveness is born, in all too many instances, the sad, and sadly intolerable, state of Irish domestic relations.

Lamenting this deplorable state, O'Connor wrote a hauntingly moving story, "The Impossible Marriage." In it Jim Graham and Eileen Clery, attracted to each other by loneliness, are deeply attached to their mothers. All too conscious of the situation, common in Ireland, where "a young man or woman 'walked out' for years before he or she was in a position to marry, often only to find themselves too old or tired of it," they decide not to wait but to get married formally; they would, nevertheless, go on living as heretofore, each caring for their mothers. The mothers react typically. Mrs. Clery exclaims: "Go off with him! . . . Go on off with him! I'd sooner go to the workhouse than be disgraced by ye." Mrs. Graham, somewhat less violent, is no less upset, for "it seemed to her that it is her dependence on Jim that forces him into this caricature of marriage." [14]

Ironically, it is precisely this caricature of marriage that Jim and

Eileen must maintain in order to salvage some happiness for themselves in the face of their mothers' selfishness. And they play at this game of marriage, in theory if not in fact, for quite some time. Even after Mrs. Graham dies, Eileen comes to Jim's house to fix her husband's dinner only after as daughter she has already done so for her mother. What is so touching, and, indeed, frightening is O'Connor's description of how, after Jim's death, some two years after his mother's, Eileen moves into her husband's house with her own mother to receive his relatives. Sadly resigned to a life in which, after her own mother dies, nothing will be left to keep her from her late husband, Eileen remains impossibly "married" to an impossible situation.

Yet such conditions, O'Connor implies, are the direct result of possessive Irish mothers who, feeling that a child's mate might rob them of the attention to which they assume themselves forever entitled, smother the happiness of their offspring in a blanket of selfishness. Out of his intuitive and profound disapproval, O'Connor has fashioned this tragic tale which grips the reader in a kind of metaphysical shudder at the appalling lives of so many young Irish people, who, more out of custom than choice, destroy their lives in slavish attachment to aged parents.

Despite the disapproval of her neighbors and community, Eileen, in her sorrow, had been intensely happy, happy in some way they could not understand. What had seemed to them a mockery of marriage had indeed been one so complete and satisfying that, beside it, even by their standards, "a woman might think everything else in the world a mere shadow." With typical irony, O'Connor once again reveals to us that small consolations, in the face of a wrecked life, are assuredly better than none. That Eileen could salvage some personal pleasure, in the midst of all her sacrifices for her mother, attests more to her sincerity and devotion than to the misconceptions of neighbors. Whatever secret joys Eileen shared with Jim, her marriage was, nevertheless, in O'Connor's word, "impossible."

Another intolerable shadow falls over Ireland, causing a low marriage rate and, among those already married, untold hardship. That, of course, is drink. An occasional drinking spree might, we know, release the passions but constant drinking deadens them or, at least, creates conditions of sexual apathy. Equally distressing is the effect of alcoholism on the average family income. Hence, countless families exist in abject distress because the father and sometimes the mother drink away the greatest part of the income. To be sure, there are probably as many total abstainers as total drinkers in Ireland, but, as a social critic has correctly noted, the "Irish either have a poor head for alcohol or else they enjoy playing the part of the jolly carouser, as if determined to live up to the conception of Irish as powerful drinkers." [15] Whatever the cause, the incidence of abuse of alcohol is, by any standard, much too high. All of which gives some edge to the oft-quoted remark which states: "Put an Irishman in a room with a woman and two bottles of stout, and he'll choose the stout every time." [16]

Nowhere in the writings of O'Connor is the horror of drink in Irish family life better described than in that passage in *The Saint and Mary Kate*, in which Mary Kate, befriended in her isolation by the Vaughans, visits them one day only to find herself warning Mrs. Vaughan of her husband's returning home drunk. On seeing him stagger in, Mrs. Vaughan lets out an anguished cry that fills their tenement with deepest sorrow:

There he is, and the week's wages spent, and tomorrow I must dip into the stocking that I was putting by to contrive a little house of my own, and now I'll never have house nor garden either, but spend my days in this stinking hole. Oh, child, child, when I think of my home in Killeagh, and the hens and the pigs and the bit of garden, I could cry down tears of blood! Seven years I've rotted here and slaved here, and seven years he's promising me he's off it now for good and all.[17]

And Mary Kate, learning quickly by listening attentively, begins to realize an old Irish truth that "behind all the love of women for men lies a secret sorrow," the sorrow of a husband's excessive drink. Because that secret sorrow permeated so much of Irish family life, it tended to create a sexual incapacity on the part of Irishmen to a point that, where the "charms of women are concerned, a son of Erin couldn't care less."

Some of this apathy may also have been due to "innocence," for, let us recall, Ireland is a country where, within the framework of the Church, chastity is still paramount. The Church is one of the greatest of the male strongholds and is "primarily responsible for the separation and imbalance of the power of the sexes." One must add that this "indifference" to the other sex may be the result also of much "ignorance." "The youth of Ireland," we are told, "have not only been given a warped view of sex but have been denied, by both their parents, and society in general, the most rudimentary practical information." [18] This "ignorance," apparently, grew out of some sort of Irish conspiracy of silence and prudery about sex that left the youth of Ireland unschooled in the pleasures of romance and marriage.

Of such "innocence" and "ignorance" among Irish youth much has been written. Perhaps, one of the most telling passages is found in Sean O'Faolain's autobiography, *Vive Moi!* Lamenting the sentimentalized pictures, especially concerning sex, given to him as to many of the young people of his day, he relates:

There is one thing I do blame, I must blame, because it caused me so much suffering as a boy—the delicate-mindedness, or over-protectiveness, or mealy-mouthedness, whichever it was, of the Irish Church, and the sentimentalized picture of life, especially in relation to sex—that it presented to us through its teaching orders and from the pulpit . . . as if they believed that if nobody mentioned sex organs we would not notice that we had them. . . . A worse result of this niceness and genteelism of my clerical teachers was that, as boys, whatever we learned, mostly incorrect, about our bodies was learned in dark corners and huddles of shame from brutal words and coarse jokes that associated all passion with filth. Whenever I think of the turbulence and agony of nubile youth, the terror of a boy at his first discovery of his manhood, of a young girl at her first experience of womanhood, I can only rage at our pious elders who so sweetly, so virtuously, so loftily and benevolently sent us naked to the wolf of life.[19]

Unprepared for the struggle with the wolf of life, many Irish youth have been, either out of "innocence" or "ignorance" or both, devoured emotionally.

Sensitive, like O'Faolain, to the over protectiveness of Ireland's pious elders, O'Connor can only lament the maimed young who, in his novels and stories, roam the streets of Dublin and the green countryside. These works bear the doleful reminder that men and women generally do not "enjoy an easy and natural relationship with each other; . . . have no designs on each other beyond the pleasures of friendship and mutual interests." The element of joy in marriage and courtship is absent. "Only the luckier few know what it is to love merrily and live together tenderly." The unlucky many face each other as opposing forces in the battle of the sexes. And all because they are, due to perverse circumstances, "naked to the wolf of life."

II

That the young lovers in Ireland could not enjoy an easy love relationship troubled O'Connor. With deepest roots in his native land, he was disturbed by the conditions that converted the pleasures of love into a battle of the sexes. Among these conditions were, as indicated, the restrictive teachings of the church. Hence, when he wrote the first of his two novels, at the beginning of his career, he entitled it appropriately *The Saint and Mary Kate.* There, as in many short stories, he set the stage for the conflict between two "innocents," who, seeking the joys of friendship and marriage, are frustrated by the church's "thunderings" against the "dangers" of sex. To his disapproval of these "thunderings" O'Connor added his disgust with the pervasive influence of the ubiquitous Irish mother.

But first the story. Mary Kate McCormick, a fifteen-year-old raised in the squalor of Cork by a mother forever "going to Dublin" and without the benefit of a devoted father, believes she has found love in Phil Drinan, eight months her senior. During their "walks" together, she learns of his obsessive piety and even more obsessive attachment to his mother. She sympathizes with the latter but finds it impossible to adjust to the first. Because he wants to become a carpenter like St. Joseph, everyone refers to him as "The Saint." Aspiring to sainthood, he is more interested in the "terrifying moment of the judgment seat" than in Mary Kate's desperate need for love. Their "love," therefore, is never consummated. Finally, he leaves her, hoping "to start over" by learning first to separate his "feelings" from his "soul" and then, presumably, to return to Mary Kate who, matured in tolerance, would welcome back her "reformed" saint.

What O'Connor is anxious to relate in this sad tale of two young Irish lovers is, among other things, that neither is prepared against the "wolf of life." Mary Kate's unpreparedness is due, in part, to the poverty, the squalor of her surroundings, to the sadness of a flighty mother about whom she knew things "that she should never have known, and knew them at an age when she should have been unaware that such things existed." And, worse yet, her drunken father was away in Dublin, causing Mary Kate "to suffer acutely from the thought of what a father's sympathy and affection would have meant to her in the crisis of growing up." Small wonder, therefore, that, starved for affection, Mary Kate, after crawling once as a youngster into the bed of Mr. Vaughan, a family friend, should pray that God "send her a father who smoked a pipe and smelled like Mr. Vaughan, or as an alternative, to take the four Vaughan children back to heaven and allow her to be adopted in their place." [20] Love for her has all the "agonizing peaks and abysses of a graph," due in great measure to her pathetic upbringing.

And Phil, apparently, could do little to help her or himself. He is a prime example of what O'Connor referred to as one of the religious "in-betweens" who is never satisfied with attendance at regular services but is compelled, whenever he passes a church, to enter for additional prayers. "Nothing mattered for him beside the terrified moment of the judgment seat." Terrified, he adds to his "in-between" piety a host of little superstitious beliefs. "The great thing," for him, "was not to cross your own tracks nor pass by the same road twice." Such a fearful person is obviously unable to satisfy Mary Kate's need for love. For what she wants is "human" love, not "divine" love, "a love that was natural and free and easy and unencumbered by the obsessive fealty to penitential excesses" or the "in-betweens of piety." Obviously, Phil is even more "naked to the wolf of life" than Mary Kate.

Religious life in Ireland, O'Connor clearly implies, with its exaggerated rigor produced inhibited characters like Phil Drinan.

The whole body of clerical and lay thought is given to penitential excesses because the conception of sin—especially inherent in courtship—is everywhere. Part of the tragedy of life in Ireland is that people seem to have lost the feeling and craving for life itself. Hence, Mary Kate, displaying a decided lukewarmness about the fierce modesty with which Phil surrounded himself, makes the "most dramatic advance of her life by announcing that she thought a lot of talk was made about nothing, and, personally, if he, for instance, wanted to kiss her she wouldn't mind." [21] But Phil, ever conscious of sin and the thought that as a result of such a kiss he would be forced to marry her, rejects her offer. Because of their unpreparedness their life remains for them simply hopeless.

This hopelessness is compounded, O'Connor reveals, by the omnipresence in their life of Phil's mother. Though she died early, Phil, seized at the graveside by the terror not only of her death but, apparently, of the "death of life," becomes devoted to her memory, "wanting everything to be kept just as it had been during *her* lifetime; with the feeling of *her* in the room he did not see how he could be lonely." And Mary Kate finds that obsession in Phil's character as loathsome as his omnipresent feeling that nothing matters in life as much as the "responsibility of meeting God in death." Hence, his remark that "I'll never marry a woman that isn't like my own mother and I'd expect it of her that she'd be as I'd be," [22] though not wholly unexpected, is disturbing to Mary Kate. She begins to feel that it is a "curse to fall in love for the first time with a boy whose tastes in women ran to motherhood." But what else could she hope for in a country filled with possessive Irish mothers? Phil, like so many other Irishmen, would turn out to be "something less than a full man," or, at best, a "married bachelor."

One cannot, however, help observe that something more profound troubled O'Connor as he portrayed Mary Kate and Phil in the agony of their courtship. He would have us understand that they represent something more than two lovers unable to meet on common ground. For O'Connor speaks of Mary Kate as one who, while attending morning mass, is really staring into the "morning world of her fancy." She is, then, "a poet though she did not write, a musician though she neither played nor sang, a painter though her pictures were herself." [23] Mary Kate becomes, for O'Connor, the symbol of the artist, nay, the "pagan," who desires the pleasures of this world far more than the next, the now rather than the hereafter. Phil is the exact opposite. Together, they seem to symbolize those two aspects of the Irish mind that have been, ever since Celtic times, "in constant conflict, namely, pagan immorality and Christian morality."

What we have in this novel, then, are two people who seem to represent vehicles of that eternal struggle between fruitful humanism and ascetic practice, between Christian morality and pagan immorality, between the sacred and the profane. This dualism is, perhaps, best expressed by Sean O'Faolain who, in *The Irish*, affirms that ever since the beginning of the Christian period such a dichotomy existed in the Irish world and mind: "There may be an overlay of Christian morality. At bottom there is a joyous pagan amorality. They believe in Hell. They also believe in the Happy Isles. They believe in the Christian doctrine of punishment or compensation in the after-life. They believe, simultaneously, in the continuance of life's normal mortal joys and sorrows for all beyond the setting sun and behind the dripping udders of the cloud." [24] This dualism was buttressed by the Jansenist tradition, which ever since the eighteenth century professed that unresolved conflict, because of the essential evil in man between redeeming grace and corrupting nature. Furthermore, Jansen identified this evil in man with concupiscence. Hence, the exaggerated concern in Ireland with lust, resulting in a generally repressive attitude toward life and, too often, a morbid view of human nature.

It is not surprising, therefore, that in *The Saint and Mary Kate*, O'Connor has Phil, after going away alone, seek by some miracle a rejuvenescence which will enable him to see life whole. Perhaps in that way he might possibly bridge these two elemental aspects of the traditional Irish mind as they manifest themselves in Irish life. On the other hand, Mary Kate, maturing suddenly, could recognize only the impossibility of his task and is left with the final suffering thought that behind "all the love of men for women lies a secret sorrow."

And that may be precisely why O'Connor portrays each as unprepared for the other, just as they are unprepared for life. They are left with thoughts of what might have been, had the dualism of their lives as Irish youngsters not been so irreconcilable. Because so much of Irish life forms and dissolves in a never ending duality of spirit and mind, all the saints and sinners, farmers and city dwellers, professionals and laborers and, in *The Saint and Mary Kate*, the young lovers—all, O'Connor believes, are, sadly and inevitably, "naked to the wolf of life."

III

Unlike Mary Kate, not all of O'Connor's characters consider the "in-betweens" of piety as "silly" and frustrating. Some embrace the life of the convent, severing the "common chord" in the solitude of the countryside among the silhouettes of "hills and trees." There they contemplate the mysteries of their faith, seeking, ostensibly, a love higher than that of man. But even those who make this choice find, according to O'Connor, the search for greater love unappealing and, ultimately, somewhat less than rewarding.

Consider, for example, two of his stories, one published early, the other late in his career, in which the choice of religious orders, however appealing, could not satisfy the needs of love. The first, "After Fourteen Years," tells of Nicholas Coleman who, after this time elapsed, returns home to visit a former girl friend, living, apparently serenely, in a convent beyond the outskirts of the town. As she appears, he notices that her "face had lost something; perhaps it was intensity; it no longer suggested the wildness and tenderness that he knew was in her." [25] They reminisce about their past, mutual friends, his life and hers. Of her life, she reveals how "one works, one doesn't think. One doesn't want to think . . . [she] hates anything that comes to disturb the routine." And all he can add is how good it is "to have one's life settled, to fear nothing and hope for nothing." On leaving her, Nicholas begins to think that perhaps her way is best. "Yes it is good to have one's life settled," he concludes again, "to fear nothing and hope for nothing."

Suddenly, however, as the train takes him farther and farther away from this place, it replies with its petulant, metallic voice:

"Ruthutta, ruthutta, ruthutta." As if, O'Connor indicates, it were saying that the convent may not be the best of lives; that one ought to do battle with the world that is bleared, smeared with toil. The sound the train makes seems to echo the sentiments of Mrs. Verschoyle, Mary Kate's friend, and a Protestant, who "smoked, dabbled in spiritualism and was more than half an atheist." Criticizing Phil for believing that by living alone in his garret without venturing out into the world, he would insure his sainthood, she exclaims: "And if you think you can be a saint or anything else in that stinking garret you're very much mistaken. You'll rot there body and soul. You're rotting already, only you don't know it. You're too perverse to see yourself." [26] Neither Phil nor the "nameless" nun can, like so many others in Ireland who preceded or followed her into celibacy, ever face in their current state the toil of life. They must, if life is to be lived fully and convincingly, leave their stifling garrets.

It takes a while before May MacMahon, the good-looking protagonist in O'Connor's later story "The Corkerys," in *A Set of Variations*, understands this elemental fact. An only child, May is so fascinated by the large Corkery family "who always seemed to be playing" that her love for Peter, one of the sons, "was part of her love affair with the family as a whole, the longing to be connected with them." [27] But the Corkerys are also a very religious family: Mrs. Corkery's brother is a Dean of the Cathedral; her sister, Mother Superior of the Convent; her son, Ian, a Dominican, and Joe studies for the priesthood. And Peter, totally dominated by his mother, is a latent homosexual who could therefore, hardly be expected to reciprocate May's love.

Loveless, May, confirming the express fears of her father Jack, who worshipped no one, enters a convent because first, she feels there the "traces of worldliness slip from her" and, second, because she "liked the proximity of Tessie and Sheela," the two Corkery girls already there. But that decision provides her with little love and less with a preparation for living than she had earlier been led to believe. What she suffers there is a series of mortifications followed by major depressions.

May is depressed further when she begins to realize that the nuns she lives with—even Tessie and Sheela—are not made of the stuff of saints and martyrs but are rather commonplace. And what depresses her most is the intuitive feeling that she is the "last Catholic in the world" because the Catholicism she "had known and believed in was now dead." Such depression eventually leads her to enter another home—a nursing home for rest and cure. Cured of her depression, May is brought to her own home by her father, who loathes the Corkerys for what they have done to her. Not long thereafter, Peter, whose mother had herself decided to enter a convent now that her children were all cared for, feels free for the first time in his life to propose, almost half-heartedly, to May. After some initial misgivings, May accepts and both of them, "having travelled so far together and such extraordinary ways," are able, after rejecting the "in-betweens of piety," to face life together with some hope of success.

That too much "in-between" piety had, in O'Connor's view, a negative effect on the loves and lives of young Irish people is clearly evident in yet another of his stories, "The Holy Door," recently dramatized for television. It tells of two girls, Polly Donegan and Nora Lolar, both pious and both terrified by the ghosts of love and marriage: Polly, because she is totally unacquainted with the facts of life; and Nora, because she is a bit of a dreamer who "could hardly bring herself to look at the statue of a saint in the eyes without wondering what he'd look like without his clothes." [28] Because, ironically, Nora finds Charlie Cashman, a hairy man, unacceptable, he marries Polly instead. They honeymoon in Lourdes, and returning home, Polly buys a gallery of holy pictures to cover the walls of her bedroom.

Childless, they make a pilgrimage to the "Holy Door," opened, according to tradition, once in seven years in Rome, which, when visited, assures a couple of having children. Of course, it doesn't help in this case. So Polly asks Father Ring whether she might think of the handsome local school teacher while Charlie made love to her. The priest consents, provided, of course, that she doesn't get any carnal pleasures out of it. But that too doesn't help. So, to prove his manhood, Charlie makes love to the maid, who becomes pregnant immediately. Embarrassed, Polly takes to drink and dies.

Faced with the alternative of marrying the pregnant maid or Nora, Charlie, at the suggestion of Father Ring, chooses the latter because he had learned from Polly the "importance of doing things with a good object." They marry and Nora has the alarming suspicion that she has gotten the "very opposite of what she had always desired."

What O'Connor desired to relate in this story, as in the other two, is that all the protagonists, like so many of their race, "had combined a strong grasp of the truths of religion with a hazy notion of the facts of life." [29] In other words, the pious and, in the case of "The Holy Door," superstitious notions they carry around are no substitute for the "natural" and true emotional relationships of marriage. Neither Lourdes nor The Holy Door can replace the maturity of genuine affections.

All of which leads us to conclude that much of O'Connor's writing on marriage and family life expresses a belief that the vast number of men and women going through life in barren and witless celibacy—all because of the church's thundering on the terrible danger of keeping company, of the easy, happy pursuits of friendship—is weird and unnatural. Unless the beauty and dignity of marriage are presented clearly and unmistakably by the church, schools, teachers, and other shapers of public opinion, the bachelor and spinster mores of Ireland will, O'Connor implies, forever doom the young to remain "naked to the wolf of life."

IV

Ireland's failure to remove a quasi-monasticism from secular life in order to allow for a mutual understanding of the sexes, especially during the formative years, is the theme also of O'Connor's only other novel, *Dutch Interior*. If somewhat less successful structurally than *The Saint and Mary Kate, Dutch Interior* is no less revealing of the nature and destiny of Irish life. For O'Connor's persistent concern—central, in fact, to all his fiction—with the relations of parents and children, with religion, love, and the flight of young people from their native soil is evident in this work. Had he chosen, however, to narrow his attention to one major crisis, as in *The Saint and Mary Kate*, O'Connor might have been more effective. What we get is a series of sketches of middle-class Irish people, drawn together by the fact that they live in the same small town. To be sure, these characters might serve as a microcosm of Irish life. But one cannot escape the conclusion that a central conflict, so necessary to all fiction, is not clearly discernible here. This novel appears too ambitious. O'Connor seems to be attempting a far larger fictional study of Irish society than he can possibly execute. There are gaps— at times, huge gaps—in the story where he just can't come to grips with the need, according to his own views, to delineate the role of the individual in that society. The individual characters seem somehow lost and it is only when he concentrates on the immediate relations between members of the Devane and Dalton families—a thing he does supremely well in his short fiction—that he succeeds if only partially, in this work. Unlike his short stories, he fails to write simply in this novel. As a result, *Dutch Interior* is the least satisfying of his two less than satisfactory novels.[30]

That is not to say that what O'Connor presents here lacks cogency to anyone vitally interested in the panorama of Irish life. And it is the important elements of that life which he wished to describe in this novel. Its curious title would seem to indicate as much. For as O'Connor explains in his "Preliminary" comments to a discussion of the nineteenth-century English and European novel in *The Mirror in the Roadway*, "Dutch interior might be chosen as the ideal of the nineteenth-century novelist." By that he means, apparently, that because the attitude of the middle classes, then establishing themselves politically, socially, and economically in England, was "fully expressed in Dutch genre painting," the novel, written especially for them, would be on its arrival "primarily domestic and civic, would concentrate on the study of society and the place of the individual in it, and on the structure of the classes, professions, and trades rather than on the mythological or historical part."[31] Hence, the name *Dutch Interior*. O'Connor, like his earlier counterparts, intended to concentrate in this work on a study of Irish society and the place of the individual in it. He wanted, obviously, to write something in the "Dutch genre."

Dutch Interior begins, then, with the childhood scenes of the brothers Gus and Peter Devane, both friends of Steve Dalton, presumably the "protagonist." As these scenes unfold, we are witness to those experiences of our impressionable childhood which seem to remain with everyone throughout life, such as those stemming from the relationship of a child to its mother. Echoes of this relationship fill, we may recall, O'Connor's autobiographical works. Here, for example, Peter walks in the rain with his mother, who has just been told by Eileen Soames, the neighborhood waitress, that, whatever fears she may have had about her end, she did, in the meantime, have her son as a consolation. As his mother's face lights up, "Peter thought with joy that soon they would be going home through the wet streets, he taking shelter under her shawl, carefully pacing to her uncertain tread and watching the pavements from under a fold of it. . . . He smiled at her. It was their secret." [32] Such secrets seem to be shared by so many Irish youngsters who, having little else in their squalor, have at least their mothers as shelters.

In fact, Stevie shares Peter's secret. He, too, adores his mother, "loving, lonely and considerate." Walking home one day with his friend, Steve feels lonely and "for the first time that day he thought of his mother, rising before dawn, and sitting alone in the cold parlor, thinking her own thoughts. And there is nothing he could do for her." [33] To O'Connor, nothing seems more painfully difficult than the Irish youngster finding himself, in his first meetings with life, alone, with no one to protect him except his suffering mother.

And Steve, like so many other Irish lads, can do little to thwart the evil that flows naturally from his father, a father who can recall the name and location of every railway station, and the population of every town in Ireland as well as Europe, but knows nothing about nor cares about the personal desires and ambitions of his sons. So when Ned, Steve's older brother, suffering from an infectious cold, is forced by their stern father to go to work in the freezing outdoors, he dies soon thereafter. Just before then, when Steve sits drawing one day, instead of doing his lessons, his father's reaction is violent: "So them are the lessons you're doing! Is that what I'm paying good money for you at school for? Is it? Go on out now . . ." And when Ned comes to his defense by wrestling with the father who grabbed the book, the old man shouts: "Out to hell

to ye I say, ye two ignorant, idle bastards, better fed than taught."
All of which does not surprise us, for lying behind the father's
"madness" is not only his total lack of appreciation of such things
as art but also O'Connor's contempt for the father who terrorizes
his home and family. It is, in fact, Ned, who, turning to Steve, sums
it up best in bitterness and contempt: "Don't bother your head
about him. . . . You'll meet plenty more like him. The world is
full of them. They think they're great; they think they're God Almighty and known every humping thing. They know nothing." [34] If
father knows nothing, mother, especially in O'Connor's life and
works, knows everything, or almost everything. And Steve's mother
is another good woman, who, liking books, inspires Steve to read.
Inspired, Steve suddenly is aware, after reading and thinking, that
in his home surroundings there exists, despite his mother, a terrible
emptiness.

If life is empty for Steve, it is equally empty for different reasons,
for Ellen Soames, who goes "walking with Johnny Collumby." Because life offers them little opportunity, they feel they will be unable to marry. So when Mr. Donoghue, a comfortable man, proposes marriage, Ellen accepts because like so many marriageable
girls in Ireland, she can ill afford to wait for her "true love," lest
she remain a spinster. On leaving Johnny, she seems to justify her
decision by convincing herself that "true love" had not been
vouchsafed to the young of Ireland: "The nuns are right. There's
no such thing as love. I don't believe in it, and I should know, seeing what it done to my family." She decides, instead, to be mistress
of her own fate.

But Ellen plays her fortunate role for only a little while. For the
other problem that plagued Ireland plagues her, namely, drink. Her
husband, Mr. Donoghue, returns home one day drunk. Rejecting
his advances, she crouches against the wall, sadly remembering her
past: "In a flash of horror it all came up before her; her mother, the
pub; an eternal pattern." And what a frightening pattern! Drink
ruined many Irish homes; it utterly destroys Ellen's.

Equally sorrowful, as these characters grow a little older, is their
lack of faith not only in family life but in the political and economic viability of their native land. Like so many of the maturing

young, they become "wild geese," who, disillusioned with Ireland, fly to greener pastures overseas or, in more recent times, to England. Gus, for one, goes to America, exclaiming: "What's happened to this place. . . ? It's rotten; you know that yourself; rotten from end to end. All this drinking and talking and joking, it's all idleness, despair, putrefaction. The bloody Irish! I feel I can't stand any more of it." [35] But, he learns, soon enough, that if he can't stand Ireland, he can stand America even less, because of the many "exploiters" he finds there. Besides, he has learned from bitter experience that "all the happiness beyond the seas is bunk. There's no such thing." Concluding, therefore, that he "could only feel right about one place," he returns home.

He does not, however, feel right again. Being home for a while, he recognizes that the noble ideals which motivated him to return can hardly be realized since his country is "behind the times." And because the best brains are continually leaving, only a "set of half-wits were running what was left." And as bad, what is left is being ruined not only by half-witted politicians but also, as O'Connor made plain in *The Saint and Mary Kate* as well as in many of his stories—by the Church. The rigid asceticism it fosters has a devastating effect, particularly on the young. The clergy are unable, it seems, to distinguish between the ephemeral nature of moral compulsion and the enduring force of a real moral training. Hence, in a lively discussion with his friends Mac and Farrel, Gus is clearly made to understand what he had himself concluded, that mere authority in the regions of moral conduct cannot have any abiding effect, especially among youth. This, in part, is their conclusion:

'Anything a child doesn't understand is bad for it,' Devane broke in with sudden earnestness. 'You see, . . .' Mac exclaimed . . . 'religion is like poetry. If you can't make it real to him, you kill the instinct in him. 'And, . . .' Farrel babbled . . . 'What happens [to] all these kids when they grow up? Tell me that! Where does all the religion go then? If one tenth of it stuck we'd have a nation of saints. And what have we? A nation of crooks!' [36]

Like Gus, Steve, too, is convinced that he is not living among a nation of saints. The authority forced on him during his youth gives way to a freedom which allows him to enjoy what was previously forbidden. Hence, when Eileen, disillusioned and unhappy with her drunken husband, invites him to "visit" with her, he does not hesitate to accept, forgetting quickly his early religious indoctrination. Their happiness is short-lived. No sooner does Eileen become pregnant and give birth to a boy than Donoghue seeks to return to his "neglected" wife. That Eileen would continue, despite his behavior, to think favorably of his return disturbs Steve terribly. Together with his friend Gus, Steve mourns their disenchantment with life, as if they were "alone at night in an empty house where nothing comes back but the sound of [their] own voices." So empty is existence for them, primarily because of their punishing past, that not only are they deadened in spirit but also prevented, in O'Connor's trenchant comment, from being able, "to eat the raw food of life; they must have it boiled down for them."

Unable to eat the "raw food of life," therefore, the characters in *Dutch Interior*, forever caught between an oppressive past and an uninspiring present, are either defeatist, fanatic, conceited, supercilious, or spiritless. No wonder the whole tone of this work is so bitter, for what, in truth, do all these people have to look forward to in a country, O'Connor knew, whose "national habit of living in the past seems to give [them] a present without achievement, a future without hope"? Hopeless, they are not only unable to take sustenance from the "raw food of life" but even find it difficult to digest it "boiled." It is inevitable that Stevie should finally conclude, in the very last paragraph of this novel, that what he has to live with are "ghosts, nothing but ghosts."

V

No characters in O'Connor's fiction seem less prepared, because of their limited circumstances, to struggle with the ghosts of life than parents and their children. To them he devotes not only the real life stories of his own parents, as in his autobiographical *An Only Child* and *My Father's Son*, but also at least some twenty fictional tales. To O'Connor, as to many a sensitive artist, the clash of generations was an unavoidable bane and, also, an essential catalyst. It is the natural function of the young to assert their independence, to challenge their elders' traditions. In turn, it is the natural propensity of parents to resist that challenge, rationally and "irrationally." Hence, in the family, parents and children—readiest targets of one another's mixed emotions, both loving and hating— are natural allies and natural enemies, mutual sources of satisfaction and frustration, pride and guilt.

That O'Connor possessed conflicting emotions towards his own parents is certain. Of the two, he favored, we need only recall, his mother. Anyone reading *An Only Child* must be immediately impressed with his intense admiration of her "humility and gentleness," her "vanity and obstinacy," and her belief in the "world of appearances," that "if something appeared to be so, or if she had been told that it was so, then she believed it to be so." In addition, he was especially moved by her strength of character, which enabled her to emerge from the deep and dirty gutter into which life had thrown her. For O'Connor she was a magnificent woman who, dreamy and romantic, survived the trauma of orphanage—seeking, throughout her life, love in a world of treachery. Hence, when she warned him, "Child, I know you're going to miss me when I'm gone," it came true. Her warning haunted him, especially after her death, for the rest of his life.

For his father, O'Connor had little reverence. Whatever respect he had was dissipated once on a Christmas Eve when the old man showed his true colors. It was then, when his mother needed money most in order to brighten the holiday for her only child, that she could not accept, as she always had with resignation, the less than adequate sum left from his weekly pay. "Lord God, what am I to do with that," she cried. Her very young son, terribly frightened, recalled: "I listened in terror because she never invoked the name of God." [37] But his father could not care less, for all that he did was lament the carrying on of his "extravagant wife and child," showing clearly his insufferable self.

This experience, repeated often apparently, etched itself so painfully in O'Connor's memory that it is reflected not only in his autobiographical works but also in his fiction. Consider, for example, his story "The Thief." On Christmas Eve, the narrator, a youngster of about nine or so, recalls how, jealous of his brother Sonny, aged seven, who "was mother's pet, always chasing after her to tell her what mischief I was up to," decides to find out whether there is such a person as Santa Claus. After both he and his brother had hung their stockings, he tries to stay awake to confront Santa himself, but falls asleep instead. In the morning, he finds that all that Santa had left him is "some sort of book folded up, a pen and pencil and a tupenny bag of sweets," whereas Sonny has received "a pop-gun that fired a cork on a piece of string." Disappointed, he switches stockings before his brother awakes. After being severely reprimanded by his mother for stealing and lying, the narrator makes one final comment which, obviously echoing O'Connor's past, is a most searing condemnation of the old man:

I understood it all, and it was nearly more than I could bear; that there was no Santa Claus, as the Dohertys said, only my mother trying to scrape together a few coppers from the housekeeping; that my father was mean and common and a drunkard, and that she had been relying on me to get on in the world and save her from the misery of the life she was leading. And I knew that the despair in her eyes was the fear that like my father I should turn out to be a liar, a thief, and a drunkard.[38]

And in "The Drunkard," another ironic tale, O'Connor's narrator actually takes a fancy to drink in imitation of the father, only to be defended, as always, by the loving, protecting mother. It all happened one day when the youngster accompanied the old man—who always attended funerals, even if it meant the loss of a half-day's pay, in order to indulge in the usual post-burial drink—to the memorial services for Willie Mack. After services, the old man took the son along to the pub, ordering lemonade for the boy and two pints for himself. No sooner does the youngster, dry and thirsty, finish his lemonade than he downs the porter while his father's back is turned. Suddenly turning sick, the boy is rushed home by the old man, fearing the derisive remarks of the neighbors who would surely accuse him, among other things, of ruining the youngster. And it is the mother, seeing them both stagger into the house, who is the most derisive of all in her comments, saying bitterly: "By this time everyone on the road knows what you are. God forgive you, wasting our hard-earned couple of ha'pence in public houses, training up your child to be a drunken corner boy like yourself!" [39] But for the boy she has only praise, thanking God for his presence in the pub so that he could serve as her husband's guardian angel. Now she must save her son from his father's "evil influence."

But a son, any son, must eventually, O'Connor understood well, protect himself from a father without benefit of his mother but by his own personal resistance. As he grows older, a son must begin that resistance with a show of independence, if, at first, only in word though not in deed. And so it seems in "The Procession of Life." After his mother died, Larry, the narrator, tells us how his father, after insisting that his grown son of sixteen report home every night at ten, locks him out when, one night, he arrives after that hour. Off Larry wanders that cold night to the local bridge, where Squinty, the watchman, all alone as usual, welcomes him, after first berating him for fearing his father. A "night woman" passing by picks him up, but as they are about to go off together, a policeman stops them. Finally, "after choking over a mouthful of the neat whiskey in the policeman's flask" and after lighting a cigarette, Larry leaves for home, unafraid of his father's threats of thrashing him because, as he boasts to Squinty, "I'd bloody well like to see him try it." [40]

Try as fathers may, they cannot withstand the inexorable "procession of life." Sons grow older and, maturing, tend to rely more on themselves, at least in their attempts to resist the blustering threats of their drunken fathers. There comes a time in their lives when they must seek a diminution of parental repression and insist on their individual choices. And all this, O'Connor seems to be saying in this story, even, or especially, in Ireland where, at least in his day, the father figure loomed large in the average household. With his usual irony, O'Connor shows how this road to maturity for an adolescent is usually lined with clandestine encounters with the law, sex, drinking, and smoking. And fathers had better be prepared not to repress these "pleasures," lest the gulf between them and their sons become deeper and wider.

Not only do children, we learn, resist their fathers as they gradually mature but, when unable to do so for whatever reason, often mock them. And that is what happens in "The Grand Vizier's Daughters." An uncle, "tall, gaunt and melancholy," is telling his nieces, Josie and Monica, about a Grand Vizier from Constantinople who has two daughters and the "devil's own temper." Warned not to spread his "subversive doctrines" about the Grand Mufti's failure to pay his share of taxes, the Vizier, because of the "boiling blood in his veins," refuses to heed the warning. Instead, grabbing the mufti by the collar of his coat and slack of his breeches, he hurls him across the room, thereby becoming the "first Mussulman in history to get hold of a mufti by the slack of the breeches." [41] When the nieces inquire why the uncle, in telling his story, fails to mention the Vizier's daughters, he contradicts himself, claiming that the Vizier had only one daughter whose engagement was terminated because of her father's drunkenness and blasphemy. The daughter moaned and cried for weeks because she was "ashamed of her father." As the uncle rises to go, Josie and Monica shout in protest that they would never dare say that they were ashamed of their father. "Daddy, daddy," Josie cried, "I'm not ashamed . . . Daddy come back to me! Come back."

Despite their protestations about their own father, who was a drunkard, they are indeed ashamed. For nothing does more to destroy the filial bonds' between fathers and children than shame, especially over a parent's drunkenness. Such daddies never really "come back." They live, instead, as a source of eternal embarrassment to their children.

And yet, despite all the shame, the derision, and the laughter, fathers could, on occasion, O'Connor contended, have a positive influence on their sons. Given the nature of Irish family life, where fathers as a rule control the destiny of their sons by sheer physical force, they did, at times, by simple persuasion and some straight talk, motivate their sons to positive action.

Witness the story entitled simply "Father and Son." Divorced from Dan, who is now married to Mildred, Min wishes to return for a weekend to see her children Bawn and Tim. Mildred, an excellent and understanding stepmother, decides that, under the circumstances, she and their little daughter, Flurry, ought not to be home that weekend. Dan disagrees vehemently, but because Mildred refuses to understand that "nothing in the world was so over as a marriage that was over," fails to convince her. She leaves. And all goes well. That night, Dan visiting Tim's room, finds the boy in tears and decides then to tell him the whole story of his broken marriage, "the good and bad, sentimental and sordid." [42] For Dan knows that "more harm was done by people trying to say what they meant than ever was done by deception." Tim, listening carefully, is impressed because what he wants from his father "wasn't fairness but a sense of the human reality, even if it hurt." It was, indeed, all over. So that when Mildred returns she confronts Dan, asking what he has done to Tim that weekend for Tim to have kissed her.

What O'Connor attempts to stress, apparently, is that fathers and sons need not confront each other in anger and disdain, as is so often the case in Irish households; instead they should speak to each other softly and faithfully of their common concerns and bonds of interest. In this particular story, O'Connor dealt with a broken marriage but the approach would apply, as well, to all other issues. Fathers need not be wolves, nor sons bleating lambs. If only they could learn that life begins with the word!

But O'Connor certainly is not oblivious to the fact that, among Irish fathers and sons, such civility is rare. Somewhere, the word, spoken softly, clearly, sympathetically, is being lost. And it may not always be due entirely to the Irish fathers themselves. Like fathers everywhere, they expect, but rarely receive, some recognition and even appreciation for their efforts. Those very expectations may be a cause for some of their bitterness and brutality. They seek a little appreciation, especially in those instances, however occasional, when, reversing their attitudes from that of demonic brutality to that of angelic concern, they are dedicated more to their offspring than to themselves. And if the still unfeeling children then do not reciprocate in kind, the failure in communication leads inevitably to a greater loss of regard between them and their children.

One such occasion is celebrated in "The Party." Old Johnny, the gas company watchman, is approached one night at Christmas time by a "stranger" who offers to guard the lights while he goes off with his friends to enjoy a drink. So Johnny and his friends, the Coakleys and Tim, spend the night drinking and wondering what moved this respectable man, Mr. Hardy, who had lost his wife some ten years earlier, to want to sit guarding street lights during the festive

holiday season. Returning at dawn, Johnny learns that the gentle-
man is less intent on watching street lights than on observing his
son and daughter, whom he had left at his house party across the
street from the watchman's box. What Mr. Hardy wants to learn
is whether his children have noticed their father's absence from all
the festivities. Confiding in Johnny, Mr. Hardy declares: "Here I
am that paid for the party, sitting out here all night, getting my
death of cold, and did my daughter or my son as much as come to
the door to look for me? Did they even notice I wasn't there?" [43]

Of course, they hadn't noticed his absence; they were too engaged with themselves and their party. But, if they haven't noticed,
the watchman in his wisdom, "a wisdom that came of the silence
and darkness when a man is left alone with his thoughts, like a
sailor aboard ship," most certainly does. Reviewing his strange
friend's predicament, Johnny offers him some wise counsel and
consolation: first, he says, "Children can be fond of you, only you'd
never see it till you didn't care whether they were or not." Second,
the watchman adds wisely: "Get some lovely little piece to spend
your money on who'll make a fuss over you and then you won't
begrudge it to them so much." [44] What the wise watchman is, in
effect, saying is that Mr. Hardy is himself selfish: he couldn't really
bear to see his children enjoying themselves while he, the widower
who gave them everything, had no one now whose pleasures he
could share. Children do care, only they do not always, for whatever
reason, demonstrate it adequately, that is, to the satisfaction of the
parents. Besides, children have their own lives to lead and cannot
devote their time to fathers who ought to seek other partners, other
places.

But fathers, O'Connor concludes, seldom understand these
things. For, toward the end of the story, when the watchman, ex-
pecting that Mr. Hardy will, in appreciation of his advice, grant
him more gifts and money, O'Connor concludes that Johnny,
though a realist, is really living in a dream. He gets nothing more.
For fathers, of all types, are generally selfish and have little use for
advice to meliorate their frustrated desire for the doting interest of
children.

What is true of Irish fathers is not true, according to O'Connor, of Irish mothers. How different are these mothers! They need not wait nor beg for the affection or attention of their children, especially their sons. In fact, it is often given to them freely, gladly. They turn from an "affection" for their husbands to a love for their sons, which, if not fully reciprocated, arouses their uncontrollable jealousy and the wily use of their subtle powers to regain it. In fact, so great is their power to hold the love and obedience of their sons that it extends even beyond the grave; even in death, the Irish mother holds sway over her brood. And if, as a result of all this possessiveness, the son turns out to be somewhat less than a man, it concerns her little. Her only concern is with "owning" her son, utterly.

To see how this possessiveness and jealousy functions in Irish life, we need but turn to O'Connor's often anthologized story "Judas." Hearing his mother's warning not to come home late, Michael John, the narrator, goes out to meet Kitty Doherty, a hospital nurse, before whom he feels inferior and inadequate. He follows her home, only to find himself further frustrated because Paddy Kinnane is also waiting for her. Though Kitty finds Michael John refreshingly different, she decides, nevertheless, against going out with him. Walking home in the moonlight, he hears the street clock and reminds himself of his mother's warning to come home early. Lying in bed, dejected at his inability to win his girl, Michael John reflects on what follows the memories of Kitty that the moonlight had brought him:

But every time I tried to imagine her face as she grinned up at me, waiting for me to kiss her, it was the mother's face that came up instead, with that look like a child when you strike him for the first time—as if he suddenly saw the stranger in you. I remembered all our life together from the night my father died; our early Mass on Sunday; our visits to the pictures, and our plans for the future and . . . it was as if I was inside her mind while she sat by the fire waiting for the blow to fall. And now it had fallen, and I was a stranger to her, and nothing I could ever do would make us the same to one another . . .[45]

Because Michael John harbors thoughts of escape from his mother by loving Kitty, he becomes, for her, like a "Judas," the destroyer of the eternal love between mother and son. Nor is she entirely blameless for giving him the nature of a permanent child who could never conceivably extricate himself from under her over-bearing presence. Small wonder, therefore, that after dreaming strangely of a different love, he runs helplessly crying to his mother who, "sitting up in bed under the Sacred Heart lamp," could only refer to him as "child, child, child . . . my little boy." Of his own hopeless, helpless condition, created by his Irish mother, herself Judas-like in her jealousy, Michael John concludes sadly:

She spread out her arms to me. I went to her and she hugged me and rocked me as she did when I was only a nipper. "Oh, oh, oh," she was saying to herself in a whisper, "my storeen bawn, my little man!"—all the names she hadn't called me in years. That was all we said. I couldn't bring myself to tell her what I had done, nor could she confess to me that she was jealous: all she could do was to try and comfort me for the way I'd hurt her, to make up to me for the nature she had given me. "My storeen bawn" she said. "My little man!" [46]

And all this suffering for being out late one single night! A jealous Irish mother, O'Connor emphasizes, can reduce a son to utter hope-lessness, nothingness.

What is so remarkable to O'Connor about this power of the jealous Irish mother to subjugate her sons is that it prevails beyond the grave. As if by some magic, she hold sway over them even after she has long gone from this earth. Witness "The Stepmother." Mr. Desmond, a "big, jolly and emotional" man, though heart-broken at the natural loss of his wife, does not wait long before remarrying to a "tidy little piece" who is "mad on amusement." While making the rounds of amusements with her husband, the new Mrs. Desmond has his children, Bob and Sheela, take turns minding the house. One day, Mrs. Desmond scolds and cuffs Sheela for insubordination; whereupon, Bob, anxious to restrain her while simultaneously protecting Sheela, kicks her in the shins. When the father comes home and demands, in his fury, to know why Bob cuffed his stepmother, the latter answers, "Because she's not our mother." [47] This, in turn, so infuriates the old man that he beats his teen-age son mercilessly. The stepmother, after first calming her husband, inquires of Bob why he kicked her. He answers forth-rightly that, on the day before her death, his mother had extracted a promise from him to the effect that if, at any time, any step-mother would ever hit him or Sheela, he'd hit her back.

It was that simple. The first Mrs. Desmond still maintained a hold over her children, demanding and receiving a loyalty to her beyond the grave. She insisted that their fealty would be hers for-ever. And Mr. Desmond, oblivious to all else, is as oblivious to this plain fact that his first wife's influence pervades his home, even though the second Mrs. Desmond is, on the whole, kind to her stepchildren. And, frustrated in her attempts to win their loyalty, she can only comment in desperation to Bob that she hoped "God would forgive your mommy anyway." Jealous Irish mothers, O'Con-nor would have us know, "never die nor do they ever fade away." Their influence and dominance over the lives of their children lin-gers on, if not forever, then for too many years after they have gone from this earth.

But this lingering power of Irish mothers over the lives of their children is not one-sided. Irish children, O'Connor knew, recipro-cate in kind. In fact, so great is this love of children for their mothers that, except for their immediate brothers and sisters, they resent and reject anyone who would invade the privacy or primacy of that love. Her children not only "rise up to call her blessed" but rise up in "arms" against anyone who would dare share that blessed-ness. In addition to her love, children, in return for their attach-ment, insist also on their mother's undiluted attention. Hence, when Larry and Susie, in "The Pretender," note with what fre-quency Denis Corby, who lost his father and has no "proper Mother," comes to visit their home, they are terribly suspicious.

One day, it suddenly dawns on Larry that, though Denis "was quite ready to play with Susie and [him], it wasn't for that he came to the house. It was Mother, not us, he is interested in. He even arranges things so that he doesn't have to come with us and could stay behind with her." [48] Their panic, especially Larry's, who is his mother's favorite, worsens when Denis begins gradually to replace them as their mother's pet. Unable to control himself, Larry strikes Denis twice and has to be restrained by his mother from hurting him further. Of course, the mother could have been the real "pre-tender," for, despite her assertions to the contrary, she might have been hiding something from her legitimate children, especially since Larry comments finally that Denis has "a cool cheek to imagine we were his brother and sister." But that does not diminish Larry's and Susie's anxiety about maintaining their mother's love and attention all for themselves against the "usurper" in their midst.

And yet, despite the strong ties that exist between sons and mothers or fathers, it is obvious that a son, if he is ever to assume his own appropriate role in society, must establish his own identity. However difficult it might actually be in his own country for an Irishman, be he boy, young man, or bachelor, to divest himself of his mother's jealousy or father's autocracy, he can survive, O'Connor keeps reminding us, only if he becomes his own unique person. And only if he does so will the Irish male master his own destiny.

For that is precisely what happens to Jimmy Garvin, apparently a "real mother's darling," in "The Paragon." Because "all he ever needed to make him happy was a book," he won all honors at school and entrance to the University. His aunt suggests that he visit his father who has deserted the family, and the mother agrees because she wants to show off to her former husband how she has raised her son to become a "paragon." Jimmy is so impressed with his father after a while that he begins to feel that his success at school is really all his own doing. He soon starts to neglect his studies and to do poorly at school. The mother, arguing that the father has "deliberately set out to corrupt him just to destroy whatever she had been able to do for him," loses confidence in her son, considering him a "cracked paragon." Relations between mother and son become strained. Once, he even berates her, shouting: "Maybe I am a blackguard, but if I am, that's my fault, not his. He only did what he thought was best for me. Why do you always assume that everybody but yourself is acting with bad motives." [49] This manner of talk scares even Jimmy who, to that point, has become so accustomed to obedience, gentleness, and industry that he could not even imagine how he had come to speak to his mother in such a tone.

Something has, obviously, happened to Jimmy that he cannot

explain: he becomes a stranger to himself. For one who enjoys staying at home every evening studying, to talk this way to his mother or to perform so poorly at school or to pick up the school teacher Anne Rudy, with whom he goes off to Crosshaven on weekends is baffling to everyone and especially to himself. Part of the explanation for such behavior O'Connor supplies by having the narrator tell us: "What neither of them saw was that the real cause of the breach was that his mother wanted him back, wanted him all to herself as in the old days, and to forget that he had ever met or liked his foolish, wayward father, and that this was something he could not forget, even for her." [50] In other words, what O'Connor is presenting here, in the person of Jimmy, is the dilemma that every young man, especially in Ireland, must feel in growing up: choosing between two worlds of experience. He may opt for, on the one hand, the sweet, serene life at home with his mother or, on the other, the "wayward" life of his father. And he alone has to make that decision, despite the consequences to either parent. He must do what is best for himself by himself.

In this story, the last, interestingly, in the collection entitled *Domestic Relations*, Jimmy finally marries Anne Rudy and, surprisingly, gets his degree. But, before going on his belated honeymoon, he visits his father in jail, where, because of charges of embezzlement, no one, not even his second wife and child, comes to see him. Jimmy, apparently, would like a little of both worlds. However, what results is something uniquely his own; once he rejects some of the obsequiousness demanded by his Irish mother and the waywardness affixed by his father, he alone would direct his destiny as a young man separate from either. That, apparently, was O'Connor's answer to the dilemma of the young men in the Ireland of his day. For he has the narrator sum up Jimmy's experience in a significant final comment, a comment that seems to serve as the quintessence of O'Connor's views on the role of young men in the troubled world of Ireland's domestic relations: "I was thinking of the troubles that Jimmy's discovery of his father had brought into his life but I was thinking, too, of the strength it had given him to handle them. Now whatever he had inherited from his parents he had combined into something that belonged to neither of them, that was his alone, and that would keep him master of his destiny till the day he died." [51]

VI

If a young man were really to master his personal destiny, O'Connor further argues, it surely could not be done through celibacy, the inherent love of which "reigns in every Irish heart." One dare not, neither man or woman, become subject to the transcendental character of the celibate life which, we know, runs through the world of the Irish child—in the home, in the church, in the school, and in the whole social milieu. Although it has been one of the basic precepts in establishing their scale of values, Irish boys and girls, O'Connor warns, must reject the "religious state of celibacy even when not taking orders." To shape one's future, he or she dare not remain a bachelor or spinster but should act, rather, in consonance with the idea that marriage is the natural goal of all human beings.

For one of the terrifying results of celibacy is, of course, the agony of loneliness, a loneliness which O'Connor, in the words of Sussie in "Don Juan's Temptation," tells us sadly grips so many of the young: "I sometimes think young people are the loneliest creatures on God's earth. You wake up from a nice, well-ordered, explainable world and you find eternity stretching all around you, and no one, priest or scientist or anyone else, can tell you a damn thing about it. And there's this queer thing going on inside you that gives you a longing for companionship and love, and you don't know how to satisfy it." [52] The conflict between a "well-ordered world" and "vast eternity," between the loneliness of celibacy and the desperate longing for companionship is central not only to O'Connor's life as an only child but also to his art and, as we shall see, his criticism.

Of all the stories dealing thematically with loneliness, none seems more moving, because so real, than "A Life of Your Own." Jane Harty, a pharmacist living alone at the edge of town because she long ago decided that it was the "only way to live a life," one day finds her home ransacked by, she suspects, an anonymous "telephone caller." Then she suddenly finds the words "I love you," written over her bed. Ned Sullivan, a friend, suggests that she ought to move to Dublin or London, not because he feared for her life but, because of these "ghosts," she could no longer afford "to live naturally in a place like this." Opening the window one night, she seems to see a vague shape in the darkness, and she beckons it it to come in with assurances that the guards, previously summoned, had gone and that no one else is home. But this figure, real or imagined, that she thought must be looking up at her, refuses to accept her call. Afraid lest, by accepting her call for companionship and love, he would end their loneliness and celibacy, he did not enter her home. He is, apparently, trapped in his own crazy character as she in hers.

And is not his refusal "crazy" indeed! For what did she want, this terribly lonely girl in a small Irish town, but, as O'Connor comments, "to come to terms with him, to lure him out of himself and make him realize that there was a world of warmth and friendship where he could be at home." And if, as her townspeople think, she would deliberately choose the wrong man or the man she could not have in order "to hurt herself worse," it is all the more "crazy." But this is certain: because of this experience of recognizing that she "no longer had a place of refuge from the outside world," since there is someone out there in a similar or worse predicament than her own, she "would never be able to live alone; never again would she have a life of her own." [53] Seeking love and companionship, she, like so many other Irish girls, must change her life, renounce her celibacy, reject that loneliness that would surely lead to illusion, disillusion, and disintegration.

What is true of this lonely pharmacist is equally true of the spinsters Joan, Nora, and Marie in "Music When Soft Voices Die," who, instead of reaching out for partners in true companionship or marriage, engage in endless debate on such hypothetical problems as what they would do if, suddenly pregnant, they would be forced to farm out their "illegitimate" children or, in another instance, what their reactions would be if someone were to "steal" their husbands. The deliberations are lusty and humorous but, simultaneously, bitterly ironic. For only Marie finally marries, while the other two fail because, as the narrator comments, they "never met with men astute enough to grab them." [54]

These spinsters, O'Connor seems to be saying, orchestrate their speech to serve as a musical moment in a life that, in its celibacy, is slowly fading away into a dying nothingness; and their talk, however engaging, is totally irrelevant to their real situation, which is filled with loneliness. They alone hear their musical sounds but fail miserably to integrate these sounds with those of others who, equally celibate, might offer them the love and companionship they need so desperately. The voices of Joan and Nora vibrate, to the sure, in the memory of their sister Marie and the narrator; there, though sounding soft and musical, they nonetheless come from hearts all sorrowful and cloyed and forever lonely.

An even greater curse afflicts those who would deliberately invent excuses to refuse the hand of marriage, even when that hand is filled with wealth. Consider, for example, the pretty young chemist in "The House that Johnny Built." She comes upon the scene after Johnny Desmond, a man of means, builds a beautiful house with the finest of furnishings in order to offset, in part, his disappointment at being refused in marriage by Dr. Brown, a local physician and a woman of "style" and "nature." Lonely, he proposes to the young chemist at their first dinner on the day of her arrival because she, too, had the "style" and "nature" he is looking for. But she, for her own reasons, also rejects him out of hand.

Her rejection is not at issue. It is the reasons she gives that form some of the fatalistic answers so many young people in Ireland use freely to rationalize their avoidance of marriage. First, she claims, "Dad wouldn't allow it. He says I mustn't marry till I'm thirty." [55] As if marriage were something of so little consequence that it could be readily postponed until that age, or, for that matter, beyond it to fifty and, then, for life. "I'm too young," she cries. This is but another form of celibacy, if only by parental fiat.

Second, she argues, "I couldn't really . . . I'd sooner not get married at all, but if I have to I'll marry the fellow I'm going with. I'm not sure that he's suitable at all; I don't think he has the right attitude—I have terrible doubts about him sometimes—but I could never think of anyone else." [56] Whether she had another boyfriend is not at all material. What is material and, in this instance, highly operative is her tacit admission that she'd rather not marry at all. And all that after Johnny has offered her the house and so much more. Small wonder, therefore, that Johnny concludes that "there was a curse on him; that his luck was broken and his beautiful house and furniture were all for nothing." For nothing, indeed, when such excuses are the fabrications upon which the young act or do not! So, when Johnny dies, within a year, the townspeople think it was "chagrin that killed him." But Dr. Brown, his first love, knows better for, in her opinion, he "really died of a broken heart." And since O'Connor concludes, "Women are great on broken hearts," he is being gently ironic, poking fun at the softness of women who, since they tend to propose romantic explanations, destroyed the house that Johnny built. And all because the curse of celibacy lay heavily on their Irish hearts.

VII

Of course, not every Irish heart need be cursed. For a curse, we know, can sometimes be lifted. And to lift it one is not required to perform rites of mysticism or exorcism. There is a simpler way— the rite of marriage. Hence, young people, whether moved by the church doctrine of the sacraments or by a simple need for companionship, can create an atmosphere in the home that would exclude the dread of loneliness. In fact, many Irish actually succeeded, despite so many frustrating attitudes toward the opposite sex, in fashioning homes of genuine companionship; while others, needless to say, failed. And it is with those who failed and the reasons for their failure that O'Connor is concerned in his art as in his life.

To judge failure properly, however, one must, we know, have some idea of success. And if it is marriage one must judge, then there should exist somewhere a criterion by which that judgment can be made. Fortunately, there existed, for O'Connor, just such a model—an old couple he knew exceptionally well and revered even more. His admiration for them was indeed boundless. They more than approximated the ideal of home life formulated by de Valera. They were known as "The Tailor and Ansty."

"The Tailor and Ansty" lived in the townland of Garrynapeaka, in the county of Cork. No two people were ever so unlike. The "Tailor," whose official name was "Mr. Buckley," was "interested in everything under the sun and his mind, like a bee, sucked the nectar of every notion. . . . He had a sense of continuity and flow. . . . He sat in his corner, the master of circumstance and the captain of his soul." [57] "Ansty," an abbreviation of Anastasia, who could neither read nor write, was "interested in nothing but her immediate surroundings and the echoes which linger in her mind without interest." Her thought and interest were "a series of full stops and exclamations," using earthy language to whomever she would be talking, regardless of their attitude. When a new edition of the life and tales of these kindly folk was prepared for publication by Eric Cross, it was only natural that O'Connor in his "Introduction" would, in a significant passage, extol their virtues and recognize the differences between them, while praising all the while the "charm" of their marriage: "It is hard to describe what constitutes charm in a married couple but they had it . . . their marriage should probably be described in capital letters. They were Man and Woman, forever squabbling and making up, eternally equal and separate; Ansty always anxious, busy concrete, the Tailor always placid, indolent and abstract." [58]

However difficult it might have been to describe specifically just what constitutes "charm" in a married couple, O'Connor would surely agree with Cross, whom he calls the old couple's "Boswell," and who, summing up his own impressions, writes of the relative merits of this loveable old pair:

All these comparisons are only comparisons of surfaces and appearances. Beneath all the seeming asperity of her appearance Ansty has a heart as big as the Tailor's. After the period of the rigor of her scrutiny and the shrewdness of her tongue, Ansty has an affection as great, a gratitude as deep, a kindliness as gentle as has the Tailor. Her home and all that she has and all that she can do for you are yours, gladly given, for Ansty and the Tailor, though they are two aspects of the same medal, are made of the same metal.[59]

What are obviously important are not the differences between the "Tailor and Ansty," for no couple, however long their union, ever lose their personality differences, but rather their unified generosity of spirit, the gratitude and kindness that constitutes the "metal" holding their lives together.

Their life together, then, is O'Connor's model. By the standards set by the Tailor and Ansty, he tends to judge the failures of his countrymen in their marriages. To be sure, O'Connor understands that the old couple is unique since they may have achieved their idyllic existence either because of pure luck or, perhaps, some special divine blessing and, hence, beyond comparison with any of the young folk beginning their lives together in his day. Nevertheless, the stories and tales and traditions surrounding their life, as recorded for posterity, are sufficiently relevant for O'Connor to serve as a basis for his judgment and art. That is not to say, of course, that, in his stories, O'Connor offers any manual for successful marriage. That is not the function of the artist. Better, it is O'Connor's interpretations and revelations of Irish family life that intrigue and sadden the reader. For O'Connor's portrait, when seen in its entirety, reveals men and women, disillusioned and frustrated, who marry eventually and then for all kinds of unapproved reasons—pity, money, jobs, position—but hardly ever for the simple one of genuine love and companionship. As a result, these couples lack any of the "charm" attributed to those old folks of Garrynapeaka townland.

The story of Frankie Daly in "Unapproved Route" is a case in point. Frankie offers to marry Rosalind after she is deserted and left pregnant by the waster Jim Hourigan. All because he pities her, arguing that "there's no humiliation where there hasn't been any offence. The offence is in deceiving others, not in being deceived ourselves." [60] But despite Frankie's advice and concern, she feels deceived and terribly unhappy. Nevertheless, they finally marry because Frankie feels that she needs his attention to overcome her personal misfortune. However, he makes a terrible mistake:

He really thought when he heard her lonely weeping that it was merely the ambiguity of her position that caused it, and not the humiliation of being rejected and hounded into marriage with someone else by a tramp like Hourigan. Frankie was a decent man; he didn't realize that in circumstances like those no woman can ever be happy, even with the best man in the world—even with the man she loves. Love, in fact, has nothing to do with it. To ignore that is to ignore a woman's vanity, the mainspring of her character.[61]

And Frankie ignores that fact that it is Hourigan's rejection which troubles her and not the "ambiguity of her position," for no sooner is she confined than she sends a note to Jim, informing him of the impending birth of his child. Frankie, drawing within himself, feels terribly hurt, a wound she could hardly understand. She protests that she would never consent to a divorce. Nevertheless, when Hourigan, responding to her note, reappears, Frankie just knew he was seeing her for the last time. He ". . . realized with a touch of bitterness that there are certain forms of magnanimity which are all very well between men but are misplaced in dealing with women, not because they cannot admire them but because they seem to them irrelevant to their own function in life." [62]

Frankie's mistake is that he married for the wrong reason; he substituted "magnanimity" for love. His "magnanimity" meant little to her for a number of reasons: first, her vanity takes precedence over all else and only Jim's acceptance of her could satisfy it; second, a marriage motivated by his grand spirit is of small value when what she seeks is happiness with the man she first loved; and, third, she does not want to be pitied, even with his love. For her, happiness is all; for Frankie it is merely an incident which, if taken away, would still leave him no poorer than before. Sensing that, under these circumstances Frankie could not provide her with what she seeks, she turns to Jim for her happiness. Theirs, O'Connor believes, is the "unapproved route."

Just as O'Connor disapproves of mere "magnanimity" as the basis of a happy marriage, so too does he reject the transforming of marriage into a "cause." The attempt, for example, to make a partner in marriage a substitute for a former one lost in war or by accident or for one who fled to far-off places will not create the "charm" O'Connor admires in the "Tailor and Ansty." At least, that is what he reveals in "The Orphans." Hilda Redmond loses her husband Jim in war. After she begins to "walk out" with Jack Giltinan, Jim's brother Larry appears. That awakens in Hilda memories of her late husband which, having "sunk into the background of her thoughts, were now very much in her mind again." [63] Despite her engagement to Jack, Larry proposes to her, hoping to create thereby some link with his dead brother to whom he is deeply attached. What Larry wants is "a brother as well as a wife—a brother probably more than a wife—which he could find only in her." Hilda cannot resist, but not without first warning him they "have their own lives to lead."

But all this is, in O'Connor's appropriate phrase, "an unhealthy situation." When people marry not for love, but out of a desire to recapture a lost or dead past, they will hardly ever become, as were the "Tailor and Ansty," two "aspects of the same medal." Since Hilda serves for Larry as a living link with his dead brother and, beyond that, with a mother and home he has long ago forgotten, she becomes a substitute brother and mother but never a true wife. "It might be years before he came to care for her as the sort of girl she was." Hence, she was now only a woman with a cause, serving her husband the best way she knows but not in the way O'Connor believes young men and women ought to be related to each other in marriage.

If a "cause" cannot insure a successful marriage, neither can the "law." To engage lawyers, for instance, to settle marital differences or to use the courts as a vehicle for conjugal happiness is absurd. Aside from the fact that husbands are hardly ever favored in the courts or that judges, according to O'Connor, suffer from "mother fixations," the law can do little to effect harmonious relations between young folk—unless they themselves find some common ground for reconciliation.

One need read only "Counsel for Oedipus" to be convinced of these somewhat apparent revelations. After Mickie Joe Dougherty, the lawyer for Tom Lynam, who is charged with cruelty and adultery, tries to defend his client against these charges by Mrs. Lynam, represented by Kenefick, the litigants go outside the courtroom. There, notwithstanding the fact that Mrs. Lynam has been exhibited in the testimony presented in court as a "grey, grim discontented monster with a mania for power," [64] husband and wife are reconciled. Despite a warning to Tom by his attorney that if he returns to this woman, she will only make his life miserable again within forty-eight hours, he remains adamant, arguing that if she does, "we'll settle it between us." Angry that his professional advice is ignored, Micki Joe again warns his client that living with her is suicide. Tom rises to her defense as they leave together, "she, small and sprightly, he tall and morose." They alone will have to determine their future marital life, because courts of law deal with the legalisms of marriage but never with the human elements that unite people even in their misery.

If law cannot adequately solve marital problems neither can "phrenology." For the use of phrenology is the mistake Jerome Kiely makes in "Jerome," when he attempts to find out from Mr. Creedy, the phrenologist, whether Hilda, his girlfriend, will make "a success of him." And even if he knew, Mr. Creedy wouldn't tell because Jerome must find that out for himself through trial and error and an intense desire to rise to the occasion of married life, "instead of sneaking around trying to find out from other people what she's like." [65] Unless Jerome will equal her "sublimity, ideality and optimism," any comment about her would be utterly meaningless. It is not her function, says the phrenologist, to "reform" him; he must "reform" himself to her level. Unfortunately, Jerome may never be equal to her, for those qualities are not easily attainable from others; one must grow and develop them oneself. The phrenologist, like the lawyer, doesn't have the formula for acquiring the "charm" of marriage; it rests within people themselves.

"Sublimity, ideality and optimism," the qualities that make up, in part, the essence of "charm" would, therefore, disallow the activities of, say, a "Don Juan," or the male as rake and flirt. This becomes obvious as we review the life of Spike, the motorman in "Don Juan (Retired)" who recalls some of his escapades of former years. He is called upon in Casserly's pub, by his friends Jimmy Matthews and Joe French, to prove his amazing "performances" of the past. They lay bets that he "couldn't get off with a decent woman in this whole town." Spike accepts the challenge and before long makes a "conquest" behind the wall. But when Joe pays his debt, Spike wonders whether he ought to accept it since his conscience dictates otherwise. The conquest seems easy, natural, and insignificant, since women, in his view, have no "moral standards" whatsoever. And he ought better to remain retired. True love demands the "standards" Hilda has successfully achieved.

To achieve these "standards," O'Connor cautions, neither partner in marriage ought to expect of life something it cannot give. One of the things it cannot give is absolute security. Too much planning is as ineffective as too little, as Sheila Hennessey, in "Expectations of Life," learns to her belated sorrow. After "walking steady" with Matt Sheridan on and off for ten years, she suddenly decides to marry Jim Gaffney, a comfortable widower some twenty years her senior, while preserving her claim on Matt, for women "hate to let one man go even when they have sworn life-long fidelity to another." [66] Jim turns out to be as untidy and casual about money as Sheila is meticulous. She tries to get him to make a will and to take out some insurance so that she can expect a bit of security when, because he is so much older, Jim would presumably leave her a widow; but, he, set in his ways, refuses. Instead, anxious to enjoy life now, he adds comforts to the house, wondering why Sheila, a "born fidget," does not "try to live more in the present."

Forever planning for the future, she succeeds in arranging a match for Matt, her former boyfriend, with Kitty O'Malley, who dies after the birth of their second child. Sheila feels that he will never remarry, at least until she is herself free to have him. But, because life cannot be neatly arranged and the best laid plans go awry, Sheila herself falls deathly ill. Suddenly, she realizes that she might have enjoyed herself just sitting on her terrace, behind the picture window Jim had specially installed, to savor the simple pleasures of home, of marriage, of the present, instead of "fidgeting" about Jim's money and her financial security and planning other people's lives. But, on her deathbed, she proceeds to suggest that Jim remarry after she's gone, despite his criticism of her being the "sort who can't be happy without someone to plan for." Of course, Jim doesn't marry again and, unlike Matt, doesn't seem too overcome with grief when Sheila finally dies.

Again, O'Connor seems to be revealing that married life is pierced with misery when love is adulterated with mixed motives, in this instance, the desire for financial security. Of course, this preoccupation with money matters, prevalent everywhere, may have particular significance in Ireland, where, ever since the Great Famine, families have faced endless financial insecurity. Nevertheless, O'Connor still insists on the achievement of that peculiar "charm" in marriage which marked the life of the remarkable old couple of his county Cork. Hence, Sheila turns out so sadly. She would have liked to possess both Jim, who has everything in securities, and Matt, "who has everything in order." She wanted, apparently, both love *and* security and ended up with neither. Not that both are impossible, but in the usual order of things, there are limitations to the expectations of life. One of them would surely limit the importance of material wealth, and place the greatest premium on unalloyed love as the touchstone of a durable marital life. O'Connor depicts, in his novels and stories, young people who have chosen differently, pursuing, instead of "charm," other and possibly less significant interests in marriage.

And these interests are, in O'Connor's fictional world, in direct conflict with the ideal of Irish life so glowingly presented by de Valera, among others, for his countrymen to follow. Few of O'Connor's characters achieved that ideal, primarily because he saw life differently, not as a "dream" but, rather, "steady" and "whole." Hence, his world is terribly different from the one de Valera envisioned for his struggling countrymen. Yet O'Connor's world is no less engaging because, far more than the then prime minister, he is conscious of the fierce conflict between the "ideal" and the "real," between life as it "should be" and life as "it is." What it is, of course, is somewhat frightening, albeit artistically ennobling, because in O'Connor's interpretation, those who carry on Irish domestic life are, alas, "naked to the wolf of life."

FIVE

A Cargo of Impure Art

To write criticism you must have certain simple facts established. You
must know what the author wrote and when he wrote it. You must
have some rough and ready idea of his intentions when he wrote it.
        —Frank O'Connor, *Towards an*
         Interpreation of Literature

. . . 'belletristic triflers' like myself . . .
        —Frank O'Connor, *The Fountain of Magic*

    Unlike his fictional characters, O'Connor prepared him-
self diligently for a life ultimately devoted exclusively to literature.
Not only did he write stories, novels, plays, and poems but, in
addition, produced five books of literary criticism: *Towards an Appreciation of Literature*, *The Mirror in the Roadway*, *Shakespeare's
Progress*, *The Lonely Voice*, and *A Short History of Irish Literature*. Like the proverbial talkative Irishman, he became drunk with
words. Not all of his words make critical sense, for, as one modern
critic noted, "a kind of brilliant fog enshrouds his pages, whereas
criticism must be read by flashes of transient illumination." And
yet, he is, at times, illuminating and, at all times, approaches literature with a certain candor and freshness which makes his criticism,
like his life, a source of interest and delight.

O'Connor's interest in literature came very early in life. Terribly
poor and uncertain of ever being able to obtain a formal education,
he decided to educate himself. For he knew instinctively that, in
order to overcome the squalor of his surroundings he would need
an education. Besides, forever dangling between his mother's gentle
and his father's coarse manners, he decided, while still young, that

he would have none of the latter. This squalor and coarseness he would surmount by reading assiduously. "Always very fond of heights," it struck him that "reading was only another form of height." [1]

To climb these new heights and to go where glory awaited him, O'Connor began with a strong preference for school stories, especially such penny weeklies as the *Gem* and the *Magnet* because "the characters in them were getting a really good education, and . . . some of it was bound to brush off on [him]." [2] And yet he was fully aware that the really good education those youngsters received would not easily "brush off" on him because of the many things which he, unlike them, did not have: "like an old fellow who did not drink and an old one who didn't work . . . long trousers, a short jacket and a top hat, bicycles, footballs, and cricket bats." In desperation, he would make believe at having some of these things by playing cricket, for example, "with a raggy ball and an old board hacked into shape for a bat before a wicket chalked on some dead wall." That was, interestingly, the start of his search for "glory."

Another factor which directed O'Connor to the world of books was his loneliness. An only child, he sought relief for his loneliness by reading books. For as he read, he was able to imagine a life far better than his own, a life with "friends" and "companions" who would help mitigate that loneliness. In fact, he admits as much at the beginning of his very first published book of criticism, *Towards An Appreciation of Literature:*

My parents were poor and I was an only child. That meant that from the beginning I was thrown very much upon myself, so I learned to read when I was still very young. The only papers I could afford or come by were English school stories. . . . They dealt with young fellows whose fathers had titles and cars and who had lots of money to spend in the tuck shop. . . . they created standards of behavior in my mind which could not be fitted in to the life about me. I don't honestly think that those standards were ever standards of money or rank. I liked the public school code so far as it was reflected in them, and I still like it. I liked boys who didn't tell lies, and who didn't split on one another when they were caught out. . . . I cannot think of any form of literature in which the reader is safe from the ideals of character and conduct which transcend everyday experience.

He came to literature, then, as he fancied a great many other people came to it, "because they need companionship and a wider and more civilized form of life than they can find in the world about them." [3]

To be sure, there was more to this climb to new heights than only personal reading, however varied and interesting. There were, for instance, friends—men like Sean O'Faolain (a few years older than he, a fellow librarian and poet at Sligo, who first made him read Yeats, Pound, and Eliot), George Russell, and Daniel Corkery —all of whom helped him overcome his lack of formal education. And were it not for these people, as well as some others he mentions in *An Only Child* and *My Father's Son*, O'Connor, who left school before he "got so far as long division" and became twenty "before he found out what the simplest grammatical terms meant," might have found himself misplaced in the city of literature as he once was in the city of Cork. He was, indeed, lucky to have met so many men of talent by the time he was "twenty-odd."

That he was able, given his own desire and perseverance as well as these friends, to become, without a formal education, one of the best short-story writers of our time, is no mean accomplishment. And yet, he was not blind to the fact that, however great his fictional art, his lack of systematic training forced him into faults which "would remain with him till the day he died." Among these faults, he states, were a "lack of method, an opinionatedness, and the inability to do the simplest thing without first pulling down the house to get at it." [4]

Nor can one escape the conclusion, on reading his criticism, that although his house of fiction—at least, the short story—is strong, solid, and on a sound foundation, his house of criticism, with some exceptions of course, is on somewhat less solid ground. What one discerns immediately is that he had no consistent approach to his writing about literature. Flashing insights abound everywhere, to be sure, but there seems to be little critical consistency to his thought. An inchoateness marks his critical writing, despite some splendid ideas. He was not temperamentally inclined, nor did he ever intend, to cultivate an "intellectual approach" to his interpretation of literature. In many ways, therefore, his criticism is, to use a favorite word of his, but in a somewhat different context, "impure."

But, if we assume the very obvious and fundamental notion about literature that words intrinsically have not one but multiple meanings, to be read on various levels, then, whether they are of one or many ages is rather immaterial. What is material is that, because words do have meanings, they give to literature its greatest attribute, a means to the understanding of man and his world. Since that idea seems to run consistently through history, shouldn't that make literature "pure" rather than "impure"? O'Connor's use of the term is somewhat unclear.

Let us consider further the other part of his definition of literature, namely as a "cargo of communications and information." [5] If we read him correctly—at times difficult to do because he is so diffuse—O'Connor obviously had a number of things in mind. First, that in fiction, the novelist must be so direct and clear that the reader need not be required to delve into the "meanings" of words, nor into circumstances of plot, nor into the intricacies of character development, beyond their immediate recognition. The writer, according to O'Connor, communicates but does *not* express, relates but does *not* imply. He would discredit, for example, as "impurities" the "psychological" or "intellectual" interpretations of a work or, for that matter, the power of any "artifice" that would keep the reader at a distance from reality. What he seeks is a "realism of presentation." Hence, when questioned during the *"Paris Review* Interview" whether by ignoring, say, the "psychological" interpretation, one would as a result be considered "old-fashioned," he replied:

. . . *I am old-fashioned! It's the only old-fashionedness you can come back to. You've got to come back eventually to humanism, and that's humanism in the old sense of the word, what the Latins and Greeks thought about human beings, not the American sense of the word, that everybody is conditioned . . . people are as you see them, and no psychiatrist is going to tell you anything fundamentally different. . . . People are as they behave . . . you're faced with the problem of which are you going to accept: the evidence of your own mind, of your own feeling of history, or this thing which says to you, "You don't under-stand how a human being works." [6]*

Similarly, O'Connor attacked the belief, widely held, that the unseen and unrevealed, the subconscious, have a bearing on the truth about a fictional character. When asked further in the same "Interview" about this very matter, he replied, no less emphatically:

. . . to me that's all represented by Joyce, talking about epiphanies; in fact, you can never know a character. At some point, he's going to reveal himself unconsciously and you watch and then you walk out of the room and you write it down, 'So-and-so at this point revealed what his real character was.' I still maintain that living with somebody, knowing some-body, you know him as well as he can be known—that is to say, you know ninety percent of him. What happens if you're torturing him or he's dying of cancer is no business of mine and that is not the individual. What a man says when he's dying and in great pain is not evidence. All right, he'll be converted to anything that's handy, but the substance of the character remains with me, that's what matters, the real thing.[7]

O'Connor, it seems, would too readily subscribe to Ford Madox Ford's remark that the "writer must have his eyes on the reader. That alone constitutes technique." An author's "private world of values" should be of little concern in his efforts to "communicate" with his reader.

Small wonder, therefore, that under the term "communication" O'Connor should also include the matter of style. That, too, de-pends on a direct relationship between writer and reader. What O'Connor laments is the increasing trend in modern fiction of a new attitude to style, which became particularly noticeable in Joyce and Faulkner, "at which style ceases to become a relationship be-tween the author and the reader and becomes a relationship be-tween the author and the object." [8] All of which leads him to disapprove of such moderns as Proust, Joyce, and D. H. Lawrence, who, however admirable their many virtues and vast contributions to contemporary literature, failed, in O'Connor's view, to "com-municate" with their readers. While dredging the essential realities of literature from the subconscious mind, they were not for O'Con-nor writing novels but autobiography of one sort or another. They were not relating themselves directly to the reader with the words, but relating words to an object: the object being themselves, or, rather, their unconscious selves.

And, one must add that when O'Connor refers to the "reader" he does not mean only the cognoscenti or others trained in academia, but also the middle and lower classes. He insists that the writer should address himself to all those both in the cities and the countryside who "had lost their traditional life and not found a civilized one to replace it." Literature dare not turn to the labyrinthian unconscious as the source of its creativity. On the contrary, the contemporary writer must say something to man in words which "communicate" meaning to his "spiritual emptiness" and help ease the "burden of his solitude." O'Connor, like Chekhov, wants literature to refashion man so that, as a result of mankind's spiritual and scientific progress, "in a thousand years' time life on this planet will be really worth while." [9]

Of course, works are never as "simple" as O'Connor would have us believe with this argument—not even O'Connor's or those of the authors he admired, and esteemed, and loved. Every literary work of any power, we know, even if the author has composed it, in O'Connor's view, with a specific audience in mind, is, in fact, an "elaborate system of controls over the reader's involvement and detachment along *various* lines of interest. The author is limited only by the range of human interests." [10]

In any event, of further interest to O'Connor, because he insists that the writer must turn his mind to man in society, is the matter of "moral judgment." A painter, he argues, "can paint a good looking prisoner without bothering his head about whether or not he approves of poisoning in principle, but there is always something freakish about a writer who refrains from moral judgment or feeling." [11] This very example would seem to indicate clearly that the "morality" O'Connor is referring to is based on the assumption that the major moral problem facing man is the regeneration of the individual and that his personal regeneration will ultimately lead to a regeneration of mankind. A work of art, therefore, must evoke "that feeling (quite distinct from all other feelings) of joy and of spiritual union with another (the author) and with others (those who are also infected by it)." Tolstoy called this the "infectiousness of art."

Furthermore, this "infectiousness of art" is increased by the degree of "sincerity" in the artist. For as Tolstoy, one of O'Connor's favorite nineteenth-century novelists, argues: "As soon as the spectator, hearer, or reader, feels that the artist is infected by his own production and writes, sings, or plays, for himself, and not merely to act on others, this mental condition of the artist infects the recipient." [12] And isn't this, indeed, what O'Connor means when, in his criticism of the "Naturalists," among whom he lists Joyce— erroneously, to be sure—he states that their attitude in writing fiction is blatantly false because they seem always to be saying: "Here is an episode. This is where it begins; this is where it ends; now watch me do it." [13] The artist must endeavor never to remove himself, like a "god paring his fingernails," from his work of art and from the reader, or recipient of that work. And he can only achieve that, according to O'Connor, by "moral judgment" which, if communicated sincerely, "will destroy in the consciousness of the recipient the separation between himself and the artist."

O'Connor's general views of literature may be traced directly to his encounter with the nineteenth-century novel, which eventually became for him "incomparably the greatest of modern arts." Growing up alone, he found that reading these novels not only provided him with the "companionship" he desperately needed but also "communicated" to him a sense of individualism, of the individualistic view of the world, in one of the most individualistic periods in English history. Because the stories in these novels "consist of a large variety of character and incident clustering round the figure of hero, bound together loosely or less loosely by an intrigue and ending with wedding bells," [14] they appealed to a youngster seeking meaning to a life that might otherwise have become meaningless.

Besides, O'Connor, like everyone else, whether young or old, loved a story. And mankind, like a child, wants to be told a good story. If anything, the nineteenth-century novelists could tell a good story which they made immediately and easily interesting. Since these novels are about people, there could be, for O'Connor, "nothing better in the world." If, as a story about people, the novel is told "in the way in which it comes chronologically, you've got the best thing you can get in fiction." Further, since writing and reading were "fun," these novels were good because they were enjoyable.

One must, of course, inevitably add yet another reason for his enjoyment of the nineteenth-century novel, the fact—so typical of O'Connor—that his mother, he tells us, "also loved novels, particularly Victorian novels." [15] As a dutiful son, he could do no better than imitate his mother. Like her, too, he was interested in the "life of ordinary people," who, we know, fill the pages of Victorian novels, given as they are to the panoramic portrayal of whole societies. Or, as David Cecil—O'Connor's favorite critic on the novel as was Bonamy Dobrée on Restoration drama—reminds us, in the Victorian novel, "a hundred different types and classes, persons and nationalities, jostle one another across the shadow screen of our imagination." [16]

It is hardly surprising, therefore, that O'Connor's second book of criticism, *The Mirror in the Roadway*, deals exclusively with the nineteenth-century novel.

II

Of all the peculiar merits of nineteenth-century fiction, in which O'Connor read extensively, the one that appealed to him particularly was that it covered a wide range of subject and mood. That range was, in part, extended further by the demands of the reading public of that time, which, though not necessarily interested in art, was seriously interested in life. For O'Connor, it is in the fiction of that period that life, at its best and worst, is mirrored completely and most satisfyingly.

While reading heavily in that century, O'Connor came to the conclusion, repeated in both *Towards an Appreciation of Literature* and *The Mirror in the Roadway*, that the writing of literary history must *not* be done by countries but by periods:

In studying the novel it is necessary to remember that the only natural classification of European literature is by periods, and that any English novelist is likely to have more in common with a French novelist of his own period than with an English novelist of a different period.

This does not mean that all the novelists of one period are equally in-
fluenced by one another. . . . All it means is that the influences are
there to unite the novelists, and that we must never forget that the
nineteenth-century novel is a nineteenth-century art and a European art,
and that all its variations are merely local and relatively unimportant.[17]

To be sure, O'Connor would agree that writers who live in the
same country and are subjected to the same geographical and social
conditions will tend to have certain characteristics in common. For
instance, "Swift, Wilde, Yeats and Joyce have certain characteristics
like insolence, introspection and a tendency to wear a mask which
are not uncommon among writers brought up in Ireland." [18] But
this, to O'Connor, is really incidental. What is not incidental is
that if one were to classify novels of any age, one would have to
do so by periods, *not* countries.

Hence, when invited to give a course in the nineteenth-century
novel at Harvard during the summer sessions of 1954 and 1955, he
prepared lectures on a wide range of novelists of the three major
European countries of the period, England, France, and Russia—
where the novel, in his opinion, could be traced to a common in-
fluence. These novelists included: Jane Austen, Stendhal, Dickens,
Balzac, Gogol, Thackeray, Turgenev, Tolstoy, Trollope, Flaubert,
Dostoyevsky, James, Hardy, Chekhov, Lawrence, Proust, and Joyce.
When delivered to his classes, these lectures were impressive. As
Richard T. Gill, at the time a reading assistant to O'Connor at
Harvard, recalls:

Standing before a lecture audience with his silver-grey hair, his dark eye-
brows, his eyes peering through dark-rimmed glasses that always looked
too small for the strong masculine voice, he was an arresting figure.
When he spoke the response was immediate, for his voice was most
impressive. It was not just the depth of it . . . but the cadence and
rhythm of his speech and also his cultivated and yet unaffected accent
and choice of words.[19]

Reading these lectures in book form, however, one is inclined to
agree with an otherwise sympathetic reviewer who commented that,
as critic, O'Connor is "very uneven indeed, by turns precise, obscure, stimulating, almost pretentious, wise and downright perverse." [20]

The title of this book, *The Mirror in the Roadway,* is, of course,
borrowed from a phrase by Stendhal, who, in turn, attributes it to
the historian Saint-Réal. That the novel is "a mirror riding along
a roadway" means that "whether the novelist reflects the sky or the
ground depends on his angle of vision, and yours as well. You must
not blame the man with the mirror when the road is muddy; and
when it leads through the mire of political controversy, you must
heed his sense of direction." [21] But, as we shall see, O'Connor may
have added another meaning to this definition, for, on a number
of occasions, instead of being "directed by the novelist," O'Connor
as critic would rather pass through the mirror to the novelist himself, thereby abandoning verifiable comment for conjecture and psychological meddling in the life of the author, which diminishes
somewhat the effectiveness of his criticism.

Holding up his mirror to the nineteenth-century novelists O'Connor sees their central concern is the "curious relationship between
imagination and truth." By "imagination," he means, it would
seem, the aesthetic experience that is based on impersonality, dis-
interestedness, and detachment, a detachment from ordinary circumstances and accidental personal interests. "Fictionality" and
"invention," to use different words, are the distinguishing trait of
their imaginative works. This "subjectivism" is the source both of
their individuality and of mankind's whole adventure into the realm
of the spirit. Fictional art, then, becomes a voyage of discovery and,
although a play of the mind—attending, selecting, and combining
—it is by virtue of its idiom, a "communication."

What is equally, if not more, communicative is the element of
"truth" in fiction. Though again imprecise in his definition, we can,
from certain fragmented statements in this work, learn to some degree O'Connor's understanding of this term. He tells us, for example, that "truthfulness with regard to facts and truthfulness with
regard to characters are inherent elements in the nineteenth-century
novel." [22] From which we might infer, one supposes, that the treatment the novelist gives his material is "realistic" or "prosaic" rather
than "romantic." The nineteenth-century novel, he tells us further,
"became the great thing it was largely because it was the form in
which the scientific temper of the modern world could best act as

control." O'Connor's use of the term "scientific" as regards "truth" must surely *not* mean truth as used in scientific discourse, since in the arts, the emotive power of words stirs us and evokes certain attitudes within us that would preclude the use of the word's literal meaning in any such context. What O'Connor probably means is truth as the equivalent of "internal necessity" or "rightness." That is "true" or "internally necessary" which completes or accords with the rest of the experience which cooperates to arouse our ordered response. "Truth" becomes an "internal necessity" or "convincingness" or an "impression of reality." [23]

It is not surprising, therefore, that to O'Connor the ideal of the nineteenth-century novelists would be the work which concentrates on their impressions of the reality of society and man's place in it. Or, to use O'Connor's own term, the most authentic novel concentrated on the "domestication of literature," or, better still, what he calls, as previously indicated, a "Dutch interior." It concerned not the "mythological" or "historical" or "romantic" past, but the classes, professions, and trades that paced the roadway of the novelist's art.

To the "domestication of literature," the significant nineteenth-century novel also added the element of "morality," since, in O'Connor's view, "moral passion is literature's main contribution to the arts." [24] Because the novel of that period so often catered to the merchant classes with their strong puritanical tradition, the morality that motivated it revolved around their interests in "money rather than in rank, in character rather than in breeding, in honesty rather than in honor." And though this tends to place the crises of the nineteenth-century novel within a narrow moral range, it is, nevertheless, "this simple, clear, workmanlike ethic—as simple as a schoolboy's code of honor—that gives it its characteristic note of deep human feeling, as satisfying to our unspoiled moral taste as is the gleam of titles in a Dutch painting to our unspoiled aesthetic sense." [25]

To be sure, though O'Connor speaks of morality as "literature's major contribution to the arts," he does not surely refer to any narrow definition of the term. Like any other free spirit, he did resent bitterly the "moralistic" views of "censors" who would, with their

usual display of moral indignation, declare, say, *Esther Waters* an
impure book, or *Madam Bovary* an apology for adultery. O'Connor
would dismiss such comic, stupefying, enraging interference as con-
temptible. But, as novelist and critic, he could hardly avoid preoccupation with morality in fiction, since he found literature to be
a profoundly serious art affecting all of man's humanity to man.
Hence the novel, respectful of human life and dignity—Tolstoy's
Sebastopol would be O'Connor's prime example—is the *normal*
medium for the expression of human sentiment and the obvious
repository of moral values.

Moral values aside for the moment, let us see how O'Connor ap-
plies the major reflection in his mirror, the "curious relationship between imagination and truth" or, as he alternately refers to them,
"instinct" and "judgment," to the novelists and novels of the nineteenth century. Foremost among the novelists of that period who
best exemplify for him these two fundamental approaches to the
writing of fiction are Jane Austen and Stendhal: the former representing the "flight from fancy"; the latter, the "flight from reality."

Because she reacted against the Gothic, as Cervantes did against
the medieval romance, Jane Austen shows O'Connor the "temper
of the true novelist who is always reacting against romanticism in
fiction." Those of her heroines who indulge their imaginations at
the expense of their judgment are severely criticized. She limited
herself, as one of her characters explains in *Northanger Abbey*, to
"fifty miles of good road, a half day's journey." The roadway she
travelled, therefore, was deliberately narrowed, not allowing the
"imagination" to misdirect her reliance on "judgment" as her central guide. For "truth" depends ultimately on that judgment. Since
she closely observed a society she knew and understood, a society
bounded by "fifty miles of good road," the "common feeling of
common life became her standard." Her own consideration of what
constitutes the ideal novel O'Connor summed up as "some work in
which the greatest powers of the mind are displayed, in which the
most thorough knowledge of human nature, the happiest delinea-
tions of its varieties, the liveliest effusions of wit and humor are
conveyed to the world in the best chosen language."

O'Connor points out that Jane Austen's critical intelligence demanded that the element of emotionalism or "strong feelings" not be the determining factor in the writing of fiction. Hence, Emma's imagination, which is set to work by everything unusual, always functions unnaturally. So that when Mr. Knightley, her admirer, tells Emma's old governess what Emma's principal fault is, he reveals: "She will never submit to anything requiring industry and patience and a subjection of the fancy to the understanding." [26] Austen's source of attraction, O'Connor believes, is in the general vigor of mind, in the art of representing life and character, and in the lack of sympathy for what is picturesque and passionate.

Unlike Austen, Stendhal remained wedded to his imagination. "My judgment," he once said, "was absolutely the sport of my emotions." All his life, O'Connor claims, Stendhal was a prisoner of his imagination, without the intellectual detachment of the truly great novelist. *The Red and the Black* is the ideal example of the "Romantic temperament," so that in the conflict between "instinct" and "judgment," Stendhal's judgment for O'Connor tended to take the form of irony: "An irony whose growth in this major work tends to rob it of emotional impact." O'Connor views Stendhal as one "who wrote of modern people behaving in a sixteenth century way, in a seventeenth century court, surviving into the nineteenth century. . . . he was happy in his imaginative world." [27] Stendhal saw, during his lifetime, his own ideas but not reality.

This distinction between judgment and imagination is then, in brief, O'Connor's thesis. Once having revealed it in the opening chapters of *The Mirror in the Roadway* he should have, we believe, shown, in the subsequent ones, how each novelist relates either to the tradition of "imagination," "instinct," or "fancy." Or, on the other hand, to "truth," "judgment," and "reality." Unfortunately, he does not do so, except for some cursory references as in the chapters on Dickens, Balzac, and Gogol, the "fantasists" of nineteenth-century fiction. He discusses other matters and makes other observations which, however, valid, lead him astray from his high road into "impurities." And all in great measure because he lacks systematic thought, the thought of a trained critic.

Some of these "impurities" of thought are soon apparent. Consider, for instance, the chapter on Thackeray. O'Connor says some good things there. He distinguishes, for example, between the writings of Trollope, Turgenev, and Tolstoy, who repudiated the romanticism of their literary fathers in search of what Turgenev called "integral truth," and that of Thackeray, whose ability to see beneath the all-powerful prince or banker derived not from his respect for "integral truth," but from a "profound, melancholy realization of historical truth, a brooding awareness of the ultimate futility of all human endeavor 'Vanity Fair.' " Or, consider too, his general observation that Thackeray's viewpoint in *Vanity Fair* is an "exceedingly disillusioned one. The mainspring of all human actions . . . is self-interest. From the servant girl up to the Princess, the only motive to be distinguished is that of getting something for oneself." [28] Both observations are, indeed, impressive.

And then suddenly, unexpectedly, he turns the mirror from the roadway to the novelist himself. There is little question, O'Connor adds emphatically, "but that there was in Thackeray a childish strain that attracted him to women who resembled his mother, women who were soft, stupid, and indulgent. And there is no question but that the mature man in him was attracted to women of a very different type—cold, sensual, calculating women like Becky Sharp, Blanche Amory, and Beatrix Esmond." [29] Concluding the chapter in a similar vein, O'Connor states that "in Amelia Sedley and Becky Sharp, Thackeray was at last able to fuse the two sides of his character, that which hankered after cold, sensual, worldly women, and to unite them in one family, so that when Esmond marries the mother he establishes a new and intimate relationship with the daughter." [30]

Stranger, indeed, are his comments on Dostoevsky. Discussing *The Eternal Husband*, O'Connor insists that this work proves conclusively his theory of the "unnatural triangle," in which the "husband or someone in the husband's position connives at his own deception for the sake of a certain abnormal pleasure," [31] that is, for the almost physical intimacy it establishes between the adulterer and himself. O'Connor claims that Trusotsky cherishes a homosexual passion for Velchaninov, betrayed in his request that Velchaninov kiss him. He also draws attention to the attraction Nadya's youth and innocence have for Trusotsky and relates it to Dostoevsky's interest in immature girls. What O'Connor has to say would make the story all too unhealthy. Aside from the obvious distortion and unsound interpretation of this story, resulting partly from an assumption on O'Connor's part of an *a priori* thesis and partly from the possible confusion of the characters with Dostoevsky himself, O'Connor fails as well to relate this chapter to the theory he promulgates at the very outset of *The Mirror in the Roadway:* the fundamental differences between "instinct" and "judgment." Surprisingly, he engages instead, as in the chapter on Gogol, in Freudian analysis, which even if interesting, has little in common with the mirror in the roadway, at least as Stendhal understood it. He betrays a "constant willingness to pass through the mirror to the novelist himself, to abandon verifiable comment to conjecture, to speculate on the psychological processes that led to the fiction we have." [32] Such an approach, in the context of his particular thesis in this work, adds to, rather than lessens its "impurities."

But more disturbing than O'Connor's Freudian speculations may be the very thesis itself. To insist that the two forces central to nineteenth-century fiction—"instinct and judgment" or "reality and fancy"—are separate and totally separated tendencies, seems, on further reflection, another broken image in O'Connor's mirror. Not only fiction but all art is, we know, based on "violent contraries." In fact, the greater the tension between these contraries, such as, say, "reason and emotion" or "irony and sympathy," the greater the work of art. It is these "contraries," Edmund Wilson reminds us, that ultimately result in producing great literature:

One of the prime errors of recent radical criticism has been the assumption that great novels or plays must necessarily be written by people who have everything clear in their minds. People who have everything clear in their minds, who are incapable of identifying themselves imaginatively with, who do not actually embody in themselves, contrary emotions and points of view, do not write great plays at all—do not, at any rate, write good ones. And—given Genius—the more violent the contraries the greater the works of art. [33]

In all fairness, it must be said that O'Connor somewhat senses that idea himself, when, speaking of Jane Austen's major theme as the conflict between imagination and judgment, he adds that "the judgment and the instincts are always at war in her." [34] Whether she succeeds or fails when she "produces an effect that is the very opposite of what she sets out to do"—O'Connor believes she fails—is, of course, subject to argument. But what is not arguable is the notion that her art—like that of any great artist—is surely motivated by the "war" which constantly raged within her. And her tilting this "war" in favor of "reality" may be the result of her own moral judgment. But of this we may be certain: Jane Austen ultimately perceives the world "through an awareness of its contradictions, paradoxes and anomalies." [35] She, too, was responsive to the "violent contraries" of art.

Similarly, O'Connor's view that Stendhal had to be far removed from "reality," since he "looked on the novel . . . as a means of exploring his own ill-balanced character," is open to some question. Another reading of Stendhal may indicate that his sense of "realism" or "judgment" might have been somewhat keener than O'Connor would ascribe to him. For Stendhal drew on two tendencies as the source of his art: "the mechanism of Helvetius and the Romantic individualism after the manner of Rousseau." Though these tendencies lie, naturally, at the opposite poles of thought and action, they represent the essentials of Stendhal's art. This becomes clear in this comment by Léon Blum, who, pointing out the very secret of Stendhal, writes:

One feels persisting in him this juvenile mixture of forces that life ordinarily separates before they are put in action: the early presumptions of the intellect which pretends to bring all under its sway; the youthful ambitions of the heart that wished to experience all. . . . Through the effect of a double influence and of a double revolt it is possible to follow to the very end in his works the combination of a heart and of a mind that contradict each other; of an intellect that believes in the necessity of order and the effectiveness of logic, that subjects everything to rational explanation and empirical verification; and of a sensibility that thirsts for and values, only disinterested exaltation, free movement, and ineffable emotion. That this fundamental opposition compromises the solidity of the system is very possible; but it is the artist, not the philosopher, that we are looking for in Stendhal, and a work of art can conciliate opposites much better than dialectics. [36]

It is of these opposites that all art including Stendhal's is created.

If O'Connor does not always reconcile opposites in his criticism, he is not to be considered, therefore, less than interesting. On the contrary, there are many chapters in this book, especially those on Flaubert and James, as well as Proust and Hardy, which are, indeed, stimulating. For instance, his contention that James's main theme in his work is that of "innocence and corruption but that he is forever prevented, partly because of the tradition in which he was writing, from making that evil tangible to us" is certainly incisive. James's problem, O'Connor adds cogently, was "to acquire the experience of Europe without the historic limitations imposed by it, to learn but to remain free, to be ultimately deeply corrupted but not corrupting." [37] Of course, with at least one observation, namely, that, to James, art was "like a religion, not merely an alternative way of life, but an alternative to life," the reader may differ. For, James was, indeed, a man of deep understanding and deep feeling or, as one modern critic states, "the man of art may be close to the secret of things when the man of action is quite apart from it." [38] If James had the "imagination of disaster," he also had, no less certainly, the "imagination of love," which is not an alternative to life but, perhaps, life itself.

Of love in Proust, a further example, O'Connor points out correctly there is no reciprocity. For it is impossible to know, impossible to master the external world. "A woman will not, and cannot, live in the world in which we would have her—that is, the world in which we live, which we ourselves imagine; and what we love in her is merely the creation of our own imagination: we have supplied her with it ourselves." Love is for Proust but a fiction we have created ourselves. How well, therefore, O'Connor sums up Proust's artistry, of which he is critical, in these words: "Proust is saying that there is no objective reality in the things we pursue, or if there is, that this must forever remain unknown to us, but also, as a corollary, that the subject itself is illusory since it changes character in response to the stimulus or lack of stimulus offered it by the imagination; that a man who is 'good' when pursuing an illusory 'good' object will cease to be so when he ceases in his pursuit." [39] If there is no object, then equally there can be, O'Connor argues, no subject.

All of which leads one to the inevitable conclusion that *The Mirror in the Roadway*, whose subject is the nineteenth-century novel, is, despite occasional cracks in its mirror, a lively and interesting book. If there is a slight confusion of aims, a shift from a discussion of the development of certain strands in fiction to a speculative loquacity on the relation between the lives of the novelists and their novels, there also is, at the same time, an understanding of and original insight into what the novel can do as well as a deep appreciation of what it has done, giving him—and us—a basic antecedent conception of its function. What O'Connor is saying, ultimately, is that perhaps "reality is inapprehensible . . . that, in fact, truth is subjective and objective, that there is no truth greater than this." And *that* truth shines constantly from the mirror along O'Connor's roadway.

III

What shines even brighter along the roadway than O'Connor's book on the novel is his book on the short story, *The Lonely Voice*. This work, too, is based on a series of lectures he was invited to deliver, in two courses and a seminar, on the novel and short story, at Stanford University, in 1961. Like his talks at Harvard, these lectures, given during a six-month teaching assignment, were exceptionally well received. Wallace Stegner, a colleague and auditor, bears testimony to the success of these lectures:

None will forget him, for he was a great teacher. He used to protest that he was not trained for the job, but his humility was not persuasive to us. We knew, as he did, with how much authority he mounted the lecture platform and laid his books and notes on the lectern. He inhabited that raised space more as an actor than as a purveyor of information. . . . Every class hour was a challenge, from his entrance to the bell; every lecture was a performance. . . . Even he, critical of his own performance, must have had to admit that his lectures were a brilliant success.[40]

The subject matter of these lectures was as wide as his platform. He discussed mainly, though not solely, Turgenev, Maupassant, Chekhov, Kipling, Joyce, Katherine Mansfield, D. H. Lawrence, Hemingway, A. E. Coppard, Isaac Babel, and Mary Lavin. His views of these story tellers and their tales, and of the general state of the short story, however much we might disagree with some of these views, are somewhat more revealing than his views of the novel.

The point of departure of the book is O'Connor's insistence that the short story is a distinct art form. Though both the short story and novel derive from the same source, they derive in a number of different ways. First, unlike the novel, the short story does not need the "concept of normal society" to exist. Further, it does not depend on the process of identification between the reader and the character or hero because it does not have a "hero." It is, instead, a direct discussion between the writer and the lonely reader. Second, "Time" is the novel's greatest asset; the chronological development of character or incident is an essential element, just as we see it in life; the short story, on the other hand, never uses the "totality of human life" as its frame of reference, focusing instead on the "crisis situation" or critical moment in the life of the characters so that, as a result of that crisis situation, they are never the same human beings again. Third, the short story teller also differs from the novelist in that he must be "much more of a writer, much more of an artist . . . more of a dramatist." No great story teller, with the possible exception of Sherwood Anderson, ever lacked the sense of the "dramatic." Fourth, no convention as to length ever seems to affect the short story writer's power to tell us all we need to know; his ideal is, as in, say, Hemingway's "Hills Like White Elephants," to give us precisely enough information, excluding all unnecessary exposition. Or, the form of the novel is given by length; in the short story the length is given by the form: "A great story is not necessarily short at all, and the conception of the short story as a miniature art is inherently false. Basically, the difference between the short story and the novel is not one of length. It is a difference between pure and applied story-telling. . . . Pure storytelling is more artistic." [41]

And, finally, there is, for O'Connor, another all-important distinction: the short story, unlike the novel, has not, to repeat, a hero, but a "submerged population group" or the "sense of outlawed figures wandering about the fringes of society." Because this "submerged population" changes its character from writer to writer, from generation to generation, it may consist, for example, of "Gogol's officials, Turgenev's serfs, Maupassant's prostitutes, Chekhov's doctors and teachers, [and] Sherwood Anderson's provincials." [42] And they are always dreaming of escape from their material and, at times, spiritual circumstances. Briefly, there is in the short story, at its characteristic best, something we do not often find in the novel—"an intense awareness of human loneliness."

O'Connor would readily subscribe, therefore, to Turgenev's view that we have "all come out from under Gogol's 'Overcoat.' " In that story, let us recall, a poor copying clerk, Akakey Akakevitch, a nonentity mocked by his colleagues, finally buys a new coat, only after the drunken tailor refuses to patch the old one further, since there is no place in it where a patch would hold. Robbed of the new coat, he goes to the Chief of Police and an Important Personage, both of whom abuse and threaten him. Such injuries and insults are too much for him, so he goes home and dies. His ghost searches for justice, which to a poor copying clerk has never meant more than a warm overcoat.

Everything about this clerk, Gogol seems to be saying, from his absurd name to his absurd job, represents the mediocre, the poor, the submerged who, because of his suffering and persecution, is, in his loneliness, in desperate need of a voice, a voice which should plead his case for man to be his brother's keeper and to desist from his shuddering inhumanity to his fellow man. Akakey is suffering for his fellow man, and his death is an expiation for man's sins. The voice he seeks is given him by the teller of short tales in every generation.

That unique role of the story teller becomes, ultimately, the source of O'Connor's judgment of the worth of these eleven writers, or for that matter, any writer of "short" fiction. If a writer assumes this role of giving voice to the multitude of "outlawed figures" who wander aimlessly around the "fringes of society," then he speaks not only *for* the "submerged population" but also *to* the lonely reader who approaches the short story in the mood of one who is frightened by the "eternal silence." Though without proof to its general truth, because of an admitted lack of critical or historical training, O'Connor still holds fast to this idea, central to this entire book.

Applying this idea to the writers chosen for discussion, O'Connor finds that Turgenev, who had the "essential stuff of humanity," is the first among those assuming the role of the lonely voice. In such stories as "The Singers" and "Byezhin Prairie," he shows how, for his outcasts and lonely individuals, the power of art adds meaning to the meaningless world and, in the latter story, to the meaninglessness of life itself and the terror of the human soul, alone with nature and night. Pavel's comment to his friends in "Byezhin Prairie," "You can't escape your fate," would seem to affirm the notion that all of them are fated to a gripping fear in the presence of the eternal silence. And it is that theme which, for O'Connor, heightens Turgenev's standing as a writer and his effect on an equally "frightened" reader.

Chekhov, the "greatest story teller who has ever lived," enlarged and enriched the idea of the "submerged population." One of the last of the nineteenth-century writers "to attempt a synthesis of a world that is already falling into chaos about him," he recognized that, since that synthesis was no longer possible, he would find it "in the lightning flash of the short story, and only in solitary lives." The short story, accordingly, became for Chekhov, O'Connor argues, the "art form that deals with the individual where there is no longer a society to absorb him, and when he is compelled to exist, as it were, by his own inner light." [43] Hence, plumbing the depths of human misery, Chekhov found man a passionately lonely being, trying desperately to live by that inner light. Loneliness itself is, then, his contribution to the enlargement of the lonely voice.

Two of his "terrible" masterpieces, "Misery" and "The Dependents," clearly revolve about that passionate theme of loneliness. In the first of these stories, an old cab driver whose son has died, tries to tell his rich, busy customers about his loss. None of them can spare him time, so he goes down to the stable and tells it to his old horse. In the second, an old man, unable any longer to support his old horse and dog, brings them to the knacker's yard, and, when he sees their corpses, goes meekly up to the stand and presents his own forehead for the blow. Nowhere, it would seem, is the personal destitution of loneliness better described. The lives of such men, as well as the doctors and teachers, of Chekhov's "submerged population" are most effectively portrayed because they, like all great characters in short fiction, are frightened by the eternal silence. Theirs is the tragedy of human loneliness. And all at once because of these stories, the conception of the "submerged population" is, for the reader, enriched.

Unlike Chekhov and Turgenev, some writers abandoned their "submerged populations," among them, notably, Joyce and D. H. Lawrence. What disturbs O'Connor about Lawrence—of Joyce later—is that, as he grew older, he trusted his instincts more and his judgment less, so that he developed a "mystical experience of nature, to a point where he began to look at a person as though he or she was a part of the landscape." As O'Connor argues further, "contemplation is all very well for a flower, but it will not do for a man or woman." Inevitably, therefore, Lawrence abandoned his "submerged population" of Midland coal miners, writing instead about "literary acquaintances of London, and still later, of Italians, Indians, and American millionaires . . . a people he had never seen in relation to his own mystical experience of nature," [44] let alone as a "submerged population." Whatever the cause of this abandonment—his being hurt by hierarchical society may be one—the result, O'Connor believes, makes Lawrence less than a very significant story teller. For his was no longer a lonely voice.

Unlike Lawrence, Isaac Babel did not abandon his "submerged population" of a persecuted minority in a half-barbarous society. To be sure, Babel, in O'Connor's view, "romanticized violence," since some of his "gangsters never existed at all outside of the wild imagination of this delicate, scholarly Jewish boy, who had been hunted through the streets like an old dog, and whose mind was full of pirates in gorgeous colors." [45] And if, in this assumption, O'Connor differs with Lionel Trilling's view in his "Introduction" to *The Collected Stories of Isaac Babel*, he emphatically agrees with—in fact, he follows closely—Trilling's other conclusion that Babel's preoccupation with violence "draws its intensity from the conflict within himself between the Jewish intellectual and the Soviet commissar": "In Babel's heart there was a kind of fighting—he was captivated by the vision of two ways of being, the way of violence and the way of peace, and he was torn between them.

The conflict between the two ways of being was an essential element of his mode of thought." [46]

And although O'Connor, like Trilling, argues that Babel's stories are some sort of working out of a highly personal and emotional conflict between the two modes of his being, one cannot forget that the violence Babel writes of was not in reality entirely romanticized. To be sure, the "gangsters" in his stories may have been larger than life in order to overcome a certain adolescent cowardice, but what he experienced in the Russian army and the trauma of his civilian life under Stalin was indeed real, frighteningly real. His suffering as well as his tragic end were as real as the inferno of suffering that consumed similar minority figures and populations during the Second World War. Despite his attachment, therefore, to a regime which was ultimately to destroy him, Babel was not blind to the loneliness that must inevitably overcome a sensitive soul, unable to synthesize his opposing ways of being. Alone and afraid of the eternal silence, his was, indeed, the lonely voice of a "submerged population."

Like Babel, Hemingway was fascinated by violence but, unlike Babel, he never "romanticized" it. His stories are replete with hunting, bullfighting, and war. Violence in his stories is a test of courage or of grace under pressure. It is most assuredly "real." What he saw and actually experienced, he describes sparsely, as was characteristic of his style. However, what O'Connor criticizes in his chapter on Hemingway—one of the two best in the book, the other being on Kipling—is not the violence, in whatever form, but another matter altogether. He objects to Hemingway's lack of a human, not to speak of a lonely, voice. O'Connor perceives Hemingway as first and foremost a rhetorician, anxious to substitute the image for the reality. In his writing, there is not "a human voice speaking, nobody resembling yourself who is trying to persuade you to share in an experience of his own, and whom you can imagine yourself questioning about its nature—nothing but an old magician sitting over his crystal ball, or a hypnotist waving his hands gently before your eyes . . ." [47] And any art, O'Connor contends further, "which formally is practically indistinguishable from a memorandum issued by a government office is necessarily impure."

As a result, Hemingway blurs the sharp contrast that, for O'Connor, should always exist between the two basic forms of which storytelling is compounded: between "narrative," or the subjective and persuasive on the one hand, and, on the other, the "dramatic" or the objective and compulsive. These two forms must be kept in delicate balance in every good story. However, in a Hemingway story one often finds that the "dramatic," because it is stylized in the same way as the narrative, tends to lose its fullest impact. O'Connor would rather Hemingway were more "subjective," delivering in his stories a more "passionate narrative."

To be sure, O'Connor was not unaware that, as a technician with words, Hemingway was marvellously equipped. No other twentieth-century writer was, in fact, as able and brilliant a technician. In O'Connor's cogent words: "He could take an incident—any incident, no matter how trivial—and by his skill as a writer turn it into something one read thirty years ago and can still read today with admiration and pleasure." [48] But the real trouble with Hemingway, it appears to O'Connor, is that he "so often has to depend upon his technical equipment to cover up material that is trivial or sensational." His is a "technique in search of a subject."

But what of the subject of Hemingway's books? What of Hemingway's "submerged population"—of the waiters, boxers, jockeys, bullfighters, and sundry others who appear in his pages? That element is curiously overlooked by O'Connor. In one of his unfortunate lapses of critical consistency in this book, O'Connor implies, surprisingly, that because Hemingway's submerged population is associated with "recreation rather than labor" it is somewhat less effective. Since when are waiters and bullfighters less worthy of their "lonely voice" than civil servants or doctors or teachers? O'Connor here is writing "instinctually" rather than "judgmentally." Even weaker is his failure to give Hemingway the freedom of his artistic temperament which, according to Maupassant, is the need to cultivate avidly the *manière spéciale de penser, de voir, de comprendre et de juger*. In other words, the emphatic right to personal exposition of what he considered *his* "submerged population."

Because he lacked, far more than Hemingway, a "lonely voice,"

Kipling comes in for O'Connor's sharpest criticism. In what is perhaps his best chapter, O'Connor proceeds to analyze just why Kipling, in the company of, say, Chekhov and Maupassant, is "an embarrassment." Since he posits that every great story teller must speak with a "lonely voice" or, better, must write of human loneliness, O'Connor finds that Kipling, despite his spokesmanship for the "submerged population" of British colonials, is utterly incapable of facing a "crisis alone" and, raised as "a little member of a colonial group," leaves the "impression that one was never alone or, at least, never should be alone. If left alone, nightmare succeeded." [49]

Echoing Edmund Wilson's argument in *The Wound and the Bow*, O'Connor believes that, as a result of the trauma of Kipling's early upbringing when the "desertion" by his parents left him at the mercy of a tyrannical religious domestic back home in England, it was impossible for him to describe people being alone. The British colonials, whose voice he became, were, after all, never really "submerged" since they were as a group, though always lonely, frequently industrious, sometimes idealistic and self-sacrificing, really poised for ascent, and never alone. Often in Kipling, when someone is in distress, everyone is rushing to the rescue and "at all times one seems to hear the thud of the Eleventh Hussars ("The Slashers") coming to save the hero from [his] fate." [50] Although it is the role of the story teller to write about human loneliness, Kipling prefers to speak "as if he himself were one of a gang." Lacking the lonely human voice, he plays up to his audience and doesn't speak to the reader in any private or personal way. Hence, Kipling is, in O'Connor's opinion, less than one of the giant story tellers.

All of which leads the reader to conclude that *The Lonely Voice*, despite its many merits—and there are many, not the least being O'Connor's fearlessness in criticizing even the greatest practitioners of the art of story telling—has its serious shortcomings. Among them is, for example, O'Connor's failure to include any discussion of such masters as Henry James and Joseph Conrad. For, even if one were *not* to subscribe to F. R. Leavis' dogma that the greatest of English novelists are Jane Austen, George Eliot, Henry James, and Joseph Conrad, no work on the short novel, it would seem reasonable to assume, could ever be complete without the last two of these masters. To be sure, O'Connor does devote a chapter to James in *The Mirror in the Roadway*, but, surprisingly, omits Conrad entirely from both works. And that is especially disconcerting, since, by any standards, *The Heart of Darkness*, for instance, is clearly one of the greatest short novels of modern times. If ever a story teller wrote of the *one* subject O'Connor believes short-story telling is inconceivable without—human loneliness— Conrad surely did. And there are others who might have been profitably included in this study, such as, say, George Moore, or Elizabeth Bowen, or Liam O'Flaherty, who, in O'Connor's opinion, is "one of the most exciting of story tellers." And there are still others. But that would be demanding another kind of book, a book O'Connor may have never intended to write. He never meant this to be a definitive work on the short story. Perhaps the plan was to engage here in some "old fashioned kind of criticism"—casual and conversational as befits his role as "Visiting Professor," standing at his lectern and making every "lecture a performance." If nothing else, he opened up a new and enlightening interest in such neglected moderns as A. E. Coppard and Mary Lavin and even dared to question the cult of the Joycean "divinity."

What must be nevertheless seriously questioned in this "performance" is the application O'Connor makes of the central idea in this work—the notion of the "submerged population group." Though normally no more than, as indicated above, an awkward expression suggesting some sociological cant, it is actually given some "sociological" meaning and credibility when used to explain a specific literary phenomenon, namely, the American short story.

Discussing Sherwood Anderson—all too briefly, incidentally, and then only in the "Introduction"—O'Connor shows how—from Anderson's "submerged population" of lonely dreamers of the Middle West, "of pioneering stock, confident, competent men and women who do not understand what it means to be beaten almost from birth"—the American short story developed to a point where it has become "a national art form." Then, as if trying to understand the superiority of the American short story over all others, he offers one reason—while recognizing, though not mentioning, others—the fact that

America is largely populated by submerged population groups. That peculiar American sweetness toward the stranger—which exists side by side with American brutality toward everyone—is the sweetness of people whose own ancestors have been astray in an unfamiliar society and understand that a familiar society is the exception rather than the rule; that strangeness of behavior which is the very lifeblood of the short story is often an atavistic breaking out from some peculiar way of life, faraway and long ago.[51]

But, then, why do the Irish, hardly populated by many submerged population groups, write so well and beautifully? And, why, too, the French? This smacks of real sociological cant.

A wiser more accurate view is expressed by Sean O'Faolain, O'Connor's friend and "mentor," in his excellent study *The Short Story*, where he argues that America produces interesting personalities in the short story because "American society is still unconventionalized," making it a "breeding ground of the personal and original way of looking at things, expounded with intelligence and defended with disruptive passion. . . . It is the primary thing in the short story which is, by nature, a pointing finger." [52] That, surely, makes more sense.

These serious reservations aside, *The Lonely Voice* is a work of singular merit. It follows, in its analysis of the short story, a consistency which shapes its coherent form. All the lectures, covering a wide spectrum of stories and story tellers, maintain the book's unity because racing through all of them is the search for the "submerged population" around which all great stories are said to be formulated. And if, in the "Epilogue," he tells his students that "a writer should bank down his creative fire until he knows precisely the object against which it is directed," O'Connor followed his own advice, not only in fiction but also in his criticism. For he seems to have known, despite all his fears and timidities about his "professorship," where his lectures were ultimately going.

And so did his students. As Wallace Stegner recalls vividly in his warm and admiring memoir on "Professor O'Connor at Stanford":

As with standard authors whom he could not fully agree with or respect, but whose skill so often inspired his entirely grudging admiration, he responded with robust enthusiasm to these young writers when they wrote well, even if he disapproved of everything their writing seemed to aim at. He could not resist good writing, and he knew it when he read it, however much it might offend his sense of the moral obligation of literature and however much he might doubt the total humanity of the writer. The seminar that at first troubled him with a sense of his own inadequacy was finally his enthusiasm and delight. And theirs.[53]

And all, it would appear, because his own creative fire helped light up this quest for what Pascal once said—O'Connor's epigraph for this book—*Le silence éternel de ces espaces infinis m'effraie.* O'Connor succeeds precisely because, growing up alone, he was himself frightened by the eternal silence of those infinite spaces. Since in his stories and criticism, was well as in his life, two terrible words ring out more than any others—"alone" and "lonely"— he assumed, naturally, his role of creating the lonely voice.

IV

Between the publication of *The Mirror in the Roadway* and *The Lonely Voice*, O'Connor reissued *The Road to Stratford*, in somewhat different form than originally published in 1948. This critical study, under the new title *Shakespeare's Progress*, is the result of "a few years spent in the theater" as well as in abiding interest in Shakespeare and his contemporaries. Like his other works of criticism, this book makes no pretense of scholarship—whatever scholarship it does possess is indebted, by his own admission, to Sir Edmund Chambers' *William Shakespeare* and *Elizabethan Stage*, to the textual criticism of J. D. Wilson in the Cambridge Shakespeare and to G. B. Harrison's *Shakespeare at Work, Elizabethan Plays and Players,* and *Elizabethan and Jacobean Journals*—but is based on his readings of the Bard, whom he approaches more as poet than playwright.

Because Shakespeare was an "abnormally sensitive man on whom every experience left its mark, and though we usually have no idea what the experience was, we can always observe its traces," O'Con-

nor sees this work as a sort of "allegory of his passage through life."
He traces Shakespeare's creative life as if it were a "pilgrim's progress," the story of Everyman, written by the "man of all men on
whom the story seems to have made the deepest impression." That
this approach does not happen to leave a similar impression on the
reader may not be due, surely, to the subject, but, rather, to the
author who, in this instance, does not prove himself to be the "man
of all men."

O'Connor senses the man Shakespeare to have been—since so
little formal data is available—an English genius, unusually sensitive to life about him and intuitive in his approach to things, who
started out with an interest in rhetoric, became an actor, mastered
his language, and then learned how to apply both that mastery and
his perceptions about the human situation in the construction of
a memorable series of plays in which the poet transcended the
dramatist.

One of the reasons the poet in Shakespeare transcended the
dramatist, according to O'Connor, is that "to every poet, poetry is
an end in itself. The medium is more important than the content,
or if you care to put it another way, to the poet plays are merely an
occasion for fine verse and the stronger the situation, the better the
verse is like to be." [54] Besides, as a director of the Abbey Theatre,
O'Connor discovered to his chagrin that he was unable to produce
Shakespeare's plays as effectively as, by comparison, some far lesser
moderns because there was, apparently, with Shakespeare "no collaboration between author, players, and audience" which alone
produces great theater.[55] As a result, some of Shakespeare's comments for example, are today "unintelligible to the audience, usually unintelligible to the actor, and, sometimes, unintelligible to
scholars as well." It is the same fate, incidentally, that must over-
take any art which depends on collaboration as much as the
theater does. What we find today, therefore, in a Shakespearean
play, O'Connor contends, "is no longer creation; it is criticism or
rather theatrical scholarship." Making no pretense to scholarship,
O'Connor naturally turned instead to the playwright's poetry.

O'Connor began his career, let us recall, producing a number of
original poems and some excellent translations which were later

collected in *King, Lords, and Commons.* In fact, he wrote poetry almost to the end of his life, publishing *The Little Monasteries,* a group of some twenty poems he translated, in 1963, three years before his death. Though not an outstanding poet, to be sure, he was a scrupulous craftsman who possessed no less a passion for a good line of verse than he had for a good line of prose. And, as the saying goes, "once a poet, always a poet." Hence, he looked to Shakespeare's poetry rather than to his drama, to the "medium" rather than the "content" in the appraisal of his greatness. To O'Connor, Shakespeare was first and foremost a poet and, as indicated, "to every true poet, poetry is an end in itself."

Beginning with an analysis of the poetry in the early historical plays—*Titus Andronicus* and the three parts of *Henry VI*—O'Connor notes that Shakespeare uses words like "paling," "park," "hart," "single," and "bay" with undue frequency, from which "we begin to gather the impression of a most enjoyable, misspent youth." [56] On such small and inconclusive evidence, O'Connor further accepts uncritically that Shakespeare left home "not out of his own free will" but because of a need to escape prosecution by Sir Thomas Lucy on whose estate he presumably poached deer. Of course, had O'Connor taken the trouble to ascertain the source of this story, he would have discovered that "it does not enter the Shakespearean tradition until more than seventy-five years after the poet's death and [is] hardly deserving of belief." As O. J. Campbell, the distinguished Shakespearean, once observed.

We may then regard with complete suspicion the belief that Shakespeare fled to London to escape prosecution of a country justice. It is more likely that he was lured there by reports of new triumphs of the English stage. They would tell of the building of new theaters, of the formation of new companies of actors, and of the production of enormously popular plays like Kyd's The Spanish Tragedy. What more natural for a young man of Shakespeare's temperament than to give up whatever he was doing in the country and to make for London with the hope of establishing a connection with one of the flourishing companies of actors.[57]

This aside, O'Connor does correctly conclude, without citing specific lines, on reading the poetry of these early histories, that

Shakespeare's comments on political affairs, where they are obvious intrusion, prove how vital and persistent were his interests in the problems of statecraft. O'Connor, not unaware of Shakespeare's "characteristic obsession with the idea of public order. . . . a theme that haunted him to the day of his death," argues cogently that the poet "had a real obsession with mobs." [58] But then, as a seeming afterthought, he adds that this obsession resulted from the fact that the "poet himself may have been caught up in one and found himself unable to escape." For this statement he brings absolutely no proof, which only proves that, however fond he may have been of the poetry, his other conclusions, though possibly correct guesses, are, to say the least, less than authentic.

How much more authentic O'Connor's reasoning in this regard might have been, had he paused to record the two universally held conceptions that were basic to Shakespeare's thinking. One is "the idea of degree of order which demands that everything in the universe keep its appointed place in a vast chain of being. Human society as a part of this system is a sort of ladder of obediences and subserviences. . . . To break any of the links in this cosmic chain was to upset the divinely planned order of creation. Since rebellion against a king, the apex of the social pyramid, destroyed the entire structure it was the most dangerous and heinous of sins." The other is the idea that "political situations recur again and again and in a mechanically exact form." History becomes, therefore, a vast collection of examples and warnings particularly for rulers of his time. Small wonder, therefore, that Shakespeare would be preoccupied in those early historics with political stability since, obsessed with the need for order, he wished to record that mobs, incited by unscrupulous men, will create conditions with "all coherence gone" and the placement of absolute power in the hands of villains "who will trample all civilized values under foot." [59]

What these early works reveal is not only, as O'Connor argues, Shakespeare's poetic ability but, more significantly, his mature power of characterization. Witness, for example, in *II Henry VI*, his convincing picture of Cade, of Henry, the actual ruler, of his uncle Humphrey, Duke of Gloucester, and Richard Plantagenet, the Duke of York, and his hump-backed son Richard, a veritable caecodemon. These early history plays also "mark a steady growth in the young dramatist's power of character portrayal and in his ability to depict history in scenes of mounting intensity. They also reveal a thoughtful man with strong—if conventional—convictions on the vital social and political questions of his day." [60]

Another of O'Connor's conclusions, on reading Shakespeare's poetry, concerns the authorship of *Edward III*. He is convinced, contrary to Brooke and Robertson, that Shakespeare wrote this play. As proof, he cites almost identical lines from the *Rape of Lucrece*, the Sonnets, and *Edward III*. In particular, he chooses this line from the Sonnets: "Lilies that fester smell far worse than weeds." [61] Similarly, Warwick, in the play, says: "Lilies that fester smell worse than weeds." This constitutes one of O'Connor's proofs of Shakespeare's authorship.

Another, the one that he believes clinches his argument, is a certain identity of style between *Edward III* and some of Shakespeare's plays of the same period. One of the most significant aspects of this style is the use in both *Edward III* and, say, *Richard III* of what O'Connor likes to call "reflexive conceit," whereby reflexive words are used consecutively in the poetry to imply antithesis. For example: "Thyself thyself misuses," says Queen Elizabeth to Richard III. "Myself myself confound," retorts Richard. Though there is nothing unusual about the conceit itself, O'Connor hastens to admit, there is an implication of antithesis: "Everyone and everything contains its own opposite by which it is saved or destroyed; and this harmonized with a certain duality in the Elizabethan temperament that enabled it to act and at the same time to watch itself acting, and to see in art and literature patterns by which to measure its own behavior . . ." [62] Because we find in the Sonnets such lines :"So in thyself thyself are made away"; or, "Narcissus so himself himself forsook," and in *Edward III*, the Black Prince must "himself himself redeem" and the Countess of Salisbury is not beautiful "if that herself were by to stain herself," O'Connor concludes unalterably, from these "infallible signs" that Shakespeare wrote *Edward III*.

The fallibility of this theory is obvious. Let us recall that Shakespeare's Sonnets were, at the time, circulated among friends to win for him, as for many another aspiring poet, the approval of his peers. The author of *Edward III*, therefore, may as readily as not have lifted the line for his own use. Besides, on such small evidence dare such large conclusions be reached? It is simply not convincing. And had O'Connor merely consulted the small, but very solid volume on Shakespeare by Marc Parrott, published some thirteen years before *The Road to Stratford*, he would have read:

Of the many plays ascribed at various times in whole or in part to Shakespeare there is, with possibly a single exception, none that deserves consideration. This exception, Edward III, contains a romantic episode of the wooing of the Countess of Salisbury by the young king, which has some slight resemblance to the style of Shakespeare in his first period, and contains a line,
   Lillies that fester smell far worse than weeds,
that appears in one of his sonnets. But his sonnets, as we know, were circulating in manscript at the time this play appeared, 1596, and it is not impossible that the unknown author simply lifted the line to adorn the play.[63]

If, from his theory of the "reflexive conceit," O'Connor draws an impossible conclusion concerning the authorship of *Edward III*, he may be on firmer ground in eliciting from it a different, and possibly acceptable notion concerning the development of Shakespeare's mind. What the "reflexive conceit" may indicate, according to O'Connor, is that, in the early stages of his career, Shakespeare owned a "profoundly subjective nature which tends to regard other people merely as extensions of itself, and tears itself asunder in the attempt to argue that there are no extensions of human personality, that from the beginning to the end it remains forever alone and aloof." [64] But something happened—just what that is, is open to wide conjecture—which prompted, apparently, a profound change in Shakespeare's thinking about, and understanding of, man and his world.

Shakespeare began, O'Connor believes, to move away from the "narcissisism that is at the base of all Elizabethan life and art" and diverted that love of self outward to a "love" of others. Suddenly, there is a breaking free and objectification of self, a splitting of the personality or, in O'Connor's apt phrase, a "cracking of the shell."

O'Connor sees, for example, a movement in his works from the characterization of a Richard III to a Richard II who possesses both personal inadequacies and individual charm. In O'Connor's words: "At this period I feel in Shakespeare a duality that is almost neurotic, as though he might quite easily have walked into a room and found himself sitting there. To me it is as though at last the antithesis has become flesh: *I* does not cease to think and feel with the same blind human passion, but on the very summit of frenzy, *I* suddenly becomes *you* and between them a universe is born." [65] And what better example of this "antithesis that has become flesh" than the story of Prince Hal and Falstaff in *Henry IV*. For where else does Shakespeare describe as well that shift from the *I* to the *you*, from a "narcissistic" Prince, influenced by a Falstaff, the embodiment of vanity and jocose irresponsibility, to a responsible leader anxious to convince his dying father that his wildness is a thing of the past, that he is at last ready to assume the fated responsibilities of a king and be the mirror of all royal virtues, an epic hero of superior moral fiber.

Furthermore, O'Connor's Shakespeare saw a Falstaff, vain and selfish, as someone *not* apart or "outside" but "within" or the other half of every man, of each human personality. That is the "antithesis," the struggle within every human being: how to change from zealous self-aggrandizement to an equally zealous involvement in the fate of others. As O'Connor argues: "But surely, the important thing to remember is that there is a Falstaff in each of us, and that it is to this Falstaff that Shakespeare appears. . . . wherever in literature we find those great doubles: Quixote and Sancho, Bouvard and Pechuchet, Dedalus and Bloom, Morell and Marchbanks in Shaw's *Candida,* or Laevsky and Von Koren in Chekhov's *The Duel,* they are never different characters, but different aspects of the same character." [66] To this otherwise sound judgment, O'Connor adds, however, a statement or two which minimizes its effect for the reader and again forces one to question O'Connor's readings of the "poet" in Shakespeare. In the very midst of this argument, O'Connor comments further, without a trace of proof, that there was a "Falstaff within (Shakespeare) himself," and that Hal and Falstaff were different aspects of the "author" and that they were meant to "externalize a conflict within himself." Such remarks, however possibly true but presented without any formal evidence, only add a little more impurity to O'Connor's interpretations—even to the soundest ones.

That O'Connor viewed some of Shakespeare's characters as only different aspects of the Bard's own character is apparent also from his interpretation of *The Merchant of Venice*, which together with *A Midsummer Night's Dream* and *Romeo and Juliet*, he considers the "masterpieces" of the early period. Shylock is that part of Shakespeare, as in every human being, who has felt the "insolence of office and the spurns that patient merit of the unworthy takes." For who among men has not felt the desire for revenge, even to the extreme of murder. Shylock, therefore, whose hatred is transformed into murderous villainy, becomes, for O'Connor, a "poor man wronged" and is the embodiment of Shakespeare's attempt to search out the "Shylock in each of us," including himself, and to make us "bring in a verdict against judgment and conscience." But to this judgment, O'Connor again fails to offer proof, just as he brings none to his opinion that the relationships between Bassanio and Antonio are "half lover-like" and are a "striking echo of the Dark Lady tangle."

Somewhat less tangled is O'Connor's reading of *Hamlet*. He concludes that the Dane is an "intellectual afflicted with melancholia." However, nowhere does O'Connor probe any deeper than that to tell us some of the possible causes of that melancholia. He never ventures the possibility that skepticism and pessimism, for example, which captured the minds of many Englishmen at the turn of the seventeenth century resulted from, among other things, the "new astronomical theories calling into question orthodox beliefs as to the nature of the universe." Or, that, because decay was enthroned as the god of the universe, man became the slave of mutability. Or, the "strange notion that the earth was nearing its end." The only other thing, besides Hamlet's melancholia, that O'Connor discusses is the changed attitude toward death we find in this play. Shakespeare, it would appear, moved away from the rationalist's view that death is the end of all and, as the final end, leaves all of life meaningless, to a different view, that it is "the only power that can quit us of the contradictions, the burnings and freezings." This antithetical view closes with the graveyard scene, leaving Shakespeare to "devise dramas of the mind," presumably to concentrate, henceforth, only on plays which are, in O'Connor's opinion, essentially poems.

Against the other major tragedies of this period—*Othello, Lear,* and *Macbeth*—O'Connor voices sharp criticism, most of it based again on his "instinct" or intuition, leaving his "judgmental" views hidden from the reader and, possibly, himself. *Othello,* for instance, he believes to be "high tragedy based on the scenario of a comic opera" because the handkerchief motif is taken from "court comedy . . . and quite insufficient to support the weight of the tragedy he builds on it." [67] This convention is farcical, not tragic, insists O'Connor, and this play, like the other two, "is susceptible to a curious staginess that detracts from their tragedy." Hence, Shakespeare reverts here to a flood of poetry which, however passionate, makes *Othello* "uninteresting."

Furthermore, for O'Connor *Othello* lacks the basic dramatic interest we have come to expect of all tragedy: the struggle between "destiny and character, the way in which destiny is foiled and recovers; in which the original simple doom is thwarted." [68] Shakespeare was only interested. O'Connor argues, "in saying what he had to say and Iago the puppet was the only medium through which he could say it." Of course, Shakespeare might have answered by saying that Othello is essentially a noble idealist manipulated into an emotional frenzy and driven to crime by the consummately clever and evil villain, Iago. In such a case, any trick would inflame the Moor. Besides, what Shakespeare is presenting is the conflict between the romantic idealist and the cynical realist whose sole motive is self-interest and from "whom idealistic striving, particularly in the relations between the sexes, is for him romantic folly and self-deceit." A romantic Othello is a noble child of nature, whose mature mind is formed by the mystery of that nature, hence no match for a devilish Iago.

And Lear, O'Connor considers simply a "fool," and the entire play a "tissue of nonsense masquerading as tragedy." He believes that the "moment is past when we can be moved by the meeting between the deluded father and his wronged son, and no tragic dramatist in his right mind would ever deliberately have sacrificed such a scene merely to extract another rabbit from the dramatic hat." [69] Taking this approach, O'Connor would hardly recognize in Lear, therefore, the tragic faults of pride and anger, or the struggle in the entire play between good and evil, or that the play represents the final, eloquent assertion of the triumph of man's spirit over the powers of darkness. O'Connor finds fault, rather, in Shakespeare's characterization of Lear, who lacks the "ambiguity which defines such characterization of Richard II, Shylock, and Falstaff." Something in O'Connor opposes the "storm of misanthropy which blows through these later plays."

So all these later plays become for O'Connor "baroque comedies." They all have the characteristics of "Baroque art": "the sensationalism and emotional attitudes, 'as if they had died of the toothache'; the sentimentality, particularly in the portraits of women; even the desire to shock." Futhermore, following Chambers, O'Connor recites that somewhere between the writing of *Macbeth* and *Pericles*, Shakespeare suffered a mental breakdown, requiring, among other things, some assistance in writing his plays. Hence, *Measure for Measure* is the work of two hands.

All of which, of course, does not explain how, if so ill, Shakespeare could write the perfectly normal *Antony and Cleopatra*, which O'Connor himself considers the "greatest" of the tragedies. And what particularly fascinates O'Connor about this play is that Shakespeare has reverted to the "realistic" thinking he employed in the writing of *Hamlet*. So that, in all the display of romanticism in *Antony and Cleopatra*, Shakespeare is keenly aware of the "absurdities of the reasons for war . . . balancing the ecstasies and rages of the middle aged lovers with the cosmic consquences of their behavior." [70] But this, it would appear, is the mark of a sane, not a sick man, which makes O'Connor's conjecture once more unclear and unproved, and, once more, based on "instinct" or undigested borrowings rather than "judgment."

About the last plays—*Timon of Athens, Cymbeline, The Winter's Tale,* and *The Tempest*—O'Connor says little, and in light of his "poetic" reading, all too little. As indicated, they are, in O'Connor's opinion, "baroque" dramas which are "not realism but expressiveness." They leave him with the impression of a dramatic personality who is "disintegrating in the continuing disintegration of language." Because of this decline in creative power, a poet and "instinctive" writer like Shakespeare caused the "shadows of fantasia to take over control and reduce the writer almost to a state of somnambulism. In the later comedies it is not the fantastic nature of the themes which produces the sense of unreality but the subjective unreality which makes the themes to appear fantastic." [71] But one cannot help wondering, despite O'Connor's voiced disapproval, whether *Cymbeline*, however lacking in materials that might raise it above melodrama, or a dramatic romance like *The Winter's Tale*, or a pastoral drama like *The Tempest*, could be classified as "somnambulistic."

Aside from his harsh criticism and even harsher reading, often the result of his "instinctual" rather than "judgmental" conclusions, O'Connor fell prey to the temptation that overcomes so many who try, but hardly ever succeed, in taking the Bard's works "as revelations of crises in his inner life," or "reflections of his experiences in the world." Of course, O'Connor was partly influenced in some of his readings of Shakespeare by Edmund Chambers who, although one of the most distinguished Shakespeareans, occasionally allowed his imagination to intrude on his criticism. And because O'Connor's imagination is most fertile, he allowed more intrusions into his readings than even his mentor. And that hinders the reader's, as well as the writer's, progress toward a best understanding of the poet and playwright or, as O'Connor preferred it, the "playwright as poet."

Stranger even than some of O'Connor's misreadings of the "poet" Shakespeare is his misunderstanding of another of his mentors, J. Dover Wilson, who develops, among other things, a Bunyanesque conception of Shakespeare's career, beginning with the Bard's life as a callow, and even apish youth who journeys through life until we get a glimpse of him as Pilgrim, at the very end, in the holy hush of *The Tempest*—"no prophet upon the heights but a penitent upon his knees." So, when O'Connor announces, at the beginning, that Shakespeare's Progress is the story of Everyman, the reader has every reason to expect that he would have his Pilgrim in a penitential posture at the end of his study. Unfortunately, what we get is not Shakespeare the "Pilgrim" but Shakespeare the "Somnambulist," with little progress along the way. Obviously, the allegory is in its application.

What O'Connor alluded to here but never developed is the third of the historical "afterimages" to which Shakespeare has been subjected. The first is that, being one of the very best of his kind, he was deserving of mass homage to his relics; second, that he was a member of the society of lords of his day, something, presumably, men most desire; and, third, that he was a sinner who finally found grace. But all of these afterimages, we are reminded by Alfred Harbage, one of the soundest Shakespeareans of our day, are fictive and defective:

> The true defect of the afterimages, apart from their fictive quality, is that they displace a conception at once less vulnerable and more useful. The veneration of relics makes Shakespeare seem terribly dead. His social elevation removes him somewhat from our sphere. The interpretation of his works as autobiography reduces the universal to the particular. Some of the sonnets are amongst the greatest poems in the language, and to insist that they were inspired by a crush on this person or that does violence to our instincts. Dramatic characters shrink when identified as particular friends, enemies, or political candidates of the artist; we prefer Hamlet as Hamlet to Hamlet as the Earl of Essex. And the treatment of plays as episodes in a salvation story spells critical disintegration: if this early comedy is an indiscreet 'experiment,' this middle tragedy a 'symptom,' this late romance a 'testament,' where are the works of art? [72]

But O'Connor, preoccupied with Shakespeare's poetry and its derivatives, as well as his own misleading pronouncements on authorship of the plays, neglects, at times, the dramatic art.

Not only does O'Connor neglect the art, but he also forgets to define his use of the term "Everyman." And here, too, one must turn to Harbage for a clearer definition because O'Connor, unfortunately, does not provide one. Quoting a letter from Keats to his brother, in which the poet writes that "a Man's life of any worth is a continual allegory . . . a life like the scriptures, figura-

tive . . . Shakespeare led a life of allegory: his works are the comments on it," Professor Harbage adds:

*What Keats is saying is that Shakespeare's significant life was not the
literal one of specific personal experience, but the allegorical one of
which his plays are the expression. Those who strive to individualize
him by picturing a woebegone lover, the politician manqué, or whatever it may be . . . are reducing his 'figurative,' his large allegorical,
significance. Shakespeare may best be thought about as Everyman, and
his biography as the life's journey of Everyman. His nature was such that
the important episodes in that life's journey were not his experiences as
self but his experiences as Man. . . . Everyman is not average man,
whatever that may be, but the abstract of what makes men men. The
only one fitted for the allegorical journey of Everyman, of man as man,
would be ourselves at our best.*[73]

What is, finally, good in *Shakespeare's Progress* is that O'Connor
does not stand in the long line of worshippers who have made of
Shakespeare some sort of secular saint of whom one must speak, if
at all, in hushed tones. He criticizes him severely. As in all his other
works of criticism, he speaks his mind freely, and is as little loathe
to criticize Shakespeare as he does his friends "Willy" Yeats and
"Jimmy" Joyce. Nothing to him is sacrosanct. His is a free spirit
and an open mind. At times, he leaves his mind or his "judgment"
to dwell in his heart or his "instinct." When that happens, of
course, as it does often, while he progresses along the road to Stratford, this book becomes merely another addition to his "cargo of
impure art."

V

Purer and better by far than *Shakespeare's Progress* is *A Short
History of Irish Literature*, primarily because O'Connor knew more
about the latter than the former. Like *The Mirror in the Roadway*
and *The Lonely Voice*, this book is the result of a series of lectures
he was invited to deliver—this time on his native soil—at Trinity
College, Dublin, and St. Patrick's College, Maynooth, just a few
months, as it happened, before his death. What moved him to record his lectures was, again, the feeling that a closer acquaintance

with Irish literature "might be an inspiration to another generation, enabling them in the words of Samuel Ferguson 'to live *back* in the land they live *in*, with as ample and as interesting a field of retrospective enjoyment as any of the nations around us'." [74] Troubled by the fact that the "great monuments of our past are almost as filthy and neglected as they were in Ferguson's day and infinitely less complete," O'Connor took on, as he did once before in writing *The Big Fellow*, the role of teacher, not only in the classroom but beyond its confines, to future generations who might one day understand, proudly and properly, the meaning of being part of the "indomitable Irishry."

Part of that "indomitability" results from a people whose minds dwelt so much on the past that they could not bear to think of it as being no better than the present, which gives all of Irish literature, in O'Connor's phrase, "a backward look." And it is that "back ward look" which here occupies O'Connor's attention, bringing to it his characteristic wit, openness, and intense feeling. Though obviously incomplete—containing large gaps and great condensation —it may, nevertheless, very well be one of the best *short* histories of Irish literature recently published. And, as in all his criticism, O'Connor is candid, expressing his opinions frankly and freely and, at times, not without some bias. All of which makes this work highly readable.

What is, first, so interesting in Irish literature, according to O'Connor, is that it had two great periods in its history: the first covers the seventh to twelfth centuries; the second, the first decade of the twentieth, when Yeats and Synge returned to those primitive beginnings in their art. In the beginning, we need recall, Irish literature was largely based on an oral tradition. The tribal social organization of nobles, professional men, and peasants was possessed of a type of mind which is largely the mind of primitive men everywhere: "To primitive man the greatest possible nightmare is the loss of his identity, which may occur at any time as the result of a loss of memory. If he does not know who his father, grandfather, and great-grandfather were or the names and events associated with the place where they lived, he is nobody." [75] To assure that they would never become "nobodies," the Irish, O'Connor contends, never relied on books but rather on an oral tradition or, stated differently, on "what the Old Man said." Hence, in those times, the professional class of "artists" was interested in producing less of the man with the "best brain" and more of the man with the "best memory."

To avoid, with the lapse of time, the inevitable lapse of memory, the sagas, told from memory, were eventually recorded by the Christian missionary monks in Ireland who owned the best memories. From the first, however, only ill-assorted fragments exist which, because those with memories lacked an intense critical apparatus, were freely linked together until they established links of their own. Because church tradition is basically literary, as opposed to that of the professional classes, which is basically oral, these missionaries, in addition to their recordings from memory, introduced to Ireland the concept of a "Book," but a "Book" that "must be rescued whole and from the mists of history and the blunders of the original uncritical transcribers and latter day scholars." [76]

Among the works rescued, though not, of course, whole, was *the* central Irish saga, an appalling text composed sometime in the seventh century—"The Cattle Raid of Cooley." The author's purpose would seem to have been, according to O'Connor's reconstruction, to tell a story of war begun because of a wily woman's whims and to warn against women in positions of authority. Besides the woman, there are sly, courageous men and bulls which are the pretext for war as well as symbols of masculinity. And yet, despite an archaic air, this work would seem to deal with a contemporary situation about which the author had some strong feelings and a powerful imagination that was able to fix it in unforgettable sequences. O'Connor's description and evaluation seems logical and outstanding:

The Connachtmen succeed in driving the Ulster bull back with them and then the real battle takes place—the battle of the two virilities, the undefeatable bulls. After fighting for a day and night in a Roscommon lake, the Ulster bull emerges triumphant with the wreck of the Connacht bull on his horns, and as he passes, homesick and dying on his lonely journey across Ireland, he tosses the fragments of the Connacht bull to the four quarters and drops dead on the frontier of his native land.

It is one of the great climaxes of literature. Nowhere else in literature that I know has war been so vividly imagined; yet some sort of murderous irony pursues irony: Gulliver's Travels is a favorite children's book; Ulysses is the last refuge of crossword-puzzle fiends; and only very serious linguists will ever be able to penetrate properly the jungle of "The Cattle Raid of Cooley." [77]

"The Cattle Raid of Cooley," as well as some of the other poems and prose works he discovered of that period, O'Connor considers "primary literature." A literature is primary when "it is in the main original, not derivative, and expresses the joys and fears of man confronted with an unfamiliar universe." To be sure, O'Connor readily admits that this is not a critical standard, since "neither French nor English literature is autonomous and primary" and yet they are major literatures. Hence, the test O'Connor proposes for Irish literature as regards its primary status "is not how far it resembles English or French, because this is something that did not happen until the sixteenth century, when Ireland shared in a common Renaissance culture, but of whether or not it gives us shock. . . . the shock of man's fundamental experience set down as though for the first time." [78] Since early Irish literature achieved that "shock of man's fundamental experience set down as though for the first time," it is primary and great. Hence, O'Connor would demand of all Irish writers "to look backward to look forward," so that they too might achieve in their writing the "shock of man's fundamental experience."

Part of that experience, O'Connor argues further, in telling the story of Irish literature *and* history at the same time is the political tone that pervades it. "I know no other literature," he flatly contends, "so closely linked to the immediate reality of politics," with the first great masterpiece of this literature written in English being Swift's *A Modest Proposal.* Hence, the entire Norman conquest proved a disaster not only for Irish history, for the "Normans could not rule the country themselves but were strong enough to prevent anyone else's ruling it," but for Irish literature as well, since a country without a political center is a country without a head. Headless, the aristocratic culture was bereft of intellectual content, resulting in a curious melancholia that underlay much of the Irish religious poetry of that time. "It is the melancholy of people who have made a feudal compact with a lord whose behavior is ultimately irrational but against whom they cannot rebel." [79]

Unable to rebel against the feudal Normans, the Irish were equally helpless against Cromwell and his hordes who destroyed, finally, what was, until then, the "cultural nationality" of Ireland. For at the turn of the seventeenth century, Irish literature becomes Anglo-Irish literature, the result, among other things, of an extension of the knowledge of English which acted as a sort of *lingua franca*. Though, to be sure, the literature of the late Middle Ages and Tudor periods is also Anglo-Irish, nevertheless, as O'Connor points out, there is a difference: "the main element in those periods was Irish. By the time we reach the eighteenth century, the dominant, indeed, the only significant element is English." And it was the Cromwellians, mainly the English lower and middle classes, urbanized, anti-Royalist and anti-Catholic, who, unable to understand the existence of a "cultural nationality not impinging on a political entity," destroyed both. By the eighteenth century, therefore, the "old aristocracy hardly existed at all and professional poetry did not exist except as a peasant imitation." [80]

Though some of these social conditions may not have changed, nor, for that matter, might they ever, the Irish, again because of a confluence of political and literary events, were propelled into the nineteenth century. At approximately the same time that Wolfe Tone, their greatest figure, was developing a policy whose aim was "to unite the whole people of Ireland, to abolish the memory of all past dissensions, and to substitute the common name of Irishmen in place of the denominations of Protestant, Catholic and Dissenter," [81] James Macpherson was publishing his supposed translations from "Ossian," which became part of the romantic movement and a success all over Europe. In addition, Charlotte Brooke published, in 1789, *Reliques of Ancient Irish Poetry*, which—though some poems were real and others forgeries—together with Macpherson's translations, had an inordinate effect on Irish history and literature. Because the Irish language had, by this time, been effectively curtailed, these two works gained in importance since "they represent the beginning of a new cultural nationalism to replace that which was lost in the Cromwellian invasions." These works, especially Charlotte Brooke's, opened the way for Ferguson, Mangan, and Yeats. And, most importantly, they inspired Ireland "to look backward again"—a task to which, O'Connor repeats, every Irish writer must dedicate himself.

Ironically, it was only this "backward look" that was left to the Irish when, in 1801, the "Act of Union," linking Ireland to the United Kingdom, put an end to the Independent Irish Parliament of Ireland as well as to the pride of "literary independence." For, among the most destructive effects of this "union" was the near extinction of the Irish language, "the one mark of cultural identity left to the people and the loss of which left the way open for the synthetic nationality that still afflicts [them]." To overcome some of that political and cultural affliction, two writers, Petrie with his *Dublin Penny Journal* and Samuel Ferguson, in his *Oghan Inscriptions in Ireland, Wales, and Scotland,* and *Congal* sought to revive Ireland's identity by the total acceptance of a common past. They argued for the "recovery of the mislaid but not lost records and acts and opinions and condition of our ancestors—the disinterring and bringing back to the light of intellectual day [of] the already recorded *facts*, by which the people of Ireland will be able to *live back* in the land they live in, with as ample and as interesting a field of retrospective enjoyment as any of the nations around us." [82] Divorced from this identity, Ireland would remain culturally deprived. Unless, as O'Connor constantly argues, there is a return to that past, or, as he calls it, a "looking backward," there can hardly be a "look forward."

In the second half of the nineteenth century there occurred a highly significant "looking backward," resulting in an incomparable Irish intellectual "forward look." When, after the famine, the Irish became a nation of town-dwellers, forcing them to sever a great part of their connection with the Irish language, usually associated with the countryside, two works, by foreigners no less, helped the Irish focus their "look backward." One was the *Grammatica Celtica* by the Bavarian schoolmaster Johann Caspar Zeuss, in 1853, in which he postulated that "Irish and Welsh were both part of the great Indo-European group of languages from which Latin and Greek came"; the second was Matthew Arnold's Oxford Lectures

On the Study of Celtic Literature, which argued that comparative philology had changed the attitude of educated Englishmen toward Ireland (though in fact that change was really effected by the Concordat) making the language of the "beaten race" and, presumably its people, at least "philologically" respectable. To be sure, there were other factors which promoted the "look backward." Yet these writings played a significant role, O'Connor believes, in changing the views of many who would not consider the Irish, henceforth, as "aliens in speech, in religion, in blood." [83]

Ultimately, however, change must come from within. Respectability for the "beaten race" could not really be effected by foreigners, however intellectually formidable, or by strangers, however distinguished as scholars. It must come from one's own people, one's race, one's own countrymen. Fortunately for the Irish, it finally did come—at the beginning of the twentieth century—with the arrival on the literary scene of William Butler Yeats and James Joyce. These two giants of modern literature achieved during their lifetime and, most certainly, by the time of their death, the transfiguration of Ireland's past. They gave their countrymen the literary respectability and acclaim denied them in previous centuries. The Irish were no longer "aliens" in the world of letters: they could now look significantly backward and forward.

To O'Connor, who referred to them as "Willie" and "Jimmy," Yeats and Joyce represent the "idealist and the realist, the countryman and the townsman, the dead past and unborn future." And their lives were also, for O'Connor, the embodiment of the words of the Second Synod: "He who can succeed, even if he imperil himself, shall teach and show himself everywhere, and he who cannot, let him be silent and depart." [84] Yeats stayed; Joyce departed—one to become the greatest poet, the other the greatest novelist of the twentieth century. And each, in his unique way, gave Ireland its greatest "forward look" and leap, helping to bring a bit closer the day when the "gray goose quill will rule the world."

Furthermore, these giants fulfilled in their writings what O'Connor considered to be the enduring conflict in all of Irish literature: between "thesis" and "antithesis." Or, stated differently, the conflict between imagination and intellect, feeling and fact, instinct and judgment; and, between those who spend a considerable part of their life in country and those who, for whatever reason, live in towns or, simply, the "country-bred" versus the "townees." In short, between the "aristocratic" thesis and "middle-class" antithesis. Yeats, of course, represented "thesis"; Joyce, "antithesis."

To be sure, O'Connor, anxious to avoid stereotyping either of these writers, finds both elements in each. Hence, he tells us that, although Yeats, influenced after an accidental meeting with the Fenian leader John O'Leary in 1886 to use Irish material in the way of Ferguson and Mangan, was still a first-rate intellect; an intellect which, in a fit of delighted exasperation, O'Connor describes as the only one that "could deduce a universal truth from two fallacies and an error." [85] Of Joyce, O'Connor also hastens to add that "intense objectivity and intense subjectivity alternate in his work, and in his later work he makes a desperate effort to fuse the two sides of his mind." [86] Both, then, are apparently "thesis" *and* "antithesis."

In any event, of the two, O'Connor decidedly favors Yeats, who is the presiding genius of this book. Aside from his close personal relationship, O'Connor sees Yeats as the only person who would be "prepared to create the 'religion of the world' from a few folk tales and to recreate the literature of Ireland from a handful of translations, most of them inaccurate." [87] And who else but Yeats, involved in his manifold activities, could, out of his blunders as well as from his successes, develop a universal scheme of religion, aesthetics, and politics? This, O'Connor outlines in brief: "To escape the vulgarity of Victorian religion one turns to mythology and magic; to escape the commonplace of journalism one goes back to peasant speech; to break the tyranny of actor-managers one simplifies acting and stage design, and to re-energize the theater one brings back the miracle and mystery play." [88]

Despite all his systems, needless to say, it is Yeats's poetry which ultimately preserves his genius. And yet, surprisingly, O'Connor devotes, even in a "survey," far less attention to the poetry than a reader would normally come to expect. Far less than, say, William York Tindall's masterly analysis in his essay in the Columbia University series of "Essay on Modern Writers." Nevertheless, O'Connor succeeds in making one or two observations that deserve attention. He remarks, for example, that Yeats's "poems and plays spring from a continuous soliloquy, an increasing interior monologue, interrupted only by voices from outside." [89] These voices, to be sure, are not always easy to detect nor is it easy to determine precisely what they are saying, but they do form a major element in his unwritten biography. Hence, the circumstances of Yeats's poetry may be obscure, not the poems themselves.

Furthermore, O'Connor argues that Yeats "does not seem a great love poet, but as a poet of friendship he is incomparable." [90] To Yeats "friendship never ends," since he had the "sort of tolerant, amused, enduring affection and a long memory for little kindnesses that go with great friendship." He was a man with no memory for injuries or imaginary injuries done to his friends, especially those he had "discovered," like Lady Gregory or Synge.

And it was the death of Synge, significantly, which, according to O'Connor, ended not only their friendship but also a most remarkable period in Irish literary history. The years between 1900 and 1910 were one of the most exciting decades in that history because so many distinguished works of fiction, poetry, criticism, and drama were then being written, published, and produced. And all, O'Connor concludes, because of the "old sorcerer Yeats, who, without a penny, had conjured up a decade of cultural achievement that suggested not some English provincial town but some state in Renaissance Italy." [91] Synge s death put an end to that state and Yeats, despondent, considered Ireland once again a "blind and bitter land" that "was made when the devil spat."

That bitterness, however, did not last long. Though he still bemoaned the death of "Romantic Ireland" in that great poem "September 1913," Yeats became reconciled to his country, especially after the Rising of 1916, when, like all sensitive Irishmen, he "accepted responsibility when there no longer was any call for him to do so." And his reconciliation was strongest with the theater—a historical fact, O'Connor bemoans, not given adequate attention in foreign studies of Yeats—for in drama, following the advice he himself once gave to Synge, Yeats chose the "commonplace phrase to restore the tone of the human voice speaking." Hence, O'Connor devotes a few pages to one of Yeats's dance plays *The Only Jealousy of Emer.* Again, though the analysis is adequate, O'Connor, unlike, say, Lennox Robinson, leaves much unsaid about the more formidable of Yeats's plays written during Yeats's renewed romance with Ireland.[92]

If O'Connor's analyses of Yeats's work are obviously wanting, there is enough value there, however, to impress the reader with the one unmistakable conclusion: O'Connor was a Yeats man to the marrow. In the two chapters in this book as well as in the articles that had previously appeared, within a year or so of Yeats's death, in the *Yale Review* and *The Bell*, O'Connor is awed by this man of genius, whose "subtle, casuistical and elegant manners" made him always appear as a "striking European figure." In fact, O'Connor was so impressed with Yeats from their very first meeting that he never ceased to be awed by him till the very end of his life. O'Connor recorded those first impressions:

There was something about him that suggested the bird: the strange inhuman cock of the head; the bird's sloping eyes, which at times seemed to be at the side rather than the front of his face; his long nose, which he tweaked; his laugh which was abrupt and remote. . . . Sometimes he laughed without moving his lips, his eyebrows raised, only his eyes smiling, and the laugh dwindled into a sad thoughtfulness as though dying upon the air. Sometimes he laughed excitedly, jerking and moving about, shaking himself within his clothes, stammering slightly; but it was always the eyes that smiled. When he was very happy and forgot himself, animation flowed over him in waves. . . . He sat forward, arms on his knees, washing his hands over and over, the pose broken sometimes by a loud harsh throaty laugh like a croak and the throwing back of the bird's head, while he sat bolt upright holding on to the lapels of his coat; sometimes by a tweaking of his nose, most characteristically perhaps by a sudden raising of the index finger for attention. But he was always alert, dramatic and amazingly brilliant. . . . He was a really lovely man to watch.

And even in Yeats's extreme old age, when he looked most wretched and discontented, O'Connor, still overawed, noticed that "quite suddenly a blaze of excitement would sweep over the face like sunlight over a moor, and from behind the mask a boy's eager, tense face stammered and glared at you . . . most exciting to see." [93]

All this excitement did not, however, blind O'Connor—to his everlasting credit—to the fact that, despite Yeats's genius, his extraordinary power with words, his great intellect, he had serious personal shortcomings. He was a "bully" who attempted to silence those who disagreed with him. He employed the wily ways of a "politician" when he tried and often succeeded in out-maneuvering his opposition on the Board of Directors of the Abbey Theatre. O'Connor was also troubled by the Yeats who, allowing his intellect to remain in abeyance, would suddenly declare that "science had shot its bolt and there were no major discoveries left to be made." But of all his shortcomings, O'Connor deplored most the fact that, in his last phase, Yeats was a supporter of the fascistic O'Duffy, even writing marching songs for him and his fanatical hordes. And, despite a meager attempt at defending him by stating that, "as a Fascist, [Yeats] was the least fanatical of men," O'Connor found Yeats's conduct deplorable and, ultimately, unforgivable.

Trying to probe these troublesome aspects of Yeats's personality, most painful, at times, being, for example, his belief that literature was some sort of "cooperative activity" which allowed him to appropriate lines of others, forcing George Moore to comment once that "Yeats had got off with the spoons," O'Connor offers an explanation which may or may not prove psychologically adequate: "Yeats was a Catholic, typically a Catholic: there was something about him that reminded you at times of a Roman prelate; fascist and authoritarian, seeing in world crises only the breakup of the 'damned liberalism' he hated; nationalist, lover of tradition and hater of reason and 'mechanical logic.' " [94] But it is not that aspect of Yeats, however strange and disappointing, that occupies the major part of O'Connor's attention. What O'Connor stresses is that Yeats was a "happy" man: "Coming to his door, hearing that rumble of verse being chanted, was like hearing bees on a summer day—a lucky, busy, wicked old man, praising his blessings. Everything came right: fame, theater, friends, wife, daughter, son—one finds them enumerated again and again in his verse." [95] All that moved O'Connor, as did the basic genius of the man which he defines as being "often a light by which we occasionally see ourselves and so refrain from some commonness of thought or action that time allows." [96] Because Yeats was able to stem, for a time, some commonness of thought or action among his associates, O'Connor remained a "Yeats man."

A Yeats man, indeed, but not, apparently, a Joyce man! An intimate friend of the former, O'Connor had only a casual acquaintance with the latter, having, by his own admission, met him only "a couple of times." O'Connor thought Joyce an "extraordinarily handsome man despite his having the biggest chin [he] had ever seen on a human being," and "shy" and terribly "arrogant," adding that Joyce was "a surgeon, not a writer." In fact, reviewing Stanislaus Joyce's *My Brother's Keeper* in the *Nation*, O'Connor comments casually that he counts himself among the "Joyce atheists." [97] Indeed, the entire review would seem to confirm his atheism. For, among other things, he favors Stanislaus over "Jim" and finds it difficult to understand, though ultimately agreeing, why Stanislaus would want to stress Jim's "gentleness, good humor and consideration for his awful father." O'Connor is everywhere critical—in the two chapters in this work as well as the single chapters in *The Mirror in the Roadway* and *The Lonely Voice*—as we shall see, of Joyce the writer. And, though O'Connor readily concedes that "nothing that I or anyone else can say will change the fact that *Ulysses* is one of the great monuments of Irish literature," he found it difficult, nay, impossible, to become a "Joyce man."

Joyce, you see, was the "antithesis" to Yeats's "thesis." "Thesis," let us recall, is in O'Connor's view the tradition of the folk life, country life, of nature with her abundance, fantasy, and the "deliberate . . . suspension of the critical faculty to justify a blind indulgence in . . . intuition." It is the folk art, the primitive art of poetry and drama, as Yeats once commented:

> John Synge, I, and Augusta Gregory, thought
> All that we did, all that we said or sang
> Must come from contact with the soil, from that
> Contact everything Antaeus-like grew strong.[98]

"Antithesis," on the other hand, is the "art life, the town life," which, in Yeats's words, "is sterile when it is not married to nature": "The whole ugliness of the modern world has come from the spread of towns and their ways of thought, and to bring back beauty we must marry the spirit and nature again. When the idea which comes from individual life marries the image that is born from the people, one gets great art, the art of Homer, and of Shakespeare, and of Chartres Cathedral." [99] Since Joyce was a "townee" who did not "marry his spirit to nature," he symbolizes "Antithesis." Elaborating further this Yeatsian distinction, O'Connor adds: "Shakespeare and Yeats were highly unscholarly men of feeling, full of happy reminiscences of a country childhood; Jonson and Joyce were men of enormous reading and curious scholarship, who were happiest in Bartholomew Fair and Nighttown. Shakespeare and Yeats appealed most to the country-bred; Jonson and Joyce to the scholars and townees." [100]

Of the two, O'Connor favored Yeats for any number of reasons. It may have been due to their long friendship; their cooperative efforts on behalf of the Abbey Theatre; or, because O'Connor, by his own admission, was an "emotional man," making him spiritually more akin to the poet; or, because, unlike Joyce, neither he nor Yeats left Ireland permanently; or, simply, that, aesthetically, O'Connor favored "thesis," as he understood it, over "antithesis."

Or this favoritism may have been due to the fact that O'Connor could never adjust to the "surgical" quality of Joyce's style, which apparently troubled O'Connor deeply and which may have been the ultimate reason for his becoming a "Joyce atheist." For central to all of O'Connor's criticism of Joyce—repeated, incidentally, almost verbatim, in *The Mirror in the Roadway* and *The Lonely Voice* as well as in *A Short History*—is the argument that he developed a peculiar style, best described as *mechanical prose*, by which certain words are "repeated deliberately and mechanically to produce the feeling of hypnosis in the reader." As an example, O'Connor chooses this passage from *A Portrait of the Artist as a Young Man*, italicizing those words which seemingly help prove this point:

*The soft beauty of the Latin word **touched** with an enchanting touch the dark of the evening, with a **touch** fainter and more persuading than the touch of music or of a **woman's** hand. The strife of their minds was quelled. The figure of a **woman** as she appears in the liturgy of the* church **passed** silently through the darkness: a white-robed figure, small and slender as a boy and with a falling girdlè. Her voice, frail and high as a boy's, was heard intoning from a distant choir the first words of a **woman** which pierce the gloom and clamor of the first chanting of the passion:

Et tu cum Jesu Galilaeo eras—

And all hearts here **touched** and turned to her **voice,** shining like a young star, shining clearer as the **voice** intoned the proparoxyton, and more faintly as the cadences died.[101]

The impression such prose seems to leave on O'Connor is that Joyce wrote "with a list of a couple of hundred words before him, each representing some association, and that at intervals the words were dropped in, like currants in a cake and a handful at a time, so that their presence would be felt rather than identified." [102]

What disturbs O'Connor even more about all of this is that Joyce introduced something new in literature. What it amounts to is that "style ceases to be a relationship between author and reader and becomes a relationship of a magical kind between author and object. Here *le mot juste* is no longer *juste* for the reader, but for the object. It is not an attempt at communicating the experience to the reader, who is supposed to be present only by courtesy, but at equating the prose with the experience." [103] In effect, Joyce, influenced by Flaubert, and in turn, influencing Hemingway, is replacing the experience by the prose or the reality by the image. What we get, therefore, is not fiction as O'Connor understands it, a fiction based on the relationship between author and reader, but rather a "rhetorician's dream."

Of course, what O'Connor fails to recognize is that Joyce's style and understanding of the art of fiction may be due to a different vision of reality. When reality becomes, in our time, so terribly complex, as William York Tindall cogently observes, "a story or novel can no longer be the simple narrative of the past." Hence words are used not simply to state but to evoke. And their effect "depends upon suggestion rather than statement," so that they "express overtones of experience while they fix its meaning and quality by rhythms." [104]

Needless to say, O'Connor would not be convinced. When questioned, therefore, about his association with Joyce, of which, naturally, he could say little, O'Connor turns abruptly to making a distinction between the "university" novelists, like Joyce and Virginia Woolf, and the "natural" novelists, among whom, one supposes, he counted himself:

The university novelists have been having it their own way for thirty years and it's about time a natural novelist got back to the job and really told stories about people . . . this conception of character has disappeared entirely, the conception of character that I am talking about. You see, I don't believe there's anything else in the world except human beings, they're the best thing you're ever likely to discover. . . . 'Well, this is all finished with' . . . there aren't individuals any longer. . . . [105]

Rhetoricians, apparently, have somehow lost faith in the individual, at least as regards fiction. They no longer develop characters so as to involve the reader in the description of the experience and "make him feel as author and character were supposed to feel." Instead, "experience is replaced by a verbal arrangement intended to leave [the reader] free to feel or not, just as he chooses, so long as he recognizes that the experience itself has been fully rendered." [106]

What troubles O'Connor finally about Joyce's style is that, having mastered the technique, he ceased being the genuine storyteller who, in *Dubliners*, was able so brilliantly to recreate the "submerged population" of Dublin. And the depiction of a "submerged population" in O'Connor's view, is, let us recall, the very essence of great short-story writing. What, then, happened? Why, after "The Dead," did Joyce cease forever to write short stories? To O'Connor, dissatisfied with Joyce's rhetorical passion, the answer appears simple:

One of his main passions—the elaboration of style and form—had taken control, and the short story is too tightly knit to permit expansion like this. And—what is much more important—it is quite clear from "The Dead" that he had already begun to lose sight of the submerged population that was his original subject. . . . They are not characters but personalities, and Joyce would never again be able to deal with characters, people whose identity is determined by their circumstances. [107]

Small wonder, therefore, that disappointed also in Joyce's failure to remain a story teller, O'Connor remained a "Yeats man." Forgetting all the while, of course, that Joyce's magical approach to language as opposed to the logical was often used by Yeats in precisely the same way; overlooking, too, the elements in the modern condition of man which drove writers like Joyce to fashion their new approach to fiction.

Nevertheless, we must bear in mind that, whatever the reasons for his preference of Yeats over Joyce, O'Connor saw both as *the* masters of Irish as well as world literature. And, both, together with the other "Olympians"—Stephens, Synge, AE, O'Casey, O'Flaherty —are the dominant figures of the "backward look." Remember, O'Connor concludes, without that look Ireland, more than any country, "has nothing and is nothing" and can hardly hope to be, in the "coming days . . . the indomitable Irishry" of history and literature.

SIX

The Abbey Is There

Drama is the most ephemeral of the literary arts, being based upon a collaboration between author, audience and performers.
—Frank O'Connor, *Towards an Appreciation of Literature*

You see, you couldn't work four years in a theatre unless you either fell in love with it or ignored it. I am in love with it, that's all.
—Frank O'Connor in a letter to Sean O'Faolain

No "backward look," we know, could possibly avoid taking in the stellar role played by the Abbey Theatre in the creation of modern Irish literature. In addition to its founders—Yeats, Lady Gregory, and Synge—the Abbey attracted some other Olympians: George Moore, Edward Martyn, Shaw, Hyde, Lord Dunsany, AE, Colum, O'Casey, Lennox Robinson, Higgins, Hunt, and, of course, O'Connor. For the Abbey became, especially during the period between Synge and O'Casey, not only the symbol of the Celtic Renaissance but of a specific tradition in playwriting, acting, and producing. That tradition, making the Abbey one of the great art centers of the western world, served as a catalyst that stimulated these brilliant dramatists, as well as distinguished actors and "imaginative audiences," to its existing stage.

It might prove worthwhile, therefore, to review briefly the nature of that tradition and of O'Connor's specific contribution to it, adding thereby to his "cargo of impure art." After that fateful meeting in 1898 between Yeats and Lady Gregory, when the talk turned to theater, they issued their first manifesto which, though now seem-

ingly pompous, served as the foundation of the Irish Literary Theatre, the forerunner of the Abbey:

*We propose to have performed in Dublin, in the spring of every year,
certain Celtic and Irish plays, which whatever be their degree of excel-
lence will be written with a high ambition, and so build up a Celtic and
Irish school of dramatic literature. We hope to find in Ireland an uncor-
rupted and imaginative audience trained to listen by its passion for
oratory, and believe that our desire to bring upon the stage the deeper
thoughts and emotions of Ireland will ensure for us a tolerent welcome,
and that freedom to experiment which is not found in theaters in
England, and without which no new experiment in art or literature can
succeed. We will show that Ireland is not the home of buffoonery and
of easy sentiment, as it has been represented, but a home of ancient
idealism. We are confident of the support of all Irish people, who are
weary of misrepresentation, in carrying out a work that is outside all the
political questions that divide us.*[1]

What this and subsequent manifestoes clearly present are the
two fundamental premises that moved Yeats and Lady Gregory
and, shortly thereafter, persuaded Synge, a somewhat shadowy
young man then living in Paris supposedly preparing himself to
become an English interpreter of French literature, to join this ambitious project: first, that literature is essentially national, with its
roots in folk culture and, second, that every writer should put his
roots down in his own country and draw this strength from the
spirit of his race. Or, as Yeats, defining his idea of an Irish Literary
Society some years before the meeting with Lady Gregory, asked
rhetorically: "Can we not unite literature to the great passion of
patriotism and ennoble both thereby?" What Yeats and his com-
patriots wanted, then, was a "union between the everlasting principles of love of truth and love of country that speak to man in solitude and in the silence of the night."[2]

If these principles spoke to Yeats—in the noise of the day as well
as the silence of the night—they did likewise to Synge after he was
persuaded by Yeats to leave Paris and to go to the Aran Islands "to
live there as if [he] were one of the people themselves." There he
would find his roots and also strength from the spirit of his country.
After one visit, in June 1898, Synge, apparently, found them. In

fact, he made five more visits, recording his impressions in *The Aran Islands*. What Synge was convinced of was that literature was based upon and addressed not to the intellectual elite but, rather, to the national folk. As Joseph Wood Krutch lucidly comments:

The successful artist must return to his own country, and that involved something more than a matter of geographical location. To return to the spirit and the imagination of the simple people of one's race and to draw from that spirit and that imagination both one's theme and one's language. It meant works which would appeal to, as well as be inspired by, the folk. That, in turn, meant the abandonment of such abstract social, moral, and philosophical questions as were concerning the modern drama of Europe in favor of the two things which are really interesting and understandable to a whole folk—namely, the incidents of its own daily life on the one hand, its folk tales and legends on the other.[3]

Out of all these premises and principles came not only the creation of a remarkable theater but a number of masterpieces and a host of plays which gave the Abbey a distinct and distinguished repertory. One of these masterpieces was Synge's *Playboy of the Western World*, which, despite the violence of the audience reaction when it was first presented in 1907, does seem, interestingly enough, to be in accord with the abstract principles formulated by him, Yeats, and Lady Gregory. The language, though technically prose, has the flavor of poetry, for it is based primarily on the speech of those who habitually thought in Irish and whose idiom resulted from mentally translating Irish constructions into English. The subject of the play is the daily life of the people whom it represents, and yet "it is also, at the same time, a fable, with its conflict between the father and the son, suggesting one of the recurrent themes of the folk tale." [4] It appeals both to the peasant and to the international intelligentsia.

What is, in addition, so interesting about this new approach to theater, as Krutch correctly observes, is that it represents a challenge to what we have come to consider as "modernism" in drama. "It simply turns away from 'modern ideas' and assumes that such modern ideas are not the business of literature at all, since its true business is to be True and Beautiful not instructive, or analytical or propagandistic." It is, in effect, an anti-modernist movement which made the Abbey the "center of an influence resisting the dominant influence of Ibsen, Shaw and the rest."

And for a few years—three at least—from the time of the first performance in 1899, the experiment proved successful. In fact, Yeats was so encouraged that he was moved to write:

We have brought the 'literary drama' to Ireland, and it has become a reality. . . . In Ireland, we had among our audience almost everybody who is making opinion in Ireland, who is part of his time, and numbers went out of the playhouse thinking a little differently of that Ireland which their work is shaping; some went away angry, some delighted, but all had seen that upon the stage at which they could not look altogether unmoved. . . . On the whole, therefore, I have a good hope that our three years of experiment, which is all we proposed to ourselves at the outset, will make literary drama permanent in Ireland during our time, and give the Irish nation a new method of expression.[5]

Nevertheless, despite Yeats's dream of permanence, the Irish theater constantly shifted its emphasis between its literary and national goals, between the cosmopolitan ideas advocated by, say, Martyn and Moore and the narrower aims of the founders, between a Theater of Beauty and a Theater of Realism. Ultimately, however,

the whole pull of modern drama and modern literature was in a direction opposite to that taken by Synge and that . . . pull proved irresistible. It has been in the direction of realism, of sociological concern, of dissonant sonorities, of an obsession with irreconcilable conflicts, and, therefore, in the direction of despair. Even though the Abbey Theater was founded to resist the pull, one generation was sufficient to make it 'modern' in a sense in which it had never wanted to be.[6]

What it also never wanted to happen were the defections from its ranks that inevitably result when a group of people, however distinguished and literary and artistic, begin to engage in the "business of men." Reality can only approximate the dream. The brothers Fay, AE, and Miss Horniman, the first "patron" of the Abbey, defected for personal, political, and sundry other reasons from the ranks of those who dreamed of a theater in Ireland based on "national life and national feeling." But through all the changes of personnel and policy—at times sharp and treacherous—and all the quarrels and rancor, one man remained at the helm, whether on the scene or abroad, and that man was Yeats. Or, as O'Connor once phrased it, "The old watchdog never relaxed his vigilance."

However, on reaching his seventieth birthday in 1935, Yeats, in ill health, recognized that to prolong his life he would need to spend more and more of his time in the south of France. Worried, therefore, that the Abbey, left in the hands of Robinson, Starkie, and Hayes—the latter two of whom he distrusted—might not survive, he added four directors, chosen with his "usual carelessness": F. R. Higgins, Brinsley MacNamara, Ernest Blythe, and, Hugh Hunt, whom he brought over from England, at the suggestion of John Masefield, the poet laureate, to act as producer. In one of its first decisions the reorganized Board, aware of the anticipated opposition, decided, nevertheless, to produce O'Casey's *The Silver Tassie*, on August 12, 1935. The opposition was, of course, loud and strong, not on justifiable artistic grounds, or that the play was badly written, but on religious grounds. But none of the directors expected the opposition to come from their own ranks. Brinsley MacNamara joined the "sentimental nationalists" in their attack, publishing a two-column announcement in the *Irish Independent* which criticized not only his fellow directors but also the Abbey audiences, who "for more than ten years have shown a wholly uncritical and I might say, almost insane admiration for the vulgar and worthless plays of Mr. O'Casey." [7] As a result, MacNamara was compelled by Yeats to resign from the Board immediately.

Looking around for a "gunman" because "all the successful businesses were being run by gunmen," Yeats chose O'Connor as the replacement for MacNamara. Because O'Connor had once been a soldier or "gunman" in the Irish Republican Army during the "Troubles," Yeats considered him a proper choice, especially since only gunmen could put the theater "on its feet again." Whether O'Connor the "gunman" put the Abbey on or off its feet is, by his own admission, uncertain. What is certain, however, is that on assuming his role in its immediate destiny, he tried, despite the machinations of his fellow directors, to right some of the wrongs he found in the Abbey.

The first and basic wrong was Lennox Robinson, the managing

director ever since the days of Lady Gregory. O'Connor found this "lanky, remote, melancholy man, a dead weight on the theatre." Although O'Connor admired him as a person and was forever grateful that he helped get him his first job as a librarian, he had never been fond of him. What disturbed O'Connor were his "sudden, extraordinary changes of mood when the kind adviser turned into a mean, sardonic enemy, determined on making every word rankle." [8] His real weakness as a director was the result of the "morbid streak" in him. He was himself "in a state of despondency and no despondent man can do work that requires endless improvisation." In short, Robinson was an unhappy man who mismanaged the Abbey.

Central to that mismanagement was the sneaky way in which Robinson refused young playwrights the opportunity of having their works produced, by persuading the Board that "no works of value were being submitted. . . . He not only approved dreary farces, but when a fine play came along, he would fasten on some fault and try to have it rejected." [9] This failure to encourage writers would often force the Abbey to produce European plays—"museum theatre" O'Connor called it—instead of allowing it to be "all-Irish theater," as originally intended. As his own "circumstances" grew worse, Robinson grew more obstructive.

O'Connor, exasperated with such incompetence, finally drafted a resolution to appoint Hugh Hunt director for two years. "It is," O'Connor later confessed, "one of the few decisions I have never regretted, because for two years he ran the theatre as it had not been run since Lady Gregory's day." In fact, even Yeats, long a defender and supporter of Robinson, agreed to O'Connor's decision. Walking home together one night after a Board meeting, Yeats turned to O'Connor saying in confidence: " 'There's something I want to say to you, O'Connor. You may not have realized that I was watching what you did, because I have had to oppose so many of the things you have done, but all the same I knew they had to be done. Thirty years ago I should have done them myself, but now I am an old man and have too many emotional associations. Thank you.' " [10]

Unfortunately, O'Connor's other fellow appointees were hardly any better. Higgins, in O'Connor's opinion, was even more obstructive than Robinson. Though talented as a poet, Higgins was the most devious and pugnacious member of the Board, who kept feeding tall stories about O'Connor to Yeats and stories about Yeats to O'Connor and Robinson, and about Hunt, "to anyone who would listen." And Hayes, who ultimately proved himself the most treacherous of all, was, in O'Connor's view, "an admirable director, warm hearted, appreciative and intelligent." Ernest Blythe appeared to O'Connor like a "Buddha in grey plaster." Genuinely attached to the Irish language and anxious to revive it—during conversations he was forever jotting down Gaelic equivalents to English polysyllabic words—Blythe was what one might call "a single-minded man." Had O'Connor discerned his true nature earlier, he might have been more wary of him, the one who, ironically, outlasted them all on the Board.

These, then, were the men O'Connor was supposed to work with. Himself with "no ability as an intriguer . . . [and who] could be fooled by appearances most of the time," O'Connor paid more attention to improving the Abbey than to the petty deviousness of his fellow directors. Hence, he quickly became the "vital force in the Abbey," for he was the "only director who had both the genius and intuitive ability to do the right thing." [11] And he did the right thing when he approached writers of ability, novelists or storytellers, offering to produce any play they cared to write, since experience, he believed, was not absolutely necessary. "Indeed, O'Connor was the only man whose genius might hold out against the ever-present deteriorating influences on the Abbey's integrity." [12]

Some of the influences which O'Connor held out against were none other than those of the "old watchdog" himself. Despite O'Connor's genuine admiration of Yeats as a "really great man of the theatre" and "one of the consistently noble men" he had ever met, as well as their long, close personal friendship, he differed with the master on a number of fundamental issues pertaining to the running of the Abbey. First, there was the matter of Yeats's failure to understand the nature of "realism" and its function in the theater. That resulted, in part, from the fact that Yeats's understanding of "realism" was totally colored—blinded would be a better word—by Robinson. On appointing Robinson to manage the Abbey after the *Playboy* riots, Yeats abdicated his responsibility for its direction and some of its needs. And that, says O'Connor, was the "ground of [his] quarrels with him":

[Yeats] could not realize that there was any sort of realism other than Robinson's, and, whether he knew it or not, he identified Robinson's realism with the crude attitude of those who had been able to see nothing in Synge but the sort of problem-play they really hungered for and the dull morality of the popular preacher. . . . After this, he sought for forms more and more remote from the popular, realistic theatre, and the result is [that] of the last plays. . . . Only one, the wonderful Words Upon the Window-Pane, was really within the theatre's competence.[13]

Yeats had, apparently, lost touch with the needs of a theater that must make the audience, as we shall see, an integral element of its "workshop."

Second, since Yeats was a master of the one-act play, a medium which he used magnificently, his material did not admit to a full-length play, with the result that, though lyrical and based on miracles, his plays "dealt with the moment of revelation rather than the painful evolution of character and incident." And even when "there is no miracle, the crisis is usually based on a form of conversion, of revelation." But the theater, O'Connor felt, needed "evolution" rather than "revolution." Yeats was primarily a poet for whom words and the ordering of words were always the chief care and delight but who had no keen sense of the drama. Because only that sort of play—*The Countess Cathleen*, say—made any profound appeal to Yeats, most early plays of the Abbey were mysteries. O'Connor opted for a change of form, fewer miracles, that is, and more realism.

Third, consider the matter of the acting style at the Abbey. Like Yeats, O'Connor was convinced that for the specific needs of the Abbey, the Senecan style of acting, "in which words were all important," and where "nobody speaks while moving and nobody moved while someone else was speaking for fear of distracting attention to the words," was essential. Nevertheless, he argued that, in order to get "the theater on its feet," it might be more profitable "to assume the opposite style of the later European naturalistic convention in which beautiful speeches are chopped up and fitted into bits of stage business—picking up matches, so to speak." [14] The Senecan convention is purely rhetorical and suitable for poetry, while the other is more of the Shakespearean convention and purely dramatic. And the Abbey, in O'Connor's opinion, needed more of the latter than an over-abundance of the former.

Fourth, O'Connor disagreed with Yeats on a matter of policy. While the Abbey was developing its repertory and reputation, let us recall, "two enthusiastic penniless young actors from London," Michael MacLiammoir and Hilton Edwards, opened the Gate Theatre in 1928, across the street, with productions to include drama of every period and every country, from Aeschylus to the present day. The aim of these founders was twofold: "to create a standard of presentation comparable with that of the best in Europe and to lay the foundations of a new Irish school of writers different in subject, style and setting from those of the Abbey." [15] Yeats, joined by Higgins, who gradually dislodged Robinson as his "best friend," felt that if anything, they could do better. The Abbey ought to include, therefore, continental drama in its repertory. O'Connor, on the other hand, recalling the earlier Yeatsian vision that Irish drama should "be not merely the product of a sharp eye and ear realistically rendering life, but which would also present 'intellectual excitement' resulting from deep emotions," rejected this new Abbey policy.

Besides, there were some very practical reasons for this particular disagreement in policy. First, it would require two producers—one for Irish, the other for European plays—when the Abbey couldn't afford even one; second, Irish writers would have no opportunity, if the theater depended on world classics, to supply the Abbey with new life. And this would mean, in effect, the end of the very literary movement which the Abbey represented in Ireland. Then again, as for European classics, O'Connor was convinced he "had seen them performed as well as [he] was ever to do and had decided that they might not be as classical as they were generally supposed to be. Shakespeare could be boring, so could Sheridan; one could even get too much of Ibsen and Chekhov." [16] What he wanted to maintain at the Abbey was an "all-Irish theatre" that would not be boring.

The effect of these major differences between these close friends was, despite Yeats's influence, a revitalization of the Abbey under O'Connor's guidance. In fact, as one historian of the Abbey observes, when the first company left for a tour of America, under the direction of Higgins, in 1937, O'Connor was "accomplishing more with the second company than had been done for years with the first." [17] Part of that accomplishment was the result of O'Connor's ability to attract new writers to the Abbey. And, interestingly, while looking for new dramatists, he found himself.

For, to his general administrative chores of reading, approving, and producing plays, O'Connor added the role of playwright. He wrote and produced four plays for the Abbey: *In the Train* (1937), a dramatization of his short story of the same name; *The Invincibles* (1937), about the little group of Dublin terrorists who assassinated the British Chief Secretary in Ireland, Lord Frederick Cavendish, and the Irish Under-Secretary, Thomas Burke, in 1882, in Phoenix Park; *Moses' Rock* (1938), about the effects of the Parnellite split upon an imagined small town Irish family, the O'Learys, and their friends—both of these last were written in collaboration with Hugh Hunt; and *Time's Pocket* (1938). His fifth play, *The Statue's Daughter*, was produced, incidentally, not at the Abbey but at the Gate Theatre, in 1941. This last, a comedy, deals with the present and its involvements with the past. Set in a small Irish town in which a committee of citizens had set up a statue to honor the memory of Brian O'Rourke, a dead hero of the War of Independence, the "statue becomes a focal point for the interplay of two generations, their revaluation of attitudes toward each other and towards the problems of modern Ireland, and their search for a common ground between people of different faiths and traditions." [18]

None of these plays is distinguished; nor do they enhance in any appreciable way O'Connor's reputation as a dramatist. However, they do show enough ability to suggest that had he continued in this genre, he might very well have established himself as a significant playwright. But his *métier*, after all, was storytelling, in which he excelled. To be sure, *In the Train* does capture the mood of the "submerged population" in his characterization of Helena Maguire of Farranchreensht, accused of poisoning her husband, and of her alienation from society. As Moll, another character, comments: "Helena on the train by herself and no one to talk to her! What sort of neighbors will she think we are? Where is she?" All the tragedy of life—its meeting and parting, here today, gone tomorrow—is depicted on this train ride. Or as the Drunk, running to and fro, remarks, pathetically: "There were you, all the time, sitting here, and there was I walking up the train and down the train and I looking for you everywhere. And there were you, sitting there, and me rambling about there, and the pair of us lonesome and we not able to find one another. I'm a lonesome sort of man and now I'm going back to my lonesome habitation." [19] To be sure, the frightening loneliness of the "submerged population," their utter hopelessness comes through, surely, in this mood piece, the best of the plays. But where, for example, is the evolution of character and incident with which O'Connor took the measure of Yeats? Surely not in this play.

Of a different, though not insignificant interest, is O'Connor's choice of historical subjects in *The Invincibles* and *Moses' Rock*. One can only conjecture that he was motivated to choose as he did by the "strong streak of national consciousness in him," as is abundantly clear in *The Big Fellow* and *A Short History of Irish Literature*. He may well have felt the need to provide through dramatic historical themes the autobiography of his race. Again, he assumes here the role of a teacher, anxious to portray to future as well as present generations a dramatic rendition of the past. Roger McHugh sums it up best:

The historical play thus may have offered both a creative challenge and an opportunity for a critical examination of conscience and of values, involving such questions as violence, the right of the majority to be wrong, the nature of integrity in politics, church involvement in political matters. The impact of the violence of the Invincibles and of the Parnellite split upon the Irish people may have provided the necessary objective correlative for the expression of O'Connor's own experience.[20]

Whatever the motivations, these plays, though good in part, are not outstanding; but, in their own way, they added new interest in the Abbey repertory while winning "much praise for themselves, [for] having raised the dignity of Ireland."

Possibly worthy of equal, if not greater praise than his plays are his critical views of the theater. Invited, as Terens Lecturer in Fine Arts at the University of Hull, in 1944, to deliver three lectures at Town Hall, Grimsby, O'Connor formulated his ideas of the drama, based in part on his experience at the Abbey. These lectures, first published in *The Bell*, appeared, in pamphlet form some three years later under the title *The Art of the Theatre*. At times, he states the obvious; at other times, he advances something new; at all times, he is, as in the rest of his criticism, interesting because of his forthright views and opinions.

Before proceeding to discuss the three major elements of the drama—audience, writer, and actor—O'Connor, convinced that drama is the "last of our public arts," draws a distinction between "public" and "private" art. The latter, he contends, when it does not tend toward the private symbolism of a Picasso, Joyce, or Eliot, moves toward "common realism" or the "realism" of the modern novel; whereas the former, speaking chiefly to the "human soul in the mass" is "bound to speak imaginatively through myth and fable," which in turn depends on poetry. And one of the literary ironies of our age is the fact that there has been a transposition of the relative importance of the arts: "because storytelling, which can easily be accommodated to the printed page and the solitary reader, has now become the greatest of the modern arts," while poetry, still the most important of the arts and originally meant for the masses, has, alas, "grown more limited in its appeal." [21] How ironic since, in O'Connor's view, poetry is still the greatest instrument of the theater as a public art!

The role of the audience in the public art of the drama, O'Connor further laments, started to diminish somewhat when the action of the theater began to be confined solely to the proscenium. When an audience, especially when the "lights are quenched," is reduced to the "position of passive spectators," it develops a "peepshow mentality." Because the drama is no longer a "public" but a "private" art, it loses some of its imaginative significance. Unlike the cinema which depends on the "art of persuasion," drama is based on the "art of illusion," on "make believe." For, after all, Venice or Arden, for example, exist only in the collective imagination of the audience, something that cannot be transferred physically to the stage. Hence, it is only in the willingness of the audience to join in the "making" of a play, in the "make believe that the bare platform at the end of the hall is Venice that you have the first and most important principle of play construction." [22]

The vital role of the audience in the "public art" of drama, as opposed to the "private art" of storytelling, is further apparent when we begin to realize that in storytelling, the theme, beginning in a shadow, gradually becomes clearer "through a succession of minor revelations till at last the reader becomes aware of what the author had originally known." In the theater, on the other hand, the audience must, at any given moment, know all the facts. Yeats, for example, would always caution young playwrights: "You must never keep a secret from your audience." Hence, O'Connor concludes:

[The playwright] knows by instinct that drama begins at the precise moment when he allows the audience to share in a knowledge which he withholds from one or more of the characters. Where he does play upon the curiosity of the audience is never on the point of who or what a character really is, but the point at which the revelation is to be made, and what effect it will have on the other characters; and it is always a sign of a great dramatic craftsman that he never for an instant forgets that he and the audience are linked by that knowledge.[23]

Because the playwright, therefore, fuses the audience into the actual construction of the play, the "audience, like the dramatist and the players are an integral portion of the play."

What gives the dramatist as integral a part as the audience in the play is the fact that through him contemporary feelings and ideas find their way to the stage. Without him, the drama lacks not only form but life. One of the reasons for the success of the Abbey, O'Connor contends, was that Yeats, realizing that he could do nothing in a theater controlled by actors, "established one in which actors didn't count." What O'Connor, like Yeats, expected of writers is that they, too, be conscious always of their audience, "whose passions and prejudices [they] must consider either to conciliate or flout." Because a writer must forever be conscious of his audience, he cannot, like Tennyson and Browning, write his play in his study. Every line he writes should, to use O'Connor's metaphor, "explode like a fragmentation bomb and hit a thousand people simultaneously." A line must be understood by all of them at once. A good dramatist, O'Connor believes, "is largely a writer not for all time but for a day, a craftsman, a specialist, if you like—a hack." [24]

All of which leads him to reach a conclusion which, as previously noted, he was destined to repeat in *Shakespeare's Progress* and *My Father's Son,* and, so often in between, that he "almost ceased to believe it himself": "A theatre is a collaboration between audience, players, and writer, and there can be no collaboration if the scene is set in Russia of fifty years ago and if nobody now living can even imagine what life was like then. There can be no collaboration if an author has been dead for four hundred years and his way of writing, his dirty jokes, his topical allusions, have become largely unintelligible." [25] The "classics," therefore, cannot, according to O'Connor, really be successfully produced on our contemporary stage. They belong, instead, in the universities "which might do worse than give us well-studied performances of the classics."

Though the writer might, in our time, be reduced to a "hack," he is also given the responsibility, O'Connor hastens to add, of writing dialogue not only as an accompaniment to an action but as "an accompaniment to an action more intense than any he can devise anywhere." If he is a true poet, "it gives him a variety, a profundity, and a swiftness of imaginative demand and an immediacy of emotional response." The trouble with poets who write "poetic plays" is, however, that they often consider the poetry an end in itself, and not merely "the greatest instrument of the theater." Poetry is not external to the theater to be applied like rouge, and "for first-rate dramatic poetry one has to turn not to professional poets but to realists like Ibsen and Synge." [26] Hence, most modern prose tragedies fail, O'Connor believes, because the "language is entirely incapable of sustaining the action." While a storyteller need not be a poet, a dramatist must always be one.

Finally, then, the actor. At first sight, of course, he obviously serves as a sort of go-between between playwright and audience who interprets, as an orchestra a score, his part to the audience. But he cannot, however well he interprets the lines, tell us what a character, say, Othello, was actually like. Hence, O'Connor insists, an actor cannot go to history or literature for a model of what the character really is: "Every artist is bounded by his own experience and it is out of this experience he must draw his inspiration. . . . The artist [painter, storyteller, dramatist or actor] does not copy any model, for the conception of the character must exist before one can even think of a model, and afterwards it must live an independent life." What sort of person the model is doesn't matter. The model may not resemble in any way the character portrayed, yet the actor will succeed in his performance "only when [he] has passed the part, speech by speech, through a *living* human being, [only then] will [he] begin to realize that a certain line must be said in a certain way even though the whole tradition of the theatre be against [him]." [27] In so far as he interprets, the actor is a musician; but as a creator he must also, like any other artist, observe and meditate, and then present the character in the image of his creation.

In the old days of the Abbey, O'Connor recalls, when an author wrote a play, he first discussed it for hours with the players in the green room. Sometimes these discussions were heated, covering both the ideas and the lines and how they should be interpreted. What is so significant about this procedure is that it made of the Abbey a "living theatre,'" an interplay between artists who sought ideas and models for expressing them from the contemporary scene of which they were a part. O'Connor frowned on what he refers to as "museum theatre," or the Shakespearean tradition of acting, because, unlike the Abbey, which was based on an "imitation of life," "acting of star actors from the museum theatre was based on other acting, and it screeched through the texture of a play like an air raid siren through a country town." [28]

To avoid such screeching, the actor needs new plays, not necessarily of his own time but in the idiom of his time, or, old plays rewritten for him. Hence, if the theater is to flourish again as a "public art," it must have *new* plays written by artists who will be granted every opportunity to learn its ways at first hand, in a theater which is not a "museum" but a living workshop. And all with an audience that will consist not of passive individuals engaged in a peep show but of a "mass with a human soul" responding imaginatively to myth, fable, poetry, and the glories of a new tradition in the arts.

What is disturbing about O'Connor's sense of audience is that it is both rather scholastic and critically unsound. If, as he contends, the theater is an act of "mass-illusion," then why in his view are some of the plays he cites—*Oedipus, Tartuffe, Macbeth,* and *The Importance of Being Earnest*—improbable for the modern audience? Why can't there be a "collaboration between audience, player and writer" even if the scene of a play is set in Athens millennia, or in England four hundred, or a hundred years ago? In an audience's very willingness "to join in the make believe of a play," there always has been such collaboration. And there still is!

Furthermore, the growth of theater companies, especially in England ever since World War II, the time O'Connor was publishing *The Art of the Theatre* in book form, unveiled a "noble breed of British actors who dignify theatrical art by devoting their talents and resources to producing distinguished drama meticulously and tastefully." Because audiences were often presented by these companies with a variety of versions of the same masterpieces, theatergoers were able to make comparisons which exercised their taste and judgment. Hence, as John Gassner informs us, it is even possible "to find Londoners who can recall and actually have jotted down impressions of numerous Shakespearean productions; they can compare state business and the interpretations of the main roles over periods ranging from several decades to half a century."

It becomes all the more difficult, therefore, to understand O'Connor's view that, under the best of circumstances, Shakespeare or other classics ought to be produced solely at the universities; that for "entertainment" one must go only to the contemporary dramatist; that he went to Shakespeare rather "as one looks at a picture of a girl one has once been in love with"; that Shakespeare was "fairy gold." O'Connor seems to have lost sight of the reality that

Shakespeare is far more durable than he gave him credit for—even on the contemporary stage.

To be sure, O'Connor's complaint that "writers will never learn to write for the theatre again until they get a chance to learn its ways and until they get theatres which produce *only* new plays" is—except for his "only"—valid, in a very practical way. There is surely a need, a need which the Abbey—at least under O'Connor's direction—fulfilled or attempted to fulfill for aspiring writers: to have their works produced and, thereby, learn their craft at first-hand. But, O'Connor's *"only"* notwithstanding, that need must necessarily include not only modern but classic drama as well. By working within the theater itself would they be able to refine their craft, achieving in the process a living institution of dramatic art.

That was something, O'Connor correctly observes, Browning and Tennyson, for example, were unable to achieve. They never wrote "actable plays." Removed from the paint that smeared the stage, they sat spinning the web of their drama at home as if nature and life as they really are lay beyond their range. Social and historical reality was somewhat beyond their dramatic spheres.

O'Connor's criticism, therefore, is valid essentially insofar as it touches the practical elements of stagecraft. Writers may well profit from direct contact with the daily operations of the stage: production, directing, rewriting, rehearsals. But what O'Connor overlooked in his analysis of the theater, apparently, is that drama is more than technique or comfortable idiom. For what the great modern, like the ancient dramatist, attempts is something beyond the stylistics of production or a given epoch. The dramatist is moved to declare, in the words of Chekhov—one of O'Connor's favorite writers—"All I wanted to say was 'Have a look at yourselves and see how sad and dreary your lives are.'" Human nature and conduct, then, is the dramatist's chief concern. And that concern is readily communicated to an audience—any audience that "joins in the make believe" of a significant play. It was because their genius was able to move their audiences always to look at themselves that leading ancient and modern dramatists wrote "actable plays." Most of Shakespeare's tragedies continue to be interesting, Joseph Wood Krutch wisely reminds us, "because we can never

quite make up our minds, whether their heroes are destroyed by
fate or whether their own characters or passions led them to destruction."

Hence, the plays of Sophocles, Shakespeare, Racine, Ibsen,
Strindberg, and Chekhov, because they explore human nature and
conduct intensely and truly, are really not, as O'Connor claims,
"museum theatre," even if, at times, some of the audience may not
get some of the "colloquialisms" or "jests" or "slang" or other ver-
balisms of a former age. Aspiring dramatists need not really become
"hacks"—another of O'Connor's disturbing critical notions. They
could remain poets whose imaginative probings might lend themselves readily to a collaboration between writer and audience, as
much outside as within "university halls."

Be that as it may, *The Art of Theatre* contains essentially the
practical ideas that, on assuming the directorship, O'Connor had
sought to institute at the Abbey. And during Yeats's final years
when he was resting in southern France, O'Connor actually became
the moving force in the theater. But the other directors, especially
Higgins and, secretly, Hayes, were jealous of O'Connor's ability "to
move in where Yeats had been." To them, he "seemed to be a
bumptious Corkman who, finding himself by accident on the Abbey
board of directors, was attempting to dominate it. He was receiving
all the publicity, and it would seem to an outsider as if no one else
mattered in the Abbey Theatre." [29] Yeats, on the other hand, was
happy with this turn of events, and, since it was, in reality "Yeats's
theater" O'Connor could proceed safely with the development of
the Abbey.

But O'Connor, as Yeats once remarked, was the sort of person
who "believes that for most of the time the vast majority of people
do not intend much harm to the others." [30] Living with his head
in the clouds, O'Connor did not suspect, what even Yeats sensed
before his death, that his fellow directors would "do him in" eventually. As they could do little, of course, while Yeats was alive, they
waited till the "old warrior" was dead. When Yeats finally died on
January 28, 1939, they asserted themselves. In August of that year,
they changed the Articles of Association, empowering them to dis-

miss a director. They then proceeded, on a motion by Hayes, a supposed life-long friend, to dismiss O'Connor.

That O'Connor was, understandably, deeply hurt and considerably perplexed is certain. For, in a letter to O'Faolain, O'Connor gives full vent to his troubled feelings. Discussing Hayes, he writes: "It sounds all Jekyll and Hyde to me—not to you, I know, because you never had the same adoration for him and always thought him a bit of a humbug. Literally, I didn't think the man could do wrong, and I haven't been in the least bit hurt about anything he's done—one is hurt by variations in temperature, but upside down and inside out—no." [31]

Despite these efforts to minimize the effect of these tactics and his subsequent ouster, O'Connor was bitter. In fact, he writes to O'Faolain, saying that he "wants to get even with the Abbey." Though he never did, O'Connor does, however, clarify in his correspondence somewhat more sharply than in *My Father's Son*, wherein he differed artistically with the other directors of the Abbey. What he apparently aimed at was not, surely, mere personal control but rather at attracting as many "independent writers" as possible to the Abbey and, thereby, gradually remove Higgins and Robinson in order to prevent them from making a shambles of it. In one letter, O'Connor writes:

You insist on thinking that it's all because I have a grievance, but theatre is a physical thing; I have that feeling in my bones; I don't want to rid myself of it; I know that we could be dramatists if only we had a theatre to potter around in, and the Abbey is there; beside any other theatre it has enormous resources and they are entirely in the hands of half-wits. . . . I have an instinct that if Higgins and Robinson were compelled to stop milking the theatre and if an independent producer were pushed in —even another Hunt—it would all be into the barrow of the writers. At present H[iggins] and R[obinson] don't give a damn if we start twenty movements; they're out to coin while the coining is good; they will tolerate no independent writers on the board because you or I or Johnston would propose the appointment of a producer and then where would they be. . . . But argument is impossible if you enter it with the notion that I'm simply trying to get my own back on the Abbey. It's too undignified.[32]

Besides, O'Connor, too dignified to engage in the shabby intrigues of his colleagues, formulated, instead, some of his positive
plans for the theater. Writing again to O'Faolain, he says:

I have just thought of a very simple application of Yeats's idea of a Na-
tional Theatre. You, Johnson [sic]—myself—any other good dramatist
interested—form a society called the National Theatre Society. We
collect plays and offer them As A Season to Edwards, Longford or the
Abbey; keeping control of choice plays in our own hands, so as to defeat
the gobshites. Young writers deal with Us not the fat Fred [Higgins]
or busy Hilton [Edwards]. Obviously, we should have to work in con-
junction with H[iggins] for a start, but two seasons would give us con-
trol. That is to say a theatre without a theatre and all the clumsy
appurtenances . . . But the really important thing is not to be bur-
dened with a theatre. There are obviously a lot of problems for solu-
tion; fainancial [sic] responsibility one of them, though all I think
capable of being solved. The aim, an organization of artists, acting as the
artists' agents, a percentage financing the venture. Think it over.[33]

O'Faolain may or may not have thought it over; O'Connor surely
did. And he reached the conclusion that, because the possibilities
of implementing his plans were, for many reasons, well nigh impossible, he ought to abandon his quest of theater. Needless to say, the
pain of it all remained. In another touching, revealing letter to
O'Faolain, O'Connor writes: "But the fact that I detest that gang
doesn't mean that long before I wasn't half bats about the censorship or the Gaelic plays or the Robinson intrigues. You see, you
couldn't work four years in a theatre unless you either fell in love
with it or ignored it. I am in love with it, that's all." [34] Perhaps it
was that love, too, which motivated him to leave the theater. Rather than possibly hurt it, he would go away.

Even had they not forced him to go away, O'Connor would,
nevertheless, have left the Abbey. As he later recalled: "With Yeats
permanently gone, I began now to realize that mediocrity was in
control and against mediocrity there is no challenge or appeal." Furthermore, mediocrity, "having neither thesis nor antithesis leads
only a sort of biological life." Surely that was not to be the life for
O'Connor. No longer able to trust anyone at the Abbey, a place
now "swamped with the rabble," O'Connor left the theater in a

"frenzy." Turning his back on the "biological life," he also rid himself of all other organizational ties and responsibilities.

O'Connor turned, instead, to a different life, the life of the artist. And when, in 1939, he sat down, at last, to write, he pursued that life brilliantly, publishing poems, short stories, novels, criticism, biography, essays, and travel books. In fact, during the last ten years of his life, he wrote "more than in any single period of his life," finishing his study of the short story, his history of Irish literature, three volumes of translations, the autobiographies, and two volumes of short stories. "We serve no purpose," he once wrote to Sean O'Faolain, "unless it be to create ourselves." [35] Obviously dedicated totally to his creativity, O'Connor's art and life remained one to his very end in March of 1966.

The lines from Yeats's play *The Herne's Egg* which O'Connor repeated to himself often on the night of the poet's death and which, to him, seemed so much better an epitaph than the one Yeats actually composed for himself—"Cast a cold eye/On life, on death"—might, we believe, serve appropriately as O'Connor's own epitaph:

> Strong sinew and soft flesh
> Arc foliage round the shaft
> Before the arrowsmith
> Has stripped it, and I pray
> That I, all foliage gone,
> May shoot into my joy.

Carrying his large "cargo of impure art," O'Connor, stripped by the arrowsmith, went, as Yeats said of Synge, "upwards out of his ailing body into the heroical fountains" of his joy.

Notes

References to O'Connor's works are listed here by title only. A more detailed listing is given in the Selected Bibliography that follows these notes.

I. A Portrait of the Artist as an Only Child

1. James Boswell, *Life of Johnson*, ed. Chauncey Tinker (London, 1960), p. 19. Early in his career, O'Connor seems to have been impressed with autobiographical writing. If he were to have been asked, he confesses, to choose the three greatest works of the eighteenth century in which he had a special interest, all would be biographical: Boswell's *Life*, Saint Simon's *Memoirs*, and Rousseau's *Confessions*. Since he believed, furthermore, that "autobiography is the art of the misfit" because the person writing it is "working off some unhappiness," I naturally discuss some of these unhappinesses in this as well as the end of the last chapter. See *Towards an Appreciation of Literature*, p. 44. The terms "true," "truer," and "truest" are used here in a non-cognitive sense and, hence, somewhat loosely. It will become clear in this work that I do not concentrate on the details of O'Connor's daily "comings and goings" in either Cork, Dublin or, even, America, leaving that to Professor James Matthews who, in his forthcoming authorized biography, shall, undoubtedly, deal with *all* the "externals of fact."

2. *An Only Child*, pp. 61, 63.

3. Ibid., pp. 35 ff. Except for the compliment that his father was a "fine-looking, handsome six-footer," O'Connor found little else to say in his favor. Like the typical "Mother's boy," he was "jealous" of his father "a giant of a man who had no more self-knowledge or self-control than a baby." In later life, though more tolerant and understanding, O'Connor still spoke of his father with a feeling of terror and hatred. See *My Father's Son*, pp. 81, 167.

4. *An Only Child*, p. 20. Although O'Connor seems to imply in *An Only Child* that he changed his name because he favored his mother and her family, he gave an altogether different reason for the change in the *"Paris Review* Interview." Asked specifically why he used a pseudonym, he replied:

"The real reason was that I was a public official, a librarian in Cork. There was a big row at the time about another writer who had published what was supposed to be a blasphemous story and I changed my name, my second name being Francis and my mother's name being O'Connor, so that I could officially say that I didn't know who Frank O'Connor was. It satisfied my committee, it satisfied me. The curious thing now is that I'm better known as Frank O'Connor than I'll ever be as Michael O'Donovan. I'd never have interfered with my name except that it was just convenient and I remember when I did it I intended to change back, but by that time it had become a literary property and I couldn't have changed back without too much trouble." See "Frank O'Connor," *Writers at Work*, ed. Malcolm Cowley, (New York, 1961), pp. 181–82.

5. *An Only Child*, p. 137.

6. Ibid., p. 139.

7. Ibid., pp. 145 ff. Of Corkery's influence, O'Connor observed further: "There was one man who did influence me; it was Daniel Corkery, a remarkable man. This little, limping teacher, with a little, black mustache, wrote something on the blackboard I had never seen before: 'Awaken your courage, Ireland.' It was an admonition to himself, too." See Harvey Breit, *The Writer Observed* (New York, 1961), p. 170.

8. *An Only Child*, pp. 158–59.

9. Ibid., p. 125.

10. Ibid., pp. 176, 274. Though he considered Turgenev his favorite author, O'Connor felt that Babel had a much greater influence on him. See *The Lonely Voice*, p. 188. O'Connor's preoccupation, early in his career, with Babel and Turgenev, among other Russian masters, may have been due to the fact that he not only wished to have them serve as "models" for his own fictional mode but also that their "realism in art" would replace for him the "subjective, idealistic, romantic literature of Yeats, Lady Gregory and Synge," with which he then was apparently anxious to break. In fact, Yeats commented that as "a writer from Catholic Ireland," O'Connor, like O'Faolain and Gerald O'Donovan, depended in his writing, more on "reason than fantasy." See Frank O'Connor, "The Future of Irish Literature," *Horizon*, 5 (Jan., 1942), 58. Later on in his career, however, O'Connor argued that what Irish writers needed really was "a realism which united the idealism of Yeats with the naturalism, the truthfulness of Joyce. It's really a form of poetic realism . . ." See Breit, *The Writer Observed*, p. 170.

11. *An Only Child*, pp. 155–56.

12. Ibid., p. 203.

13. Ibid., p. 204. However pervasive Corkery's influence may have been on O'Connor, the latter did not hesitate, typically, to disagree strongly with his "teacher," not only in matters of politics but also in art. Consider, for example, how, in his public lecture at the Abbey Theater Festival, held in Dublin, August, 1938, O'Connor all but demolishes Corkery's interpretation

of Synge's work. See Frank O'Connor, "Synge," *The Irish Theatre*, ed. Lennox Robinson (London, 1939), pp. 31–52. See also O'Connor's "Preface" to Bryan Merriman, *The Midnight Court* (Dublin, 1947), p. 8. See Daniel Corkery, *The Hidden Ireland* (Dublin, 1975), pp. 222–39.

14. *An Only Child*, p. 211.

15. Calton Younger, *Ireland's Civil War* (London, 1970), p. 403. By his own admission, O'Connor was never meant to be a soldier. See below, pp. 22–23. Furthermore, what interest could the Civil War possibly have for him when we learn that, finding himself captive for a time in the purely Irish-speaking village of Ballymakeera, west of Macroom, he forgot all about the "Troubles" and lost himself in an intense appreciation of Irish phonetics, a far more fascinating subject than the war which he found "intolerably dull." See *An Only Child*, pp. 230–31.

16. Since my writing this chapter a few years ago, a number of interesting letters O'Connor wrote to Sean Hendrick have come to light, though none touch directly on the "Troubles." See *Journal of Irish Literature*, 4 (Jan., 1975), 41–59. Henceforth all references to this journal are directed only to this particular issue, an "O'Connor Miscellany."

17. *An Only Child*, p. 237.

18. Ibid., p. 243.

19. Ibid., pp. 254–55.

20. Ibid., p. 251.

21. Ibid., p. 275.

22. *My Father's Son*, p. 22.

23. Ibid., pp. 50, 60.

24. Ibid., p. 61. See *A Book of Ireland*, p. 31.

25. In one of his letters to Sean Hendrick, in 1941, O'Connor, having previously invited his friend to visit him in Dublin, anticipates his refusal and ascribes it to "an advanced stage of the influence which Cork exercises on us." See "Letters to Sean Hendrick," *Journal of Irish Literature*, p. 52. See also *My Father's Son*, p. 49.

26. *My Father's Son*, p. 90.

27. Ibid., p. 101.

28. Ibid., pp. 115, 113. Although one gets the impression that O'Connor made this observation about Yeats on his own, it originally was told to him, apparently, by Padraic Colum. See *A Short History of Irish Literature*, p. 175.

29. *My Father's Son*, p. 112.

30. Ibid., p. 111. Though O'Connor did stand up to Yeats, he would not tolerate the same in others. When, for instance, Monk Gibbon, a relative of Yeats, criticized the poet in *The Masterpiece and the Man*, O'Connor took him severely to task, all of which left Gibbon surprised, hurt, and somewhat angry at O'Connor's "inconsistency." See *The Yeats We Knew*, ed. Francis MacManus (Cork, 1969), p. 56.

31. *My Father's Son*, p. 215.

32. Ibid., pp. 233, 234.

33. Ibid., p. 165.

34. Harold Macmillan, "Foreword," *Michael/Frank*, ed. Maurice Sheehy (New York, 1969), p. 51.

35. *My Father's Son*, p. 234. Though he "sat down at last to write," O'Connor never lost his compassionate interest in mankind. Hence, he could not understand how Sean O'Faolain would, during the first fifteen months of the existence of his widely read periodical *The Bell* in the early forties, "steadily refuse to recognize the war." See Frank O'Connor, "The Future of Irish Literature," p. 62.

II. Patriotic Frenzy

1. Eavan Boland, "The Innocence of Frank O'Connor," *Michael/Frank*, p. 81.

2. Padraic Pearse, "The Coming Revolution," in *1000 Years of Irish Prose*, ed. Vivian Mercier and David H. Greene (New York, 1961), p. 236. See Florence O'Donoghue, "Easter Week," *The Irish at War*, ed. G. A. Hayes-McCoy (Cork, 1964), p. 87.

3. J. C. Beckett, *The Making of Modern Ireland, 1603–1923* (London, 1972), p. 437.

4. "Proclamation of the Irish Republic" in Dorothy MacCardle, *The Irish Republic* (London, 1968), p. 155.

5. Beckett, *The Making of Modern Ireland*, p. 441.

6. Ibid.

7. Desmond Ryan, *A Man Called Pearse* in *Collected Work of Padraic Pearse* (Dublin, 1924), p. 157.

8. Pearse, "The Coming Revolution," p. 237.

9. Beckett, *The Making of Modern Ireland*, p. 442. Of Lloyd George's duplicity in the negotiations preceding the Rising, see MacCardle, *The Irish Republic*, pp. 188 ff. See also Thomas Jones, *Lloyd George* (Cambridge, Mass., 1951), p. 82.

10. Beckett, *The Making of Modern Ireland*, p. 443.

11. *The Big Fellow*, p. 28.

12. Rex Taylor, *Michael Collins* (London, 1970), p. 57.

13. *The Big Fellow*, p. 80.

14. Sean O'Faolain, *The Irish* (London, 1969), p. 152. See MacCardle, *The Irish Republic*, pp. 555 ff.

15. O'Faolain, *The Irish*, p. 153.

16. Michael Collins, *The Path to Freedom* (Cork, 1968), p. 31.

17. Ibid., pp. 32, 33, 34.

18. Younger, *Ireland's Civil War*, p. 313. See MacCardle, *The Irish Republic*, pp. 581 ff.

19. *An Only Child*, p. 209.

20. Younger, *Ireland's Civil War*, p. 394.

21. "Frank O'Connor," *Writers at Work*, p. 166. Sean O'Faolain, friend, fellow "Corkman," and ally, recalling also his soldiering days during the "Troubles," seems to have had a similar reaction. See his *Vive Moi!* (New York, 1964), pp. 174 ff.

22. William I. Thompson, *The Imagination of an Insurrection* (New York, 1967), p. 232.

23. W. B. Yeats, "The Man and the Echo," *Collected Poems* (New York, 1950), p. 337.

24. Thompson, *The Imagination of an Insurrection*, p. 233.

25. *An Only Child*, pp. 155–56.

26. Younger, *Ireland's Civil War*, p. 484. O'Connor also ascribes, to a degree, the writing of *The Big Fellow* to the inspiration of George Russell. See *My Father's Son*, p. 140.

27. A. L. Rowse, *The Use of History* (New York, 1948), p. 11. See also Paul M. Kendall, *The Art of Biography* (New York, 1967), pp. 121–23, 151.

28. *The Big Fellow*, p. 22.

29. Ibid., p. 83.

30. Ibid., p. 24. Some twelve years after he published *The Big Fellow*, O'Connor, again recalling the humanity of his hero, confirmed his original view of him: "Collins was the most humane of heroes: a tempestuous, blasphemous bully and at heart the softest creature in the world, who loved old people, children and mothers, and—as his astonished biographer learned —liable on the least provocation to burst into floods of tears. The number of times friends of his put on a coy look when I pressed them as to what Collins did then, and murmured with a look of shame, 'well, he-er-he began to cry!' is known only to God and myself." See Frank O'Connor, "Ireland," *Holiday*, 6 (Dec., 1949), 53.

31. *The Big Fellow*, pp. 87–88.

32. Ibid., pp. 53, 47.

33. Calton Younger, *A State of Disunion* (London, 1972), p. 121.

34. *The Big Fellow*, p. 135.

35. Collins, *The Path to Freedom*, p. 126. That O'Connor, too, felt the need for a distinctive and United Irish nation, sadly split during and after the "Troubles," is apparent in his article "Partition—The People Are Bewildered," written years later on May 7, 1944. See *Journal of Irish Literature*, p. 128.

36. *The Path to Freedom*, p. 121.

37. *The Big Fellow*, p. 25.

38. Ibid., pp. 169, 149.

39. Ibid., p. 181.

40. Younger, *Ireland's Civil War*, p. 443.

41. *The Big Fellow*, p. 184. Similar feelings of being surrounded by commonness overcame O'Connor at the death of Yeats, who also acted and spoke "from a vision of himself." See *My Father's Son*, p. 233.

42. G. B. Shaw, *The Matter With Ireland*, ed. Dan H. Laurence and David H. Greene (New York, 1961), p. 258.

43. Thomas Flanagan, "The Irish Writer," *Michael/Frank*, p. 150.

44. Frank O'Connor, "Foreword," *Stories of Frank O'Connor*, p. vii.

45. Lionel Trilling, "Introduction," *The Collected Stories of Isaac Babel* (New York, 1966), p. 16.

46. Frank O'Connor "War," *Irish Statesman*, August 7, 1926, p. 605.

47. *Guests of the Nation*, pp. 204, 205, 206.

48. Ibid., p. 221. Cf. "What's Wrong with the Country," *Bones of Contention* (New York, 1936), p. 237.

49. *Guests of the Nation*, p. 69.

50. *More Stories by Frank O'Connor*, pp. 27–28, hereafter referred to as *More Stories*. Cf. Caroline Gordon and Allen Tate, *The House of Fiction* (New York, 1960), pp. 248–51. Cf. Patrick Kavanagh, "Coloured Balloons: A Study of Frank O'Connor," *Bell*, 15 (Dec., 1947), 15–16. See also Murray Prosky, "The Pattern of Diminishing Certitude in the Stories of Frank O'Connor," *Colby Library Quarterly*, 9 (June, 1971), 311–21.

51. *Guests of the Nation*, pp. 92–93.

52. Ibid., p. 98.

53. Ibid., p. 146.

54. *More Stories*, p. 29.

55. Ibid., p. 32.

56. Ibid., p. 39.

III. Island of Saints

1. *An Only Child*, p. 276.

2. Brendan Kennelly, "Oration at Graveside," *Michael/Frank*, p. 166. This entire volume of elegiac essays affirms Dr. Kennelly's moving graveside tribute.

3. Flanagan, "The Irish Writer," p. 163.

4. George A. Birmingham, *An Irishman Looks at His World* (London, 1919), p. 87.

5. Ibid., pp. 94–95. In my discussion of the role the Church and the clergy play in the daily life of Ireland I am not unaware that this role changed perceptibly in our day. And, although some 95 percent of all the Irish are baptized members of the Catholic Church, and some 90 percent of all Irish Catholics still go to Mass at least once a week, and each town with barely more than one thousand inhabitants has its priests, its church, and its church-controlled school, the 'Catholic Church, in sometimes striking and sometimes subtle ways, is losing grip on how the Irish manage their

family lives and govern their impoverished agrarian republic." See, for instance, Peter T. Kilborn, "Catholic Church is Losing Hold on How People of Ireland Live," *New York Times*, July 17, 1976, p. 2.

6. G. B. Shaw, "Preface," *John Bull's Other Island, Selected Plays*, ii (New York, 1949), 467.

7. Timothy Patrick Coogan, *Ireland Since the Rising* (New York, 1966), p. 222.

8. Ibid., pp. 211–15.

9. G. B. Shaw, *John Bull's Other Island*, p. 563.

10. *A Book of Ireland*, p. 355.

11. Coogan, *Ireland Since the Rising*, p. 212. Of the power of the hierarchy, O'Connor had, on another occasion, this to say: "The supremacy of the Catholic priest in Southern Ireland is the result of historical circumstances which for hundreds of years made him the only educated person in a country parish and the man to whom the people naturally turned for leadership. When he uses that power wisely he can achieve miracles . . . Too often, he seems to use it unwisely in the suppression of perfectly innocent social activities like dancing and amateur theatricals, because it is not only poverty and bad social conditions that cause people to emigrate; it is sheer dullness and unnecessary regimentation." See Frank O'Connor, "Ireland," p. 40.

12. Coogan, *Ireland Since the Rising*, p. 214.

13. *A Book of Ireland*, p. 362.

14. Brinsley MacNamara, *The Valley of the Squinting Windows* (New York, 1919), pp. 22–23. If somewhat dated, this novel, which once helped change the whole current of contemporary Irish fiction, nevertheless presents the reader with a helpfully realistic description of Irish life not dissimilar from the one which O'Connor saw and experienced as he was coming of age. It is not surprising, therefore, that this novel, first published over half-a-century ago, has recently been republished in at least five paperback reprint editions by Anvil Books, Trallee, County Kerry, 1973. A new generation may possibly be seeking to learn more of its earlier life and times.

15. O'Faolain, *The Irish*, p. 107.

16. Liam O'Flaherty, *A Tourist's Guide to Ireland* (London, 1929), pp. 34–35. Cf. Horace Plunkett, *Ireland in the New Century* (Port Washington, N.Y., 1970), pp. 94–95.

17. Arland Ussher, *The Face and Mind of Ireland* (New York, 1959), p. 110.

18. Sean MacRéamoinn, "The Religious Position," *Conor Cruise O'Brien Introduces Ireland*, ed. Owen Dudley Edwards (New York, 1969), p. 62.

19. Ibid., p. 67.

20. O'Faolain, *The Irish*, p. 109.

21. *Crab Apple Jelly*, p. 56.

22. Ibid., p. 61.

23. *The Stories of Frank O'Connor*, p. 163.
24. *A Set of Variations*, p. 309.
25. *The Stories of Frank O'Connor*, pp. 229–45.
26. O'Flaherty, *A Tourist's Guide to Ireland*, pp. 41–42.
27. *A Set of Variations*, pp. 314–24.
28. *Traveller's Samples*, pp. 161–62.
29. *More Stories*, pp. 290–300.
30. *A Set of Variations*, pp. 258. 259.
31. *The Stories of Frank O'Connor*, p. 59.
32. *A Set of Variations*, p. 293.
33. *The Common Chord*, p. 189. O'Connor was known to have revised his stories endlessly. In fact, when asked specifically whether he rewrote, he answered: "Endlessly, endlessly, endlessly. And keep on rewriting, and after it's published, and then after it's published in book form, I usually rewrite it again." See "Frank O'Connor," *Writers at Work*, p. 168. This story, too, was, therefore, revised before he printed it. In the revised version he says rather severely of Tom: "and curses himself because he hasn't the strength to resist it." See *More Stories*, pp. 279–90. See also Frank O'Connor, "Introduction," *The Stories of Frank O'Connor*, p. v, and Harriet O'Donovan, "Introduction," *A Set of Variations*, p. v. For a brief comparative study of the revisions of one of O'Connor's stories, see Frank Coen, "Frank O'Connor's 'First Confession,' One and Two," *Studies in Short Fiction*, 10 (Fall, 1973), 419–21.
34. *The Common Chord*, p. 182.
35. *Crab Apple Jelly*, p. 35.
36. Ibid., pp. 38, 39.
37. Brendan Kennelly, "Light Dying," *Poems from Ireland*, ed. William Cole (New York, 1972), p. 85.

IV. NAKED TO THE WOLF OF LIFE

1. Quoted in Donald S. Connery, *The Irish* (London, 1972), p. 47. My interest in this, as in the preceding, chapter is in no way meant to present a cultural monolith of the Irishman from early Middle Ages to the present as a sexually repressed, mother-obsessed, drunken celibate, but rather to delineate the peculiar quality of Irish life between the Rising and the end of the Fifties as is reflected in the writings of O'Connor.
2. Conrad S. Arensberg and Solon T. Kimball, *Family and Community in Ireland* (Cambridge, Mass., 1968) p. 213. I am not unaware, of course, that of late the conditions of Irish marital life discussed in this chapter have changed, on the whole, somewhat for the better. See Mark Bence-Jones, *The Remarkable Irish* (New York, 1966), pp. 16 ff.
3. John A. O'Brien, "Disappearing Irish in America," *The Vanishing Irish* (New York, 1953), p. 99. The conditions of marital life discussed here are, to be sure, not indigenous to twentieth-century Ireland but already

existed, apparently, in the eighteenth century, if not earlier. Witness, for example, Brian Merryman's "The Midnight Court," the greatest modern Irish poem by a "supreme realist" who wrote this "perfectly proportioned work" on a contemporary subject. Not surprisingly, therefore, the narrator in the poem has this to say:

> My chief complaint and principal grief
> The thing that gives me no relief,
> Sweeps me from harbour in my mind
> And blows me like smoke upon every wind
> Is all the women whose charms miscarry
> All over the land and who'll never marry;
> Bitter old maids without house or home
> Put on one side through no fault of their own.

See "The Midnight Court," p. 19.

4. Sean O'Faolain, "Love Among the Irish," *The Vanishing Irish*, p. 120.

5. *A Set of Variations*, p. 67.

6. Arland Ussher, "The Boundary Between the Sexes," *The Vanishing Irish*, p. 148.

7. Arensberg and Kimball, *Family and Community in Ireland*, p. 369.

8. O'Brien, *The Vanishing Irish*, p. 19. Shades again of the narrator's complaint in "The Midnight Court":

> What chance can there be for girls like me
> With husbands for only one in three.

See "The Midnight Court," p. 42. See also Frank O'Connor, "Ireland," p. 36.

9. Conrad Arensberg, *The Irish Countryman* (New York, 1968), p. 67. O'Connor was impressed with the conclusions reached by this author concerning Irish life, for in his "famous" article about Ireland, O'Connor cites approvingly this earlier work by Professor Arensberg, a classic anthropological study which he calls the "best ever written on Ireland." See Frank O'Connor, "Ireland," p. 58. This particular article in *Holiday* magazine, it should be noted at once, evoked a sharp, shrill, and mean reaction on the part of the Irish government and some of Ireland's press. Consider, for example, the special column on the editorial page of de Valera's *Irish Press*, December 15, 1949, headed "The Poison Pen," in which the editors attack O'Connor as an "anti-Irish Irishman" for having had the temerity to reveal the truth about conditions in his native land at that particular time. The column concludes with this highly uncomplimentary comment: "The editors of *Holiday* owe an apology to their two fine photographers for having surrounded their magnificent pictures with the miserable utterances of a typical anti-Irish Irishman."

10. Maura Laverty, "Woman-shy Irishmen," *The Vanishing Irish*, p. 57.

11. Ibid.

12. *The Stories of Frank O'Connor*, p. 11. For a Freudian analysis of this story as well as of "Judas" and "The Man of the House," see Daniel Weiss, "Freudian Criticism: Frank O'Connor as Paradigm," *North West Review*, 2 (Spring, 1959), 5–14; and Edward C. McAleer, "Frank O'Connor's Oedipus Trilogy," *Hunter College Studies*, 2 (1964), 33–40.

13. Connery, *The Irish*, p. 196.

14. *A Set of Variations*, pp. 51, 54.

15. Connery, *The Irish*, p. 112. Cf. Plunkett, *Ireland in the New Century*, pp. 113–14 and William V. Shannon, "The Lasting Hurrah," *New York Times Magazine*, March 14, 1976, p. 73.

16. Laverty, "Woman-shy Irishmen," p. 58.

17. *The Saint and Mary Kate*, p. 47. This repeated complaint about drinking is echoed mockingly by Tim Haffigan, the "tenth-rate schoolmaster" in *John Bull's Other Island* who, confronted by Broadbent's sneering observation that "you Irishmen certainly know how to drink," replies drunkenly: "Dhrink is the curse o'me unhappy counthry." See G. B. Shaw, *John Bull's Other Ireland*, p. 506.

18. Connery, *The Irish*, p. 205.

19. O'Faolain, *Vive Moi!* (Boston, 1964), pp. 21–22. Italics mine. Cf. O'Brien, "Disappearing Irish in America," p. 107.

20. *The Saint and Mary Kate*, pp. 23, 24.

21. Ibid., p. 129. Cf. Kavanagh, "Coloured Balloons," pp. 16–17.

22. *The Saint and Mary Kate*, pp. 86, 129.

23. Ibid., p. 141.

24. O'Faolain, *The Irish*, p. 31.

25. *Guests of the Nation*, p. 238.

26. *The Saint and Mary Kate*, p. 256.

27. *A Set of Variations*, p. 167.

28. *The Common Chord*, p. 56.

29. Ibid., p. 118.

30. Some six months or so after writing this critique of *Dutch Interior*, I visited the Bancroft Library at the University of California in Berkeley to read the "Sean O'Faolain Papers," containing some of O'Connor's letters. Among them, I chanced upon two which, to my pleasant surprise, confirm the view expressed here. Among other things, O'Connor writes to O'Faolain: "You needn't be either terrified or envious of the novel—it's no good. Potentially, I still think very good: a lovely design but I can't feel it. It's too obvious—there are vast empty spaces where the implications elude me entirely, where they flap about like canvas unpegged in a high wind. That's why I say 'simplify' . . ." In another letter, again undated (all his letters to O'Faolain are undated) O'Connor writes: "Just sent off last proofs of the novel which I loathe detest and abominate." See "Sean O'Faolain Papers," Bancroft Library, University of California, Berkeley. See also Flanagan, "The Irish Writer," p. 162. Even though O'Connor considered *The*

Saint and Mary Kate "for all its intolerable faults . . . a work of art," I am personally more inclined, because of its "intolerable faults," to accept Yeats's comment to O'Connor: "My dear boy, that is a play, not a novel." See *My Father's Son*, pp. 86, 176.

31. *The Mirror in the Roadway*, p. 12.

32. *Dutch Interior*, p. 18.

33. Ibid., p. 94.

34. Ibid., pp. 65, 67.

35. Ibid., p. 250.

36. Ibid., p. 124.

37. *An Only Child*, p. 132. O'Connor's deep concern both in his life and his works with the relationship of parents and children also pervades the work of Joyce. See W. Y. Tindall, *James Joyce: His Way of Interpreting the Modern World* (New York, 1950), p. 11.

38. *Traveller's Samples*, p. 72.

39. Ibid., p. 59.

40. *Guests of the Nation*, p. 278.

41. *Crab Apple Jelly*, p. 27.

42. *More Stories*, p. 343.

43. *A Set of Variations*, p. 244.

44. Ibid., p. 245.

45. *More Stories*, p. 88.

46. Ibid., p. 89.

47. *The Common Chord*, p. 239.

48. *The Stories of Frank O'Connor*, p. 77.

49. *Domestic Relations*, p. 255.

50. Ibid., p. 256.

51. Ibid., p. 260.

52. *The Common Chord*, p. 276.

53. *A Set of Variations*, pp. 161–62.

54. Ibid., p. 151.

55. *Crab Apple Jelly*, p. 96. Cf. O'Faolain, "Love Among the Irish," *The Vanishing Irish*, pp. 114–16.

56. In the revised version of this story, O'Connor added the sentence quoted here, indicating a little more explicitly the excuses so readily given by those determined to thwart the chances of marriage and the joy of companionship because of their desire to stick to their celibacy. See *The Stories of Frank O'Connor*, p. 259.

57. Eric Cross, *The Tailor and Ansty* (New York, 1964), pp. 14–15.

58. Frank O'Connor, "Introduction," *The Tailor and Ansty*, p. 7.

59. Ibid., p. 19.

60. *More Stories*, p. 362.

61. Ibid., p. 364.

62. Ibid., p. 369.

63. *Domestic Relations*, p. 178.
64. *More Stories*, p. 235.
65. *Traveller's Samples*, p. 183.
66. *Domestic Relations*, p. 127.

V. A CARGO OF IMPURE ART

1. *An Only Child*, p. 120.
2. Ibid., p. 118. Cf. Sean O'Casey, "On Playwriting," *Selected Plays of Sean O'Casey* (New York, 1955), p. xxiv.
3. *Towards an Appreciation of Literataure*, pp. 5, 7. Though the need to overcome loneliness was, undoubtedly, the major cause of O'Connor's turning to literature and, eventually, to writing, he informs us, nevertheless, that poverty, too, affected this decision. As he once told an interviewer: "I began very early. I started producing my first collected editions at the age of twelve. I was intended by God to be a painter. But I was very poor, and pencil and paper were the cheapest. Music was out for that reason as well. Literature is the poor man's art." See Breit, *The Writer Observed*, p. 169.
4. *Towards an Appreciation of Literature*, p. 7. Sean O'Faolain, an intimate friend during O'Connor's formative years, corroborates this unflattering view O'Connor had of his own critical capability when he writes: "His imagination was a ball of fire . . . his memory was infallible, his interests more confined; his brain was first-class but completely untrained, and discipline was a word he had never heard; his intuitive processes were something to marvel at, to distrust and, if one was wise, to respect profoundly, because if you were patient enough to discard the old boots and bits of seaweed that he would bring up from his deep diving he was certain, sooner or later, to surface with a piece of pure gold. I do not think he ever reasoned out anything." See O'Faolain, *Vive Moi!* pp. 368–69. Cf. Frank O'Connor, "Public Opinion," *The Bell*, 2 (June, 1941), pp. 61–67, and the reply by Louis Lynch D'Alton, "Public Opinion," *The Bell*, 2 (July, 1941), pp. 72–76.
5. *The Mirror in the Roadway*, p. 41. See *Towards an Interpretation of Literature*, p. 33.
6. "Frank O'Connor," *Writers at Work*, p. 178.
7. Ibid. See *Towards an Appreciation of Literature*, p. 51.
8. *The Mirror in the Roadway*, p. 304.
9. *Towards an Appreciation of Literature*, p. 32.
10. David Cecil, *Victorian Novelists* (Chicago, 1961), p. 6.
11. *Towards an Appreciation of Literature*, p. 26.
12. Leo Tolstoy, *What is Art?*, trans. Aylmer Maude (London, 1946), p. 229.
13. *Towards an Appreciation of Literature*, p. 26.
14. Cecil, *Victorian Novelists*, p. 5.
15. *An Only Child*, p. 83.
16. Cecil, *Victorian Novelists*, p. 9.

17. *The Mirror in the Roadway*, p. 5. See *Towards an Appreciation of Literature*, pp. 13–17.

18. *Towards an Appreciation of Literature*, p. 16.

19. Richard T. Gill, "Frank O'Connor at Harvard," *Michael/Frank*, p. 40.

20. John Peter, "Through the Looking Glass," *Kenyon Review*, 19 (Winter, 1957), 153.

21. Harry Levin, "Toward Stendhal," *Pharos*, 3 (Winter, 1945), 52.

22. *The Mirror in the Roadway*, p. 10.

23. I. A. Richards, *Principles of Literary Criticism* (New York, 1950), p. 269.

24. *The Mirror in the Roadway*, p. 12. Cf. Wayne Booth, *The Rhetoric of Fiction*, (Chicago, 1968), p. 385.

25. *The Mirror in the Roadway*, p. 14.

26. Ibid., p. 33.

27. Levin, "Toward Stendhal," p. 22. Of O'Connor's distinction between "judgment" and "instinct" discussed here, see also Gerry Brenner, "Frank O'Connor's Imprudent Hero," *Texas Studies in Language and Literature*, 10 (Fall, 1968), 457–69.

28. *The Mirror in the Roadway*, p. 115.

29. Ibid., p. 123. I am not unaware of a similar view held by Gordon Ray concerning the relation between Thackeray's fiction and his personal life. Though it appeared some four years prior to *The Mirror in the Roadway*, O'Connor makes no reference to it. See Gordon N. Ray, *The Buried Life* (Cambridge, Mass., 1952).

30. Ibid.

31. Ibid., pp. 206 ff. In his chapter on Katherine Mansfield, O'Connor refers in passing to Middleton Murry's theory that D. H. Lawrence also had a similar "triangular" relationship with Frieda's husband. See *The Lonely Voice*, p. 131.

32. Peter, "Through the Looking Glass," p. 155.

33. Edmund Wilson, *The Triple Thinkers* (New York, 1948), p. 180. That O'Connor considered this tension of contraries as central to art seems clear when we recall that, writing of his admiration for George Russell's thought, he records that his friend subscribed to the "doctrine of the diversity of the inner and the outer." Russell believed further that it "was dangerous to try and get rid of whatever afflicted you because it might be this tension that made you what you were." See Frank O'Connor, "A. E. A Portrait," *The Bell*, 1 (Nov., 1949), 52. See also Maurice Wohlgelernter, "Brendan Behan," *Journal of Modern Literature*, 3 (Feb., 1974), 540–42.

34. *The Mirror in the Roadway*, p. 26.

35. Lionel Trilling, *The Opposing Self* (New York, 1968), p. 206.

36. Leon Blum, "A Theoretical Outline of 'Beylism,'" *Stendhal*, ed. Victor Bromberg (Englewood Cliffs, N.J., 1963), p. 109.

37. *The Mirror in the Roadway*, p. 230.

38. Trilling, *The Liberal Imagination* (New York, 1957), p. 76.

39. *The Mirror in the Roadway*, pp. 285, 289.

40. Wallace Stegner, "Professor O'Connor at Stanford," *Michael/Frank*, pp. 94–95.

41. *The Lonely Voice*, pp. 22–23, 27.

42. Ibid., p. 18.

43. *The Mirror in the Roadway*, p. 253.

44. *The Lonely Voice*, p. 145.

45. Ibid., p. 190.

46. Trilling, "Introduction," *Isaac Babel: The Collected Stories* (Cleveland, 1960), p. 14.

47. *The Lonely Voice*, p. 158.

48. Ibid., p. 164.

49. Ibid., p. 110. Cf. O'Faolain, *The Short Story* (Old Greenwich, Conn., 1951), p. 32.

50. *The Lonely Voice*, p. 112.

51. Ibid., p. 41.

52. O'Faolain, *The Short Story*, pp. 30–31.

53. Stegner, "Professor O'Connor at Stanford," p. 101.

54. *Shakespeare's Progress*, p. 33.

55. This idea that the direct collaboration between "author, players and audience" is at the heart of all drama is so central to O'Connor's thought that it is not only the point of departure of his little volume *The Art of the Theatre* but is repeated in *Towards an Appreciation of Literature*, p. 33, and in *My Father's Son*, pp. 6, 187.

56. *Shakespeare's Progress*, p. 19.

57. *The Living Shakespeare*, ed. Oscar James Campbell (New York, 1958), p. 7.

58. *Shakespeare's Progress*, p. 29.

59. *The Living Shakespeare*, pp. 29, 32.

60. *Shakespeare's Progress*, p. 33.

61. Ibid., p. 45.

62. Ibid., p. 47.

63. Thomas Marc Parrott, *William Shakespeare* (New York, 1955), p. 183.

64. *Shakespeare's Progress*, p. 55.

65. Ibid., p. 57. Cf. James Joyce, *Ulysses* (New York, 1934), pp. 183, 185, 186, 192, In fact, the entire "library scene" in Ulysses seems echoed in O'Connor's views discussed here. See *Ulysses*, pp. 182–215.

66. *Shakespeare's Progress*, p. 92. Cf. Joyce, *Ulysses*, p. 190.

67. *Shakespeare's Progress*, p. 129.

68. Ibid., p. 132.

69. Ibid., p. 133.

70. Ibid., p. 172.
71. Ibid., p. 179.
72. Alfred Harbage, *Conceptions of Shakespeare* (New York, 1968), pp. 19–20.
73. Harbage, pp. 21–22.
74. Quoted in *A Short History of Irish Literature*, p. 230. Henceforth referred to as *A Short History*. O'Connor relates that although A. E. and Yeats once had urged him to write this *Short History*, he did not get around to doing it till some thirty-five years later. See *My Father's Son*, p. 90.
75. *A Short History*, p. 11.
76. Ibid., p. 19.
77. Ibid., p. 40.
78. Ibid., p. 42.
79. Ibid., p. 90.
80. Ibid., p. 125.
81. Ibid., p. 129.
82. Ibid., pp. 134, 150.
83. Ibid., pp. 156, 157. Professor Kelleher had earlier expressed a similar view that Arnold's lectures, though dated by his facile notions of race and national temperament, were, nevertheless, a welcome advocacy of the Irish cause: "When Matthew Arnold set out to describe the characteristic of Celtic literature and to analyze its effects, he paid the Celtic world the first valuable compliment it had received from an English source in several hundred years." See John V. Kelleher, "Matthew Arnold and the Celtic Revival," in *Perspectives in Criticism* ed. Harry Levin (Cambridge, Mass., 1950), p. 197.
84. *A Short History*, p. 162. In a letter to O'Faolain in which he complains bitterly about censorship in Ireland and the "uncivilized" state of his fellow Irishmen, O'Connor writes: "I'd pack up and clear out in the morning but I wouldn't give them the sat[isfaction]. I'll try and hang on like Yeats for the mere pleasure of kicking their arses at the age of 70. Oh, how intolerably insolent I'll be!" See "Sean O'Faolain Papers,"
85. *A Short History*, p. 164.
86. Ibid., p. 199.
87. Ibid., p. 165.
88. Ibid., p. 167.
89. Ibid., p. 173.
90. Ibid., p. 175. See *My Father's Son*, p. 221.
91. Ibid., p. 176. Apparently, O'Connor was deeply impressed with the quality of friendship in Yeats, for he refers to it whenever he speaks of him. See *My Father's Son*, p. 113. That may also have been one of the reasons he was moved to dedicate *The Magic Fountain* to Yeats.
92. See Lennox Robinson, "The Man and the Dramatist," *Scattering Branches*, ed. Stephen Gwynn (New York, 1940), pp. 55–115.

93. Frank O'Connor, "Two Friends: Yeats and A. E.," *Yale Review,* 29 (Sept., 1939), 71, 72. Cf. Mary Colum, *Life and the Dream* (New York, 1947) pp. 127–41.

94. Ibid., p. 76. Of Yeats's fascistic tendencies, O'Connor tells a story, supposedly funny in the poet's eyes but which left O'Connor, either out of shame or disappointment or disapproval—or all three combined—speechless. He therefore makes no comment except to introduce this story by saying only that one "never knew from month to month what [Yeats's] next *frenzy* [would] be" [italics mine]. O'Connor then writes: "His neighbors, who he thought were Blueshirts, kept a dog. Mrs. Yeats, who was a democrat, kept hens. One day Mrs. Yeats' favorite hen disappeared and she complained to her neighbors of the dog. By return came a polite note to say that the dog had been destroyed. Yeats was delighted. This showed the true fascist spirit; but Mrs. Yeats, who was fond of animals, was very depressed. Then one evening Yeats came to me bubbling with glee. The democratic hen had turned up safe and sound and Mrs. Yeats was conscience-stricken. Another victory over the democracies!" See Frank O'Connor, "Ireland," p. 52.

95. "Two Friends," p. 77.

96. *My Father's Son,* p. 233.

97. Frank O'Connor, "Joyce and His Brother," *Nation,* 186 (Feb. 1, 1958), 102.

98. W. B. Yeats, "The Municipal Gallery Revisited," *Collected Poems* (New York, 1950), p. 318. Quoted in *A Short History* p. 194.

99. *A Short History,* p. 196.

100. Ibid., p. 195. Whereas O'Connor delineates the contribution of Yeats and Joyce to the development of the Modern Irish literary renaissance in terms of "thesis" and "antithesis," Thomas Flanagan does so by using Bally-lee Castle and the Martello Tower as symbolic loci of the differences between these two giants. He also argues that the major distinction between them centers mostly in their distinctly different approaches to the Irish language as the best medium of expressing the "matter of Ireland." See Flanagan, "Yeats, Joyce, and the Matter of Ireland," *Critical Inquiry,* 2 (Autumn, 1975), 43–67.

101. James Joyce, *A Portrait of the Artist as a Young Man* (New York, 1928), p. 228. Quoted in *The Mirror in the Roadway,* p. 302.

102. *The Mirror in the Roadway,* p. 302. See *A Short History,* p. 199.

103. *The Mirror in the Roadway,* p. 304. Cf. *The Lonely Voice,* pp. 115–18; 141. Early in his own thinking, O'Connor seems already to have been critical of Joyce's obsession with language and form. He claimed, for example, that Joyce's use of associative language is the "reader's first stumbling block" and that in *Finnegans Wake,* he has "sailed off into a world where the atmosphere—for most normal lungs—is so rare that it is scarce liveable —in." See Frank O'Connor, "Joyce—the Third Period," *Irish Statesman,* April 12, 1930, pp. 114–16.

104. Tindall, *James Joyce*, p. 3.
105. "Frank O'Connor," *Writers at Work*, pp. 176–77.
106. *The Lonely Voice*, p. 116.
107. Ibid., p. 125.

VI. THE ABBEY IS THERE

1. Lady Gregory, *Our Irish Theatre* (New York, 1965), pp. 8–9.
2. W. B. Yeats, *Letters to the New Island*, ed. Horace Reynolds (Cambridge, Mass., 1934), pp. 155, 157. See also Colum, *Life and the Dream*, pp. 117–27.
3. Joseph Wood Krutch, *"Modernism" in Modern Drama* (Ithaca, N.Y., 1966), p. 95.
4. Ibid., p. 97.
5. Quoted in Ann Saddlemyer, " 'Work Out with Dreams,' " *The World of W. B. Yeats*, ed. Robin Skelton and Ann Saddlemyer, (Seattle, 1967), pp. 79–80.
6. Krutch, *"Modernism" in the Modern Drama*, p. 100.
7. Quoted in Peter Kavanagh, *The Story of the Abbey Theatre* (New York, 1950), p. 171.
8. *My Father's Son*, p. 172. Like so many other Irishmen, especially his friend Yeats, O'Connor had a long memory for wrongs, real or imagined, committed against him. Hence, Robinson, too, became "one more man as eevil as you could find in a day's march." Many of his contemporaries shared this view. Consider, for example, Joseph Holloway, a diarist of the early years of the Abbey, who records that Robinson had the "same effect on his mind as a telegraph pole seen through the windows of a rapidly moving train." And yet, there was a period in Robinson's life before he "got his nose into the Abbey and became a conceited cad of the most overbearing and kickable type" when the likes of, say, Miss Yeats, spoke of him as a "country schoolboy," a "nice boy . . . quite boyish and gentle," and of his manner as "simple and unsophisticated." See *Joseph Holloway's Abbey Theatre*, ed. Robert Hogan and Michael O'Neill (Carbondale, Ill., 1967), pp. 160; 121–22. What apparently changed Robinson, among other things, was his compulsive drinking—a fact which disturbed Yeats greatly—and which might possibly explain Robinson's "sombre personality," pessimism, conceit, selfishness, and a far greater "interest in his own career that [in] the future of the theatre." One critic, however, argues that the "pessimism of Robinson's disenchantment with the world about him—his tendency to gloom—was his own favorite illusion. Like Yeats, Robinson felt the need to wear a mask. But Robinson's mask served to disguise the fact that he was more hopeful about life and people than he wished to acknowledge." See Michael O'Neill, "Preface," *Lennox Robinson* (New York, 1964), p. v. See also Eileen O'Casey, *Sean*, (London, 1973), p. 226.
9. Ibid., p. 175. Higgins, Hayes, and Blythe were, apparently, no less vul-

nerable to this accusation which O'Connor hurled at Robinson. In a letter to O'Faolain, O'Connor laments: "You should see them. I discussed suggestions, and pointed out that they don't go out after plays, that they cant [sic] expect me or you to go trailing around after Higgins or themselves begging them to produce our plays, and that there can be no real theatre with the literary men left out. . . . I certainly won't write plays for Blythe or Hayes; I would write plays for them or Longford but there must be a real immediate possibility of production and that can only be guaranteed by the presence on any Board there is of real literary men, yourself or Johnson [sic]." And in another letter, O'Connor states that, because the "murderous inhuman rejection slip business . . . haunted [him] all the time [he] was in the Abbey, "we should need a circular to be sent to all budding dramatists who submit plays, rather like the circular Yeats used to send out, telling them exactly the sort of play we want and the sort of plays intending dramatists should read and how they should approach their material." See "Sean O'Faolain Papers."

10. *My Father's Son*, pp. 197–98. It would appear that these feelings of distrust of Robinson were mutual, since the latter, in his history of the Abbey, devotes no more than one line to O'Connor's role in it, and that merely to record his appointment to the governing Board in October, 1935. See Lennox Robinson, *Ireland's Abbey Theatre* (London, 1951), p. 199.

11. Kavanagh, *The Story of the Abbey Theatre*, p. 171. Yeats is reported once to have said to O'Connor: "*You* will save the Abbey Theatre." See O'Faolain, *Vive Moi!* p. 357. One of his intuitive abilities to do the right thing was, he boasts in a letter to O'Faolain, to save the Abbey money: "I did brutally pull down expenses at the Abbey and saved something like £3500 in a couple of years." See "Sean O'Faolain Papers."

12. Kavanagh, p. 173.

13. Frank O'Connor, "A Lyric Voice in the Irish Theatre." *The Genius of the Irish Theater*, ed. Sylvan Barnet, Morton Berman, and William Burto (New York, 1960), p. 357.

14. *My Father's Son*, p. 200. See also Gabriel Fallon, "The Abbey Theatre Acting Tradition," *The Story of the Abbey Theatre*, ed. Sean McCann, (London, 1967), pp. 101–25.

15. "Ireland," *Oxford Companion to the Theatre*, ed. Phyllis Hartnoll, 3rd ed. (London, 1967), p. 475.

16. *My Father's Son*, p. 187.

17. Kavanagh, *The Story of the Abbey Theatre*, p. 173.

18. Roger McHugh, "Frank O'Connor and the Irish Theatre," *Michael/Frank*, p. 74.

19. Frank O'Connor, *In the Train*, in *The Genius of the Irish Theater*, p. 258. Of O'Connor's five plays, only two, *In the Train* and *The Statue's Daughter*, were ever published by him. Two other plays, *Guests of the Nation* and *The Saint and Mary Kate*, published, respectively, by the Dra-

matic Play Service (New York, 1958) and the Proscenium Press (Newark, Delaware, 1970), were adapted by other hands: the former, by Neil McKenzie; the latter, by Mary Manning.

20. McHugh, "Frank O'Connor and the Irish Theatre," p. 72.

21. *The Art of the Theatre*, p. 8.

22. Ibid., p. 9.

23. Ibid., p. 14.

24. Ibid., p. 30.

25. Ibid., p. 28.

26. Ibid., pp. 31, 33.

27. Ibid., pp. 40, 41.

28. Ibid., p. 49. Cf. *My Father's Son*, p. 191.

29. Kavanagh, *The Story of the Abbey Theatre*, p. 177.

30. *My Father's Son*, p. 182. O'Connor adds this about himself: "I had no ability as an intriguer and could be fooled by appearances most of the time . . ." See p. 186. One can only conjecture that the shock of being robbed of his innocent belief in most people may have prompted O'Connor to have Eileen say to Joan—under somewhat different though not entirely unrelated circumstances—in *The Statue's Daughter*, produced, incidentally, a mere two years after he left the Abbey: "You can't play at intrigue with these people, because every time you step off the dotted line you're knifed." See *The Statue's Daughter, Journal of Irish Literature*, p. 98. In point of fact, O'Connor actually refers to himself in a review as an "apolitical man." See Frank O'Connor, "It's Fiction All Right, But Is It Political." *New York Times Book Review*, March 31, 1957, p. 4.

31. Sean O'Faolain Papers.

32. Ibid.

33. Ibid.

34. Ibid.

35. Ibid. One cannot but note sadly that O'Connor and O'Faolain who were, in their early years, such close friends, fellow townsmen, and associates should have drifted apart to a point where almost all communication between them ceased forever. The reasons for their broken friendship are significant and highly interesting since both, as is common in such cases, give entirely different versions of what transpired between them which reflect something of their own temperaments. O'Faolain claims that O'Connor's "great gift for simplification had its corresponding weakness in oversimplification," whereas his own "preference for winding [himself] into a subject with a blend of thought and sensibility has its weakness in overcomplication." Nevertheless, they "stimulated one another." O'Faolain concludes, however, that "over the years Michael and I grew weary of one another's ways and more attached each to his own way. Ultimately the friendship died, to our mutual loss." See O'Faolain, *Vive Moi!*, p. 370.

O'Connor, on the other hand, tells us something else altogether. In a

letter to Sean Hendrick, dated May, 1944, he finds that O'Faolain seemed
to have had certain "hallucinations of grandeur" which he found difficult to
tolerate. Among a series of unrelated matter, O'Connor writes: "I gave up
writing for *The Bell* when O'Faolain started sending me letters, written by
the office boy, beginning Dear Michael and ending per and pro S. O'Faolain.
Among the forms of hallucinations of grandeur I never before heard of a
man that thought himself a limited company." See *Journal of Irish Literature*, p. 57.

What he had omitted to tell Hendrick, however, O'Connor revealed in an
earlier letter addressed to O'Faolain himself. After accusing him, ever since
the first number of *The Bell*, founded by O'Faolain, of engaging in "tricks,
evasions and sham humanitarianism," O'Connor continues: "I don't want
to have anything to do with you in the way of business, not because I think
you're tricky but because in some extraordinary fashion you're no longer
capable of doing anything except with a multiplicity of motives, one sure if
another fails. All the motives are honourable, but altogether they're awful.
. . . I do object to being treated as if I were a gull . . . the *Bell* seems
to me the reflection of a mind which is swamped in a multiplicity of motives. Don't kid yourself into the belief that it's subtlety—it's just an incapacity for disinterested action. I know you think I'm this that and the other,
but the *Bell* . . . gives me the horrors. It's literary hari-kari, very long drawn
out, and with no sense of dignity. . . . You'd prefer to cut yourself off
from artists and gratify your creative instincts by hacking and rewriting the
work of your inferiors. You and Dev [de Valera]—how you both love the
second-rate!" See "Sean O'Faolain Papers."

Selected Bibliography

Note: For a more detailed bibliography of the works by and about Frank O'Connor, the reader should consult the two excellent bibliographies presently available: Gerry Brenner, "Frank O'Connor, a Bibliography," *West Coast Review*, 2 (Fall, 1967), pp. 55–64, and "Towards a Bibliography of Frank O'Connor's Writing," *Michael/Frank*, New York, 1969, pp. 168–99. To repeat them here would obviously be superfluous. I have, therefore, listed, in addition to the *books* by O'Connor, only those general works which have been useful to me and that, in my opinion, are likely to be most useful and interesting to the reader.

A. WORKS BY FRANK O'CONNOR

I. Novels and Short Story Collections

Bones of Contention. London: Macmillan, 1936.

The Common Chord. New York: Knopf, 1948.

Crab Apple Jelly. London: Macmillan, 1944.

Day Dreams. London: Pan Books, 1973.

Domestic Relations. New York: Knopf, 1957.

Dutch Interior. London: Macmillan, 1940.

Fish for Friday. London: Pan Books, 1971.

Guests of the Nation. New York: Macmillan, 1931.

The Holy Door. London: Pan Books, 1973.

A Life of Your Own. London: Pan Books, 1972.

The Mad Lomasneys. London: Pan Books, 1970.

Masculine Protest. London: Pan Books, 1972.

Modern Irish Stories. Introd. Frank O'Connor. London: Oxford Univ. Press, [1957] 1970.

More Stories. New York: Knopf, 1954.

My Oedipus Complex and Other Stories. London: Penguin, 1969.

The Saint and Mary Kate. New York: Macmillan, 1932.

A Set of Variations. New York: Knopf, 1969.

Stories by Frank O'Connor. New York: Vintage, 1956.

The Stories of Frank O'Connor. New York: Knopf, 1952.

Traveller's Samples. New York: Knopf, 1951.

II. Non-Fiction Books

The Art of the Theatre. Dublin: Fridberg, 1947.
The Big Fellow. Springfield, Ill.: Templegate Press, [1937] 1966.
A Book of Ireland. Edited with introd. London: Fontana, [1959] 1971.
Dead Souls. Nicolai Gogol. Ed. with introd. New York: New American Library, 1961.
Irish Miles. London: Macmillan, 1947.
Irish Street Ballads. Ed. Colm O Lochlainn. "Introduction." New York: Corinth, 1960.
The Lonely Voice. Cleveland: World, 1963.
The Mirror in the Roadway. New York: Knopf, [1956] 1964.
My Father's Son. New York: Knopf, 1969.
An Only Child. New York: Knopf, [1961] 1970.
Shakespeare's Progress. Cleveland: World, [1948] 1960.
A Short History of Irish Literature. New York: Capricorn, [1967] 1968.
The Tailor and Ansty. Eric Cross. "Introduction." New York: Devin-Adair, [1942] 1964.
Towards an Appreciation of Literature. Port Washington, N. Y.: Kennikat Press, [1945] 1970.

III. Poetry

The Fountain of Magic. London: Macmillan, 1939.
A Golden Treasury of Irish Poetry, 600–1200. Ed. with David H. Greene. London: Macmillan, 1967.
Kings, Lords, and Commons. Freeport, N.Y.: Book for Libraries Press, [1959] 1969.
A Lament for Art O'Leary. Trans. from the Irish. Dublin: Cuala, 1940.
The Little Monasteries, Poems Translated from the Irish. Dublin: Dolmen, 1963.
The Midnight Court, A Rhythmical Baccanalia from the Irish of Bryan Merryman. Dublin: Fridberg, 1945.
Three Old Brothers and Other Poems. London: Nelson, 1936.
The Wild Bird's Nest, Poems from the Irish. Dublin, Cuala, 1932.

IV. Plays

In the Train. A Play in One Act from the Short Story. First performed May 31, 1937. Rpt. in *The Genius of the Irish Theatre*, ed. Sylvan Barnet, Morton Berman, and William Burto. New York: Mentor, 1960.
The Invincibles. A Play in Seven Scenes. With Hugh Hunt. Unpublished. First performed February 23, 1938.
Moses' Rock, A Play in Three Acts. With Hugh Hunt. Unpublished. First performed February 23, 1938.
The Statue's Daughter, A Fantasy in a Prologue and Three Acts. First per-

formed December 8, 1971. Rpt. in *Journal of Irish Literature*, 4 (Jan. 1975), 59–117.

Time's Pocket, A Play in Five Acts. Unpublished. First performed Dec. 26, 1938.

B. GENERAL WORKS

Arensberg, Conrad. *The Irish Countryman.* Garden City, N.Y.: Natural History Press, [1937] 1968.

———, and Solon T. Kimball. *Family and Community in Ireland.* Cambridge, Mass.: Harvard Univ. Press, 1968.

Babel, Isaac. *Collected Stories.* Ed. Walter Morison, introd. Lionel Trilling. Cleveland: World, 1966.

Barnet, Sylvan, Morton Berman, and William Burto, eds. *The Genius of the Irish Theater.* New York: Mentor Books, 1960.

Bates, H. E. *The Modern Short Story.* Boston: The Writer, 1972.

Beckett, J. C. *The Making of Modern Ireland, 1603–1923.* London: Faber and Faber, [1969] 1972.

Behan, Brendan. *Brendan Behan's Island.* London: Corgi Books, [1962] 1970.

Bence-Jones, Mark. *The Remarkable Irish.* New York: David McKay, 1966.

Birmingham, George A. *An Irishman Looks at His World.* London: Hodder & Stoughton, 1919.

Booth, Wayne. *The Rhetoric of Fiction.* Chicago: Univ. of Chicago Press [1961], 1968.

Boyd, Ernest. *Ireland's Literary Renaissance.* New York, rev. ed., London, Knopf, 1922.

Brenner, Gerry. "A Study of Frank O'Connor's Short Stories." Diss. Univ. of Washington 1965.

Bromberg, Victor, ed. *Stendhal.* Englewood Cliffs, N. J.: Prentice-Hall, 1962.

Brown, Malcolm. *The Politics of Irish Literature.* Seattle: Univ. of Washington Press, 1972.

Cahill, Susan and Thomas. *A Literary Guide to Ireland.* New York: Scribner's, 1973.

Campbell, Oscar James, ed. *The Living Shakespeare.* New York: Macmillan, 1958.

Caulfield, Max. *The Easter Rebellion.* London: Four Square Books, 1965.

Cecil, David. *Victorian Novelists.* Chicago: University of Chicago Press, [1935] 1961.

Coffey, Thomas M. *Agony at Easter.* London: Pelican, 1971.

Cole, William, ed. *Poems From Ireland.* New York: Crowell, 1972.

Collins, Michael. *The Path to Freedom.* Cork: Mercier Press, 1968.

Colum, Mary. *Life and the Dream.* New York: Doubleday, 1947.

Colum, Padraic, ed. *An Anthology of Irish Verse.* New York: Liveright, [1922] 1972.

Connery, Donald S. *The Irish.* London: Arrow Books, 1972.

Coogan, Timothy Patrick. *Ireland Since the Rising.* New York: Praeger, 1966.

Corkery, Daniel. *The Hidden Ireland.* Dublin: Gill and Macmillan, [1924] 1975.

Doyle, Lynn. *The Spirit of Ireland.* New York: Scribner's, 1936.

Edwards, Owen Dudley, ed. *Conor Cruise O'Brien Introduces Ireland.* New York: McGraw-Hill, 1969.

Edwards-Rees, Désirée. *Ireland's Story.* New York: Barnes & Noble, 1967.

Ellis-Fermor, Una. *The Irish Dramatic Movement.* London: Methuen, 1954.

Ellmann, Richard. *James Joyce.* New York: Oxford Univ. Press. [1959] 1965.

——— *Yeats: The Man and the Masks.* New York: Macmillan, 1948.

Ferrar, Harold. *Denis Johnston's Irish Theatre.* Dublin: Dolmen, 1973.

Flanagan, Thomas. *The Irish Novelists. 1800–1850.* New York: Columbia Univ. Press, 1959.

——— "Yeats, Joyce, and the Matter of Ireland." *Critical Inquiry,* 2 (Autumn, 1975), 43–69.

Forester, Margery. *Michael Collins.* London, Sphere Books, 1972.

"Frank O'Connor Miscellany." *Journal of Irish Literature,* 4 (Jan., 1975), 3–178.

Gassner, John. *Masters of the Drama.* New York: Random House, 1954.

——— *The Theatre in Our Times.* New York: Crown, 1954.

Gordon, Caroline, and Allen Tate. *The House of Fiction.* New York: Scribner's, 1960.

Greene, David H., and Edward M. Stephens. *J. M. Synge. 1871–1909.* New York: Macmillan, 1959.

Gregory, Lady Augusta. *Our Irish Theatre.* Introd. Daniel J. Murphy. New York: Capricorn, [1913] 1965.

Gwynn, Stephen L. *Irish Literature and Drama in the English Language.* London: Thomas Nelson, 1936.

———, ed. *Scattering Branches.* New York: Macmillan, 1940.

Hall, James, and Martin, Steinmann, eds. *The Permanence of Yeats.* New York: Macmillan, 1950.

Harbage, Alfred. *Conceptions of Shakespeare.* New York: Schocken, 1968.

Hayes-McCoy, G. A., ed. *The Irish at War.* Cork: Mercier Press, 1964.

Hogan, Robert and Michael O'Neill, ed. *Joseph Holloway's Abbey Theatre.* Carbondale, Ill.: Southern Illinois University Press, 1967.

Inglis, Brian. *The Story of Ireland.* London: Faber & Faber, 1966.

Jackson, Kenneth Hurlstone. *A Celtic Miscellany*. London: Penguin, [1951] 1971.

Kain, Richard. *Dublin in the Age of W. B. Yeats and James Joyce*. Norman: Univ. of Oklahoma Press, 1962.

Kavanagh, Peter. *The Story of The Abbey Theatre*. New York: Devin-Adair, 1950.

Kendall, Paul Murray. *The Art of Biography*. New York: Norton, [1965] 1967.

Kiely, Benedict. *Modern Irish Fiction: A Critique*. Dublin: Golden Eagle Books, 1950.

Knight, G. Wilson. *The Golden Labyrinth*. New York: Norton, 1962.

Krutch, Joseph Wood. *"Modernism" in Modern Drama*. Ithaca, N. Y.: Cornell Univ. Press, [1953] 1966.

Levin, Harry. "Toward Stendhal." *Pharos*, 3 (Winter, 1945), 6–70.

MacCardle, Dorothy. *The Irish Republic*. London: Corgi Books [1937] 1968.

MacManus, Seumas. *The Story of the Irish Race*. Rev. ed., New York: Devin-Adair, [1921] 1972.

MacNamara, Brinsley. *The Valley of the Squinting Windows*. New York: Brentano's, 1919.

Marreco, Anne. *The Rebel Countess*. London: Corgi Books, 1969.

McCann, Sean, ed. *The Story of the Abbey Theatre*. London: Four Square Book, 1967.

McHugh, Roger, ed. *Dublin, 1916*. London: Arlington Books, 1966.

McManus, Francis, ed. *The Yeats We Knew*. Cork: Mercier Press, [1965] 1969.

Mercier, Vivian. *The Irish Comic Tradition*. Oxford: Clarendon, 1962.

——, and David H. Greene. *1000 Years of Irish Prose*. New York: Universal Library, [1952] 1961.

Nathan, George Jean, ed. *Five Great Modern Irish Plays*. New York: Modern Library, 1941.

O'Brien, John A. *The Vanishing Irish*. New York: McGraw-Hill, 1953.

O'Broin, Leon. *Dublin Castle and the 1916 Uprising*. New York: New York Univ. Press, 1971.

O'Casey, Sean. *Mirror in My House*. New York: Macmillan, 1956.

O'Connor, Ulick. *Brendan*. Englewood Cliffs, N. J.: Prentice-Hall, 1970.

—— *The Times I've Seen: Oliver St. John Gogarty*. New York: Ivan Obolensky, 1963.

O'Driscoll, Robert, ed. *Theatre and Nationalism in Twentieth-Century Ireland*. Toronto: University of Toronto Press, 1971.

O'Faolain, Sean. *De Valera*. Rev. ed., Harmondsworth, Middlesex: Penguin, 1939.

—— *The Irish*. London: Pelican, [1947] 1969.

O'Faolain, Sean, ed. *Short Stories, A Study in Pleasure*. Boston: Little Brown, 1961.
—— *The Short Story*. Old Greenwish, Conn.: Devin-Adair, [1951] 1970.
—— *The Vanishing Hero*. Boston: Little, Brown, 1957.
—— *Vive Moi!* Boston: Little, Brown, 1964.
O'Flaherty, Liam. *A Tourist's Guide to Ireland*. London: Mandrake Press, 1929.
O'Neill, Michael. *Lennox Robinson*. New York: Twayne, 1964.
Oxford Companion to the Theatre. Ed. Phyllis Hartnoll, 3rd ed., London: Oxford Univ. Press, 1967.
Pakenham, Frank. *Peace by Ordeal*. London: Sidgwick and Jackson, [1935] 1972.
Parrott, Thomas Marc. *William Shakespeare*. Rev. ed., New York: Scribner's, [1934] 1955.
Plunkett, Horace. *Ireland in the New Century*. Port Washington, N. Y.: Kennikat Press, [1904] 1970.
Porter, Raymond J. *P. H. Pearse*. New York: Twayne, 1973.
Ray, Gordon N. *The Buried Life*. Cambridge, Mass.: Harvard Univ. Press, 1952.
Richards, I. A., *Principles of Literary Criticism*. New York: Harcourt Brace, 1950.
Robinson, Lennox. *Ireland's Abbey Theatre*. London: Sidgwick and Jackson, 1951.
——, ed. *The Irish Theatre*. London: Macmillan, 1939.
Rowse, A. L. *The Use of History*. New York: Macmillan, 1948.
Russell, Diarmuid, ed. *The Portable Irish Reader*. New York: Viking, 1946.
Shaw, George Bernard. *John Bull's Other Island*. *Selected Plays*. Vol. II. New York: Dodd, Mead, 1949.
—— *The Matter With Ireland*. Ed. Dan H. Laurence and David H. Greene. New York: Hill and Wang, 1961.
Sheehy, Maurice P., ed. *Michael/Frank*. New York: Knopf, 1969.
Sheehy, Michael. *Is Ireland Dying?* New York: Taplinger, 1968.
Skelton, Robin, and Ann Saddlemyer, eds. *The World of W. B. Yeats*. Rev. ed. Seattle: Univ. of Washington Press, 1967.
Sullivan, Kevin. "Apostolic Succession." *Nation*, 209 (Dec. 15, 1969), 668–70.
—— "The Son of Minnie O'Connor." *Nation*, 192 (April 8, 1961), 306–07.
Synge, John Millington. *The Aran Islands*. Ed. Robert Tracy. New York: Vintage, [1907] 1962.
—— *The Playboy of the Western World*. Ed. Henry Popkin. New York: Avon, [1907] 1967.
Taylor, Rex. *Michael Collins*. London: New English Library, [1958] 1970.
Thompson, William Irwin. *The Imagination of an Insurrection*. New York: Harper Colophon, 1972.

Tindall, William York. *James Joyce: His Way of Interpreting the Modern World.* New York: Scribner's, 1950.

—— *W. B. Yeats.* New York: Columbia Univ. Press, 1966.

Tolstoy, Leo. *What is Art?* Trans. Aylmer Maude. London: Oxford Univ. Press, [1898] 1946.

Tomory, William Michael. "A Man's Voice Speaking: A Study of the Fiction of Frank O'Connor." Diss. Univ. of Denver, 1973.

Trautmann, Joanne. "Counterparts: Stories and Traditions of Frank O'Connor and Sean O'Faolain." Diss. Purdue Univ. 1967.

Trilling, Lionel. *The Liberal Imagination.* Garden City, N. Y.: Doubleday Anchor, 1950.

—— *The Opposing Self.* New York: Viking, [1955] 1968.

Ussher, Arland. *The Face and Mind of Ireland.* New York: Devin-Adair, 1950.

Wilde, Lady. *Ancient Legends of Ireland.* Galway: O'Gorman, [1888] 1971.

Williams, Desmond. *The Irish Struggle 1916–1926.* London: Routledge & Keegan Paul, 1966.

Wohlgelernter, Maurice. "Brendan Behan." *Journal of Modern Literature,* 3 (Feb. 1974), 540–42.

—— "Frank O'Connor." *Journal of Modern Literature,* 1 (Spring, 1971), 883–85.

Yeats. William Butler. *Autobiographies.* New York: Macmillan, 1938.

—— *Collected Poems.* New York: Macmillan, 1951.

—— *Letters to the New Island.* Cambridge, Mass.: Harvard Univ. Press., [1934] 1970.

"Yeats Miscellany." *Journal of Modern Literature,* 4 (Feb., 1975), 529 734.

Younger, Carlton. *A State of Disunion.* London: Fontana Books, 1972.

—— *Ireland's Civil War.* London: Fontana Books, 1970.

Index